P9-DVA-722

Finnish
PHRASE BOOK
& DICTIONARY

Easy to use features

● Handy thematic colour coding
● Quick Reference Section — opposite page
● Tipping Guide — inside back cover
● Quick reply panels throughout

How best to use this phrase book

● We suggest that you start with the **Guide to pronunciation** (pp. 6-9), then go on to **Some basic expressions** (pp. 10-15). This gives you not only a minimum vocabulary, but also helps you get used to pronouncing the language. The phonetic transcription throughout the book enables you to pronounce every word correctly.

● Consult the **Contents** pages (3-5) for the section you need. In each chapter you'll find travel facts, hints and useful information. Simple phrases are followed by a list of words applicable to the situation.

● Separate, detailed contents lists are included at the beginning of the extensive **Eating out** and **Shopping guide** sections (Menus, p. 39, Shops and services, p. 97).

● If you want to find out how to say something in Finnish, your fastest look-up is via the **Dictionary** section (pp. 164-189). This not only gives you the word, but is also cross-referenced to its use in a phrase on a specific page.

● If you wish to learn more about constructing sentences, check the **Basic grammar** (pp. 159-163).

● Note the **colour margins** are indexed in Finnish and English to help both listener and speaker. And, in addition, there is also an index in Finnish for the use of your listener.

● Throughout the book, this symbol ☛ suggests phrases your listener can use to answer you. If you still can't understand, hand this phrase book to the Finnish-speaker to encourage pointing to an appropriate answer. The English translation for you is just alongside the Finnish.

Revised edition—1st printing 1995   Printed in Switzerland

Contents

4

Acknowledgements
We are particularly grateful to Mr Ilkka Lavonius for his help
in the preparation of this book, and to Dr T J A Bennet and Mrs
Rayne Bensky who devised the phonetic transcription.

Guide to pronunciation

This chapter is intended to make you familiar with the phonetic transcription we have devised and to help you get used to the sounds of Finnish.

An outline of the spelling and sounds of Finnish

The writing system in Finnish is systematic: each letter corresponds to one and the same phoneme (basic sound) and each phoneme corresponds to one and the same letter. The number of phonemes is smaller than in most European languages. Letters like **b, c, f, q, w** and **z** are only found in words recently borrowed from foreign languages.

You'll find the pronunciation of the Finnish letters and sounds explained below, as well as the symbols we're using for them in the transcriptions. The imitated pronunciation should be read as if it were English except for any special rules set out below. Of course, the sounds of any two languages are never exactly the same; but if you follow carefully the indications supplied here, you'll have no difficulty in reading our transcriptions in such a way as to make yourself understood.

Letters written in bold type should be stressed.

Consonants

Letter	Approximate pronunciation	Symbol	Example	
k, m, n **p, t, v**	as in English			
d	as in rea**d**y, but sometimes very weak	d	**taide**	tah'day
g	in words of Finnish origin, only found after **n**; **ng** is pronounced as in si**ng**er	ng	**sangen**	**sah**ngayn
h	as in **h**ot, whatever its position in the word	h	**lahti**	**lah**hti
j	like **y** in **y**ou	y	**ja**	yah

l	as in let	l	**talo**	**tah**loa
r	always rolled	r	**raha**	**rah**hah
s	always as in set (never as in present)	s/ss*	**sillä**	**sill**æ
			kiitos	**kee**toass

*To make doubly sure that the Finnish **s** receives its correct pronunciation as **s** in English set, and not as a **z** sound in present, we often use **ss** in our phonetic transcriptions. Similarly, we sometimes employ a double consonant after **i** to ensure this is pronounced like **i** in pin, and not like **i** in kite. In these cases you can quickly check with the Finnish spelling whether you should pronounce a single or a double consonant.

Vowels

a	like a in car; short or long	ah	**matala**	**mah**tahlah
		aa	**iltaa**	**i**ltaa
e	like a in late; but a pure vowel, not a dipthong; short or long	ay	**kolme**	**koal**may
		$\overline{ay}$	**teevati**	**tay**vati
i	like i in pin (short) or ee in see (long);	i	**takki**	**tah**kki
		ee	**siitä**	**see**tæ
	ir + consonant like i in pin (short)	eer	**kirkko**	**keer**koa
o	a sound between aw in law and oa in coat; short or long	oa	**olla**	**oal**lah
		$\overline{oa}$	**kookas**	**koa**kahss
u	like oo in pool; short or long	oo	**hupsu**	**hoop**soo
		$\overline{oo}$	**uuni**	**oo**ni
y	like u in French sur or ü in German über; say ee as in see, and round your lips while still trying to pronounce ee; it can be short or long	ew	**yksi**	**ew**ksi
		$\overline{ew}$	**syy**	**sew**

ä	like **a** in h**a**t; short or long	æ	**äkkiä**	**ækkiæ**
		ᴂ̄	**hyvää**	**hewv**ᴂ̄
ö	like **ur** in f**ur**, but without	ur	**tyttö**	**tewt**tur
	any **r** sound, and with the	ūr	**likööri**	**likkū**rri
	lips rounded; short or long			

N.B. The letters **b, c, f, q, s, sh, w, x, z, ž** and **å** are only found in words from foreign languages, and they are pronounced as in the language of origin.

Diphthongs

In Finnish, diphthongs occur only in the first syllable of a word, except those ending in **-i**, where they can occur anywhere. They should be pronounced as a combination of the two vowel sounds represented by the spelling. The list below shows you how the Finnish diphthongs are written in our imitated pronunciation.

The first vowel is pronounced louder in the following diphthongs:

ai = ah^i	**iu** = i^{oo}	**äi** = æ^i
au = ah^{oo}	**oi** = oa^i	**äy** = æ^{ew}
ei = ay^i	**ou** = oa^{oo}	**öi** = ur^i
eu = ay^{oo}	**ui** = oo^i	**öy** = ur^{ew}
ey = ay^{ew}	**yi** = ew^i	

The second vowel is louder in:

ie = ^{i}ay	**uo** = ^{oo}oa	**yö** = ^{ew}ur

Double letters

Remember that in Finnish *every* letter is pronounced, therefore a letter written double is pronounced long. Thus, the **kk** in ku**kk**a should be pronounced like the two **k** sounds in the words thi**ck c**oat. Similarly the **aa** in k**aa**tua should be pronouced long (like **a** in English c**a**r). These distinctions are important, not least because ku**k**a has a different meaning to ku**kk**a and **k**atua a different meaning to **k**aatua.

Compound words

Finnish uses a great number of compound words. We have indicated the separate parts as in the examples below:

rauta|tie means 'railway', the compound being made up of *rauta* (iron) and *tie* (road); similarly: *maito|suklaa* (milk chocolate), *yli|opisto* (university).

This splitting of compound words has been done to help you with pronunciation. It will also provide you with an aid to stress, one of the distinctive features of Finnish.

Stress

A strong stress always falls on the first syllable of a word. In compound words, the first syllable of each part of the word receives a stress.

Pronunciation of the Finnish alphabet					
A	aa	**K**	kōa	**U**	ōo
B	bāy	**L**	æl	**V**	vāy
C	sāy	**M**	æm	**W**	**kak**sois-vāy
D	dāy	**N**	æn	**X**	æks
E	āy	**O**	ōa	**Y**	ēw
F	æf	**P**	pāy	**Z**	tsayt
G	gāy	**Q**	kōo	**Å**	**ruot**salainen ōa
H	hōa	**R**	ær	**Ä**	æ
I	ee	**S**	æs	**Ö**	ūr
J	yee	**T**	tāy		

Some basic expressions

Yes.	**Kyllä/Joo.**	**kew**llæ/yōō
No.	**Ei.**	ayⁱ
Please.	**Olkaa hyvä.**	**oal**kaa hew**v**æ
Thank you.	**Kiitos.**	**kee**toass
Thank you very much.	**Kiitos paljon.**	**kee**toass **pahl**yoan
That's all right/You're welcome.	**Ei kestä.**	ayⁱ **kays**tæ

Greetings *Tervehdyksiä*

Good morning.	**(Hyvää) huomenta.**	(hew**vææ**) h°oa**mayn**tah
Good afternoon.	**(Hyvää) päivää.**	(hew**vææ**) pæⁱ**vææ**
Good evening.	**(Hyvää) iltaa.**	(hew**vææ**) **il**taa
Good night.	**Hyvää yötä.**	hew**vææ** ^{ew}**ur**tæ
Goodbye/Bye-bye.	**Näkemiin/Hei hei.**	**næ**kaymeen/hayⁱ hayⁱ
See you later.	**Näkemiin/Hei sitten.**	**næ**kaymeen/ hayⁱ **sit**tayn
Hello/Hi!	**Hei/Terve!**	hayⁱ/**tayr**vay
This is Mr/Mrs/Miss ...	**Tässä on herra/rouva/neiti ...**	**tæs**sæ oan **hayr**rah/**roa**°°vah/**nay**ⁱti
How do you do? (Pleased to meet you.)	**Hyvää päivää. (Hauska tutustua.)**	hew**vææ** pæⁱ**vææ** (**hah**°°skah **too**toost°°a)
How are you?	**Mitä kuuluu?**	**mit**tæ kōōlōō
Very well, thanks. And you?	**Kiitos, hyvää. Entä teille/sinulle?***	**kee**toass hew**vææ ayn**tæ **tay**ⁱllay/**sin**noollay
How's life?	**Miten menee?**	**mit**tayn may**nā**y

* Many of the expressions in this book vary depending on whether they are used formally or informally. These are shown with the formal expression first followed by the informal.

Fine, thanks.	**Kiitos, hyvin.**	kee**toass hew**vin
I beg your pardon?	**Anteeksi?**	ahn**tay**ksi
Excuse me. (May I get past?)	**Anteeksi. (Pääsenkö ohi?)**	ahn**tay**ksi (p**ææ**saynkur oahhi)
Sorry!	**Anteeksi!**	ahn**tay**ksi

Questions *Kysymyksiä*

Where?	**Missä?**	**mis**sæ
How?	**Kuinka?**	**koo**'nkah
When?	**Milloin?**	**mil**loa'n
What?	**Mitä?**	**mit**tæ
Why?	**Miksi?**	**mik**si
Who?	**Kuka?**	**koo**kah
Which? (of these/of two)	**Mikä?/Kumpi?**	**mik**kæ/**koom**pi
Where is ...?	**Missä on ...?**	**mis**sæ oan
Where are ...?	**Missä ovat ...?**	**mis**sæ oavaht
Where can I find/ get ...?	**Mistä löydän ...?**	**mis**tæ **lur**ᵉʷdæn
How far?	**Kuinka kaukana?**	**koo**'nkah kah°°kanah
How long (time)?	**Kuinka kauan?**	**koo**'nkah kah°°ahn
How much/How many?	**Kuinka paljon/ Kuinka monta?**	**koo**'nkah **pahl**yoan/ **koo**'nkah **moan**tah
How much does this cost?	**Paljonko tämä maksaa?**	**pahl**yoankoa **tæ**mæ **mahk**saa
When does ... open/ close?	**Milloin ... aukeaa/ suljetaan?**	**mil**loa'n ... ah°°kayaa/ **sool**yaytaan
What do you call this/that in Finnish?	**Mitä tämä/tuo on suomeksi?**	**mit**tæ **tæ**mæ/t°°oa oan s°°oamayksi
What does this/that mean?	**Mitä tämä/tuo tarkoittaa?**	**mit**tæ **tæ**mæ/t°°oa **tahr**koa'ttaa

Do you speak ...? *Puhutteko ...?*

Do you speak English?	**Puhutteko englantia?**	poo**hoot**taykoa **ayng**lahntiah
Does anyone here speak English?	**Puhuuko kukaan täällä englantia?**	poo**hōō**koa **koo**kaan **tæl**læ **ayng**lahntiah
I don't speak (much) Finnish.	**En puhu (paljon) suomea.**	ayn **poo**hoo (**pahl**yoan) s°°oamayah

Could you speak more slowly?	**Voisitteko puhua hitaammin?**	voa'sittaykoa **poo**hooah hittaammin
Could you repeat that?	**Voisitteko toistaa sen?**	voa'sittaykoa **toa'**staa sayn
Could you spell it?	**Voisitteko tavata sen?**	voa'sittaykoa **tah**vahtah sayn
How do you pronounce this?	**Kuinka äännätte tämän?**	koo'nkah **ǣn**nættay sayn
Could you write it down, please?	**Voisitteko kirjoittaa sen?**	voa'sittaykoa **keer**yoa'ttaa sayn
Can you translate this for me?	**Voitteko kääntää tämän minulle?**	voa'ttaykoa **kǣn**tǣ tæmæn **min**noollay
Can you translate this for us?	**Voitteko kääntää tämän meille?**	voa'ttaykoa **kǣn**tǣ tæmæn **may'**llay
Could you point to the... in the book, please?	**Voisitteko osoittaa... kirjassa.**	voa'sittaykoa **oa**soa'ttaa... **keer**yahssah
word	**sanaa**	**sah**naa
phrase	**sanontaa**	**sah**noantaa
sentence	**lausetta**	**lah°°**sayttah
Just a moment.	**Hetkinen.**	**hayt**kinayn
I'll see if I can find it in this book.	**Katson, voinko löytää sen tästä kirjasta.**	**kaht**soan voa'nkoa **lur°ʷ**tǣ sayn **tæstæ keer**yastah
I understand.	**Ymmärrän.**	**ewm**mærræn
I don't understand.	**En ymmärrä.**	ayn **ewm**mærræ
Do you understand?	**Ymmärrättekö?**	**ewm**mærrættaykur

Can/May...? *Voiko/Saako...?*

Can I have...?	**Saanko...?**	**saahn**koa
Can we have...?	**Saammeko...?**	**saahm**maykoa
Can you show me...?	**Voitteko näyttää minulle...?**	voa'ttaykoa **næ°ʷ**ttǣ **min**noollay
I can't.	**En voi.**	ay'n voa'
Can you tell me...?	**Voitteko sanoa minulle...?**	voa'ttaykoa **sah**noah **min**noollay

Can you help me?	**Voitteko auttaa minua?**	voa'ttaykoa ah°°ttaa minnooah
Can I help you?	**Voinko auttaa teitä?**	voa'ankoa ah°°ttaa tay'tæ
Can you direct me to...?	**Voitteko opastaa minut...-n luo?**	voa'ttaykoa oapahstaa minnoot...-n l°°oa

Do you want...? *Haluatteko...?*

I'd like...	**Haluaisin...**	hahlooah'sin
We'd like...	**Haluaisimme...**	hahlooah'simmay
What do you want?	**Mitä teille saisi olla?**	mittæ tay'llay sah'si oallah
Could you give me...?	**Antaisitteko minulle...?**	ahntah'sittaykoa minnoollay
Could you bring me...?	**Toisitteko minulle...?**	toa'sittaykoa minnoollay
Could you show me...?	**Näyttäisittekö minulle...?**	næ°w ttæ'sittaykur minnoollay
I'm looking for...	**Haen...**	hahayn
I'm searching for...	**Etsin...**	aytsin
I'm hungry.	**Olen nälkäinen.**	oalayn nælkæ'nayn
I'm thirsty.	**Olen janoinen.**	oalayn jahnoa'nayn
I'm tired.	**Olen väsynyt.**	oalayn væsewnewt
I'm lost.	**Olen eksynyt.**	oalayn ayksewnewt
It's important.	**Se on tärkeä.**	say oan tærkayæ
It's urgent.	**Sillä on kiire.**	sillæ oan keeray

It is/There is... *Se on/On...*

It is...	**Se on...**	say oan
Is it...?	**Onko se...?**	oankoa say
It isn't...	**Se ei ole...**	say ay oalay
Here it is.	**Tässä se on.**	tæssæ say oan
Here they are.	**Tässä ne ovat.**	tæssæ nay oavaht
There it is.	**Tuolla se on.**	too°°llah say oan

There they are.	**Tuolla ne ovat.**	too°°llah nay oavaht
There is/There are ...	**On ...**	oan
Is there/Are there ...?	**Onko ...?**	oankoa
There isn't/aren't ...	**Ei ole ...**	ay¹ oalay
There isn't/aren't any.	**Ei ole yhtään.**	ay¹ oalay ewhtæn

It's ... *Se on ...*

beautiful/ugly	**kaunis/ruma**	kah°°nis/roomah
better/worse	**parempi/huonompi**	pahraympi/h°°oanoampi
big/small	**suuri/pieni**	soori/p¹ayni
cheap/expensive	**halpa/kallis**	hahlpah/kahlliss
early/late	**aikainen/myöhäinen**	ah¹ka¹nayn/m°°urhæ¹nayn
easy/difficult	**helppo/vaikea**	haylppoa/vah¹kayah
free (vacant)/occupied	**vapaa/varattu**	vahpaa/vahrahttoo
full/empty	**täysi/tyhjä**	tæᵉʷsi/tewhyæ
good/bad	**hyvä/huono**	hewvæ/h°°oanoa
heavy/light	**raskas/kevyt**	rahskahs/kayvewt
here/there	**täällä/tuolla**	tǣllæ/t°°oallah
hot/cold	**kuuma/kylmä**	kōōmah/kewlmæ
near/far	**lähellä/kaukana**	læhayllæ/kah°°kahnah
next/last	**seuraava/viimeinen**	say°°raavah/veemay¹nayn
old/new	**vanha/uusi**	vahnhah/ōōssi
old/young	**vanha/nuori**	vahnhah/n°°oari
open/shut	**avoin/suljettu**	ahvoa¹n/soolyayttoo
quick/slow	**nopea/hidas**	noapayah/hiddahss
right/wrong	**oikea/väärä**	oa¹kaya/vǣræ

Quantities *Määriä*

a little/a lot	**vähän/paljon**	væhæn/pahlyoan
few/a few	**harvat/muutamat**	hahrvaht/mootahmaht
much	**paljon**	pahlyoan
many	**monta**	moantah
more(than)/less(than)	**enemmän (kuin)/vähemmän (kuin)**	aynaymmæn (koo¹n)/væhaymmæn (koo¹n)
enough/too	**tarpeeksi/liiaksi**	tahrpāyksi/leeahksi
some/(not) any	**hieman/ei yhtään**	hiᵉʸmahn/ay¹ ewhtæn

A few more useful words *Muutama hyödyllinen sana lisää*

above	-n yllä/yli	-n ewllæ/ewli
after (time)	-n jälkeen	-n jælkāyn
and	ja	yah
at	-n kohdalla	-n koahdahllah
before (time)	ennen -a	aynnayn -a
behind	-n takana/taakse	-n tahkahnah/taaksay
below	-n alla/alle	-n ahllah/ahllay
between	-n välissä/välillä	-n vælissæ/vælillæ
but	mutta	moottah
down	alas/alhaalla	ahlahs/ahlhaallah
downstairs	alakerrassa	ahlahkayrrassah
during	aikana	ah^ikahnah
for	-n suuntaan/-n sijaan	-n soontaan/-n siyyaan
from	-n suunnasta	-n soonnahstah
in	-n sisässä/-llä	-n sissæssæ/-llæ
inside	sisään/sisälle	sissāēn/sissællay
near	lähellä/lähelle	læhayllæ/læhayllay
never	ei koskaan	ay^i koaskaan
next to	vieressä	v^iayrayssæ
none	ei yhtään	ay^i ewhtāēn
not	ei	ay^i
nothing	ei mitään	ay^i mittāēn
now	nyt	newt
on	-n päällä/päälle	-n pāēllæ/pāēllay
only	vain	vah^in
or	tai	tah^i
outside	ulkona/ulos	oolkoanah/ooloas
perhaps	ehkä	ayhkæ
since	alkaen	ahlkahayn
soon	pian	p^iahn
then	sitten	sittayn
through	läpi	læpi
to	-n kohdalle	-n koahdayllay
too (also)	myös	m^ewurss
towards	-a kohti	-a koahti
under	alla/alle	ahllah/ahllay
until	asti	ahsti
up	ylös/ylhäällä	ewlurss/ewlhāēllæ
upstairs	yläkerrassa	ewlækayrrahssah
very	tosi	toasi
with	-n kanssa	-n kahnssah
without	ilman	ilmahn
yet	vielä	v^iaylæ

Arrival

Passport control *Passin|tarkastus*

Here's my passport.	**Tässä on passini.**	tæssæ oan **pahs**sini
I'll be staying...	**Viivyn...**	veevewn
a few days	**muutamia päiviä**	mōōtahmiah pæ'viæ
a week	**viikon**	veekoan
2 weeks	**kaksi viikkoa**	kahksi veekkoah
a month	**kuukauden**	kookah°°dayn
I don't know yet.	**En tiedä vielä.**	ayn t'aydæ v'aylæ
I'm here on holiday.	**Olen täällä lomalla.**	oalayn tǣllæ loamahllah
I'm here on business.	**Olen täällä liike|-asioissa.**	oalayn tǣllæ leekayahsioa'ssah
I'm just passing through.	**Olen vain läpi-|kulku|matkalla.**	oalayn vah'n læpikoolkoomahtkahllah

If things become difficult:

I'm sorry, I don't understand.	**Anteeksi, en ymmärrä.**	ahntāyksi ayn ewmmærræ
Does anyone here speak English?	**Puhuuko kukaan täällä englantia?**	poohōōkoa kookaan tǣllæ aynglahnt'ah

> **TULLI**
> CUSTOMS

After collecting your baggage at the airport (*lentokenntä—**layn**toa**kayn**tæ*) you have a choice: use the green exit if you have nothing to declare. Or leave via the red exit if you have items to declare (in excess of those allowed).

tullattavia tavaroita	**ei tullattavaa**
goods to declare	nothing to declare

The chart below shows what you can bring in duty-free:*

	Cigarettes	Cigars	Tobacco	Spirits	Wine
European residents	200	or	250 g. of other tobacco products	1 l. and 1 l.	
Non-European residents	400	or	500 g. of other tobacco products	1 l. and 1 l.	

I have nothing to declare.	**Minulla ei ole mitään tullattavaa.**	minnoollah ayͥ oalay mittᾱn toollahttahvaa
I have...	**Minulla on...**	minnoollah oan
a carton of cigarettes a bottle of whisky	**kartonki savukkeita pullo viskiä**	kartoanki sahvookkayͥtah poolloa viskiæ
It's for my personal use.	**Se on henkilö|koh-taiseen käyttööni.**	say oan haynkillurkoahtahͥssᾱyn kæᵉᵂttūrni
It's a gift.	**Se on lahja.**	say oan lahhyah
Your passport, please.	**Passinne, olkaa hyvä.**	pahssinnay oalkaa hewvæ

Onko teillä mitään tullattavaa?   Do you have anything to declare?

Avatkaa tämä laukku.   Please open this bag.

Teidän täytyy maksaa tullia tästä.   You'll have to pay duty on this.

Onko teillä lisää matka\|tavaroita?   Do you have any more luggage?

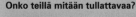

* All allowances are subject to change without notice

Baggage—Porter *Kantaja*

In the absence of porters, you'll find plenty of luggage trolleys at the airport. You might find porters at the railway stations, but they are becoming scarce.

Porter!	**Kantaja!**	**kahn**tahyah
Please take (this/my)...	**Olkaa hyvä ja ottakaa (tämä/minun)...**	**oal**kaa **hewv**æ ya **oat**tahkaa (**tæm**æ/**min**noon)
luggage	**matka|tavarani**	**mahtkahtah**vahrani
suitcase	**matka|laukku|ni**	**mahtkahlah°°**kkooni
(travelling) bag	**(matka)laukku|ni**	(**mahtkah**)**lah°°**kkooni
That one is mine.	**Tuo on minun.**	t°°oa oan **min**noon
Take this luggage...	**Ottakaa tämä laukku...**	**oat**tahkaa **tæm**æ **lah°°**kkoo
to the bus	**bussille**	**boos**sillay
to the luggage lockers	**säilytys|lokeroille**	**sæi**lewtews**loa**kayroaillay
to the taxi	**taksille**	**tahk**sillay
How much is that?	**Paljonko tämä maksaa?**	**pahl**yoankoa **tæm**æ **mahk**saa
There's one piece missing.	**Yksi laukku puuttuu.**	**ewk**si **lah°°**kkoo poottoo
Where are the luggage trolleys (carts)?	**Missä on työntö|kärryjä?**	**mis**sæ oan t°ʷurnturkærrewyæ

Changing money *Rahan\|vaihto*

Where's the currency exchange (office)?	**Missä on valuutan vaihto (toimisto)?**	**mis**sæ oan **vah**lootahn **vah**ʰtoa (**toa**ʰmistoa)
Can you change these traveller's cheques (checks)?	**Voitteko vaihtaa nämä matka|sekit?**	**voa**ʰttaykoa **vah**ʰtaa **næm**æ **mahtkah**saykit
I want to change some dollars/pounds.	**Haluaisin vaihtaa dollareita/puntia.**	**hah**looaiʰsin **vah**ʰtaa **doal**lahrayiʰtah/**poon**tiah
Can you change this into Finnish marks?	**Voitteko vaihtaa tämän Suomen markoiksi?**	**voa**ʰttaykoa **vah**ʰtaa **tæm**æn s°°oamayn **mahr**koaiʰksi
What's the exchange rate?	**Mikä on vaihto|kurssi?**	**mik**kæ oan **vah**ʰtoa**koors**si

BANK-CURRENCY, see page 129

Where is...? *Missä on...?*

Where is the...?	**Missä on...?**	missæ oan
booking office	**lippu|myymälä**	lippoomew̄mælæ
duty (tax)-free shop	**vero|vapaa myy-mälä**	vayroavahpaa mew̄mælæ
newsstand	**lehti|myymälä**	layhtimew̄mælæ
restaurant	**ravintola**	rahvintoalah
How do I get to...?	**Miten pääsen... -n/-lle?**	mittayn pǣsayn...-n/-llay
Is there a bus into town?	**Meneekö kaupun-kiin bussia?**	maynāykur kah°°poonkeen boossiah
Where can I get a taxi?	**Mistä voin saada taksin?**	mistæ voa'n saadah tahksin
Where can I hire (rent) a car?	**Mistä voin vuok-rata auton?**	mistæ voa'n v°°oakrahtah ah°°toan

Hotel reservation *Hotellin varaus*

Do you have a hotel guide (directory)?	**Onko teillä hotelli|opasta?**	oankoa tay'llæ hoatayllioapahstah
Could you reserve a room for me?	**Voisitteko varata minulle huoneen.**	voa'sittaykoa vahrahtah minnoollay h°°oanāyn
in the centre	**keskustassa**	kayskoostahstah
near the railway station	**lähellä rauta|tie|asemaa**	læhayllæ rah°°taht'ayahsaymaa
a single room	**yhden hengen huone**	ewhdayn hayngayn h°°oanay
a double room	**kahden hengen huone**	kahhdayn hayngayn h°°oanay
not too expensive	**ei liian kallis**	ay' leeahn kahlliss
Where is the hotel/ guesthouse?	**Missä on hotelli/ matkustaja|koti?**	missæ oan hoataylli/ mahtkoostahjahkoati
Do you have a street map?	**Onko teillä kau-pungin karttaa?**	oankoa tay'llæ kah°°poongin kahrttaa

HOTEL/ACCOMMODATION, see page 22

Car hire (rental) *Auton vuokraus*

All the major international agencies are represented in Finland. To hire a car you must show a valid driving licence from your country of residence. The minimum age varies from 19 to 23 and one year's driving experience is required. Most companies require a cash deposit but this is often waived for holders of major credit cards.

I'd like to hire (rent) a car.	**Haluaisin vuokrata auton.**	hahlooah'sin v°°oakrahtah ah°°toan
small	**pieni**	p'ayni
medium-sized	**keski|kokoinen**	kayskikoakoanayn
large	**suuri**	soori
automatic	**automaatti| vaihteella**	ah°°toamaattivah'htāyllah
I'd like it for a day/a week.	**Haluaisin sen päiväksi/viikoksi.**	hahl°°ah'sin sayn pæ'væksi/veekoaksi
Are there any weekend arrangements?	**Onko viikon|lopuksi eri tarjouksia?**	oankoa veekoanloapooksi ayri tahryoa°°ksiah
Do you have any special rates?	**Onko teillä mitään erikois|hintoja?**	oankoa tay'llæ mittǣn ayrikkoa'shintoayah
What's the charge per day/week?	**Mikä on päivä|maksu/viikko|maksu?**	mikkæ oan pæ'væmahksoo/veekkoamahksoo
Is mileage included?	**Kuinka suuri kilo|metri|määrä sisältyy hintaan?**	koo'nkah soori killoamaytrimǣræ sissæltew hintaan
What's the charge per kilometre?	**Mikä on kilo|metri|maksu?**	mikkæ oan killoamaytrimahksoo
I'd like to leave the car in...	**Haluaisin jättää auton...-n/-lle**	hahlooah'sin yættǣ ah°°toan...-n/-llay
I'd like full insurance.	**Haluaisin täyden|vakuutuksen.**	hahlooah'sin tæ°ʷdaynvahkootooksayn
How much is the deposit?	**Kuinka suuri on ennakko|maksu?**	koo'nkah sōōri oan aynnahkkoahmahksoo
I have a credit card.	**Minulla on luotto|kortti.**	minnoollah oan l°°oattoakoaartti
Here's my driving licence.	**Tässä on ajo|kortti|ni.**	tæssæ oan ahyoakoaarttini

CAR, see page 75

Taxi *Taksi*

Taxis are easy to spot as they all have a yellow *Taxi* or *Taksi* sign. If this sign is lit the cab is available. All taxis have meters and a surcharge is added at weekends and at night. Drivers don't expect a tip but a few extra coins for good service is customary.

Where can I get a taxi?	**Mistä voin saada taksin?**	mistæ voa'n saadah tahksin
Where is the taxi rank (stand)?	**Missä on taksi|asema?**	missæ oan tahksiahsaymah
Could you get me a taxi?	**Voitteko hankkia minulle taksin?**	voa'ttaykoa hahnkkiah minnoollay tahksin
What's the fare to...?	**... – Mitä maksaa ajaa sinne?**	mittæ mahksaa ahyaa sinnay
How far is it to...?	**Kuinka kaukana on...?**	koo'nkah kah°°kahnah oan
Take me to...	**Viekää minut...**	v'aykææ minnoot
this address	**tähän osoitteeseen**	tæhæn oasoa'ttæyssæyn
the airport	**lento|kentälle**	layntoakayntællay
the town centre	**kaupungin keskustaan**	kah°°poongin kayskoostaan
the... Hotel	**hotelli...-n/-lle**	hoataylli...-n/-llay
the railway station	**rauta|tie|asemalle**	rah°°taht'ayahsaymahllay
Turn... at the next corner.	**Kääntykää... seuraavassa kulmassa.**	kæntewkææ... say°°raahvassah koolmahssah
left/right	**vasemmalle/ oikealle**	vahsaymmallay/ oa'kayahllay
Go straight ahead.	**Ajakaa suoraan eteen|päin.**	ahjahkaa s°°oaraan aytāynpæin
Please stop here.	**Pysähtykää tässä.**	pewssæhtewkæ tæssæ
I'm in a hurry.	**Minulla on kiire.**	minnoollah oan keeray
Could you drive more slowly?	**Voisitteko ajaa hitaammin?**	voa'sittaykoa ahyaa hittaammin
Could you help me carry my luggage?	**Voisitteko auttaa kantamisessa?**	voa'sittaykoa ah°°ttaa kahntahmissayssah
Could you wait for me?	**Voitteko odottaa?**	voa'ttaykoa oadoattaa
I'll be back in 10 minutes.	**Tulen takaisin kymmenessä minuutissa.**	toolayn tahkah'sin kewmmaynayssæ minnoottissah

TIPPING, see inside back-cover

Hotel—Other accommodation

Finnish hotels maintain high standards. During the last few years many modern, tastefully furnished hotels and motels have been built. In a typical hotel (*hotelli*) you're likely to find not only a *sauna* but a swimming pool as well. Finnish Tourist Board offices in Finland and abroad supply the brochure *Hotels*, which details all the facilities provided.

motelli
(moataylli)
Accommodation for motorists, all modern and of a very good standard.

kongressi|hotelli
(koangrayssihoataylli)
These are modern, big hotels with a special emphasis on congress facilities and other services.

kesä|hotelli
(kaysæhoataylli)
These are usually student living quarters which open as hotels in the summer months (June-August); thus the name 'summer hotels'. Comfortable accommodation in modern buildings at attractive rates.

hospiz, hospitsi
(hoaspitsi)
Small hotels operated by the YMCA or YWCA.

matkustaja|koti
(mahtkoostahjahkoati)
Small, modest hotels providing basic accomodation at affordable prices.

retkeily|maja
(raytkay'lewmahjah)
Youth hostels open during the summer months only. Despite the name they welcome visitors of any age (it is worth checking with individual hostels if children are allowed). Most require membership of a national youth hostel organisation, however non-members are admitted upon payment of a small surcharge. Foreigners can buy a visitor's card from any youth hostel in Finland.

loma|kylä
(loamahkewlæ)
Finland has more than 200 holiday villages consisting of self-contained bungalows in rustic settings. Some are open all year round and are excellent for winter holiday stays.

mökki
(murkki)
Cabins found on well-equipped camping sites.

maatalo|majoitus (maatahloamah yoa'tooss)	A number of farmhouses take in guests, who have their meals with the family on a full-board, half-board or bed-and-breakfast basis and can participate in the work of the farm if they wish.	
täysi|hoitola (tæ^{ew}ssihoa'toalah)	These boarding houses may offer specialized holidays such as sports, health cures etc.	
kesä|mökki (kaysæmurkki)	Summer cottages are available for rent through the local tourist office.	

Can you recommend a hotel/guesthouse?	**Voitteko suositella hotellia/matkus-taja|kotia?**	voa'ttaykoa s°°oasittayllah hoataylliah/ mahtkoostahjah|koatiah
Are there any flats (apartments) vacant?	**Onko yhtään huo-neistoa vapaana?**	oankoa ewht^æn h°°oanay'stoaah vahpaanah

Checking in—Reception *Ilmoittautuminen—Vastaanotto*

My name is...	**Nimeni on...**	nimayni oan
I have a reservation.	**Minulla on varaus.**	minnoollah oan vahra°°s
We've reserved 2 rooms.	**Olemme varanneet kaksi huonetta.**	oalaymmay vahrahnnayt kahksi h°°oanayttah
Here's the confir-mation.	**Tässä on vahvistus.**	tæssæ oan vahhvistooss
Do you have any vacancies?	**Onko teillä vapaita huoneita?**	oankoa tay'llæ vahpah'tah h°°oanay'tah
I'd like a...	**Haluaisin...**	hahlooah'sin
single room	**yhden hengen huoneen**	ewhdayn hayngayn h°°oanāyn
double room	**kahden hengen huoneen**	kahhdayn hayngayn h°°oanāyn
We'd like a room...	**Haluaisimme huo-neen,...**	hahlooah'simmay h°°oanāyn
with twin beds	**jossa on kaksi vuodetta**	yaossah oan kahksi v°°oadayttah
with a double bed	**jossa on kaksois|vuode**	yaossah oan kahksoa'sv°°oaday
with a bath	**jossa on kylpy|huone**	yaossah oan kewlpewh°°oanay
with a shower	**jossa on suihku**	yaossah oan soo'hkoo

CHECKING OUT, see page 31

with a balcony	**jossa on parveke**	yoassah oan pahrvaykay
with a view	**josta on näkö|ala**	yoastaah oan nækurahlah
at the front	**joka on julki|sivun puolella**	yoakah oan yoolkisivoon p^{oo}oalayllah
at the back	**joka on taka|osassa**	yokah oan tahkahoassahssah
It must be quiet.	**Sen täytyy olla hiljainen.**	sayn tæ^{ew}t̄ew oallah hilyah'nayn
Is there...?	**Onko...**	oankoa
air conditioning	**ilmastointia**	ilmahstoa'ntiah
a conference room	**neuvottelu|huonetta**	nay^{oo}voattaylooh^{oo}oa nayttah
a laundry service	**pyykki|palvelua**	pēwkkipahlvaylooah
a private toilet	**oma wc**	oamah vāysāy
a radio/television in the room	**huoneessa radio/ televisio**	h^{oo}oanayssah rahdioa/ taylayvissioa
a sauna	**saunaa**	sah^{oo}naa
a swimming pool	**uima-allasta**	oo'mahahllahstah
hot water	**kuuma vesi**	kōomah vayssi
room service	**huone|palvelua**	h^{oo}oanaypahlvaylooah
running water	**juokseva vesi**	y^{oo}oaksayvah vayssi
Could you put an extra bed/a cot in the room?	**Voitteko tuoda huoneeseen lisä-sängyn/lapsen sängyn?**	voa'ttaykoa t^{oo}oadah h^{oo}oanāysāyn lissæsængewn/lahpsayn sængewn

How much? *Paljonko?*

What's the price...?	**Mitä hinta on...**	mittæ hintah oan
per day	**päivältä**	pæ'væltæ
per week	**viikolta**	veekoaltah
for bed and breakfast	**aamiaisen kanssa**	aamiah'sayn kahnssah
excluding meals	**ilman aterioita**	ilmahn ahtayrioa'tah
for full board (A.P.)	**täysi|hoidosta**	tæ^{ew}sihoa'doastah
for half board (M.A.P.)	**puoli|hoidosta**	p^{oo}oalihoa'doastah
Does that include...?	**Sisältyykö siihen...?**	sissæltēwkur seehayn
breakfast	**aamianen**	aamiah'nayn
service	**palvelu|palkkio**	pahlvayloopahlkkioa
value-added tax (sales tax)	**liike|vaihto|vero**	leekayvah'htoavayroa
Is there any reduction for children?	**Onko lapsille alennusta?**	oankoa lahpsillay ahlaynnoostah

NUMBERS, see page 147

Do you charge for the baby?	**Veloitatteko pikku|lapsesta?**	vayloa'tahttaykoa pikkoolahpsaystah
That's too expensive.	**Se on liian kallista.**	say oan leeahn kahllistah
Do you have anything cheaper?	**Onko teillä mitään halvempaa?**	oankoa tay'llæ mittæn hahlvaympaa

How long? *Kuinka kauan?*

We'll be staying...	**Viivymme...**	veevewmmay
overnight only	**vain yhden yön**	vah'n ewhdayn ew'urn
a few days	**muutamia päiviä**	mōōtahmiah pæ'viæ
a week (at least)	**(vähintään) viikon**	(væhintæn) veekoan
I don't know yet.	**En tiedä vielä.**	ayn t'aydæ v'aylæ

Decision *Päätös*

May I see the room?	**Saanko nähdä huoneen?**	saankoa næhdæ hᵒᵒoanāyn
That's fine. I'll take it.	**Tämä on hyvä. Otan sen.**	tæmæ oan hewvæ oatahn sayn
No. I don't like it.	**Ei. En pidä siitä.**	ay' ayn pidæ seettæ
It's too...	**Se on liian...**	say oan leeahn

cold/hot	**kylmä/kuuma**	kewlmæ/koomah
dark/small	**pimeä/pieni**	pimm'ᵉ'æ/p'ayni
noisy	**meluisa**	mayloo'sah

| I asked for a room with a bath. | **Pyysin huonetta, jossa on kylpy\|huone.** | pēwsin hᵒᵒnayttah yoassah oan kewlpewhᵒᵒoanay |
| Do you have anything...? | **Onko teillä mitään...?** | oankoa tay'llæ mittæn |

better	**parempaa**	pahraympaa
bigger	**suurempaa**	sōōraympaa
cheaper	**halvempaa**	hahlvaympaa
quieter	**rauhallisempaa**	rahᵒᵒhahllissaympaa

| Do you have a room with a better view? | **Onko teillä huonetta, josta on parempi näkö\|ala?** | oankoa tay'llæ hᵒᵒoanayttah yaostah oan pahraympi nækurahlah |

Registration *Kirjoittautuminen*

Upon arrival at a hotel or guesthouse you'll be asked to fill in a registration form (*matkustaja|kortti*—**maht**koostahyah-**koart**ti).

Suku|nimi/Etu|nimi	Name/First name
Koti|kaupunki/Katu/Numero	Home town/Street/Number
Kansallisuus/Ammatti	Nationality/Occupation
Syntymä|aika/|-paikka	Date/Place of birth
Tulossa/Menossa	Coming from.../Going to...
Passin numero	Passport number
Paikka/Päivä	Place/Date
Alle|kirjoitus	Signature

What does this mean?	**Mitä tämä tarkoittaa?**	mittæ tæmæ tahrkoa'ttaa

Saanko nähdä passinne.	May I see your passport?
Voisitteko täyttää tämän matkustaja|kortin.	Would you mind filling in this registration form?
Allekirjoittakaa tähän.	Please sign here.
Kuinka kauan viivytte?	How long will you be staying?

What's my room number?	**Mikä on huonee|ni numero?**	mikkæ oan h°°oanayni noomayroa
Will you have our luggage sent up?	**Toimitatteko matka|tavaramme ylös?**	toa'mittahttaykoa mahtkahtahvahrahmmay ewlurss
Where can I park my car?	**Minne voin pysäköidä auto|ni?**	minnay voa'n pewsækur'dæ ah°°toani
Does the hotel have a garage?	**Onko hotellilla auto|tallia?**	oankoa hoatayllillah ah°°toatahlliah
I'd like to leave this in the hotel safe.	**Haluaisin jättää tämän hotellin talle|lokeroon.**	hahlooah'sin jættæ tæmæn hoatayllin tahllayloakayroan

TELLING THE TIME, see page 153

Hotel staff *Hotellin henkilökunta*

hall porter	**portieeri**	**poart**i°**yri**
maid	**siivooja**	**see**voayah
manager	**johtaja**	**yoh**tahyah
porter	**kantaja**	**kahn**tahyah
receptionist	**vastaan|otto**	**vahs**taan**oatt**oa
switchboard operator	**keskus**	**kays**kooss
waiter	**tarjoilija**	**tahr**yoa'**liy**ah
waitress	**tarjoilija**	**tahr**yoa'**liy**ah

General requirements *Yleisiä tarpeita*

The key to room..., please.	**Avain huoneeseen numero..., kiitos.**	ah**vah**'n h°°oan**ays**sayn noomayroa... **keet**oass
Could you wake me at... please?	**Voisitteko herättää minut kello...?**	voa'**sitt**aykoa hayr**ætt**æ minnoot **kayl**loa
When is breakfast/ lunch/dinner served?	**Mihin aikaan tarjoillaan aamiainen/ lounas/päivällinen?**	**mih**in ah'kaan tahryoa'**llaan aam**iah'nayn/ **loa**°°nahs/ pæ'**væll**inayn
May we have breakfast in our room, please?	**Voisimmeko saada aamiaisen huoneeseen?**	voa'**simm**aykoa **saad**ah **aam**iah'ayn h°°oan**ays**sayn
Is there a bath on this floor?	**Onko tässä kerroksessa kylpy|huonetta?**	**oan**koa **tæss**æ **kayr**roaksayssa **kewl**pewh°°oanayttah
What's the voltage?	**Mikä on jännite?**	**mikk**æ oan **yæn**nittay
Where's the shaver socket (outlet)?	**Missä on parran|ajo|koneen pisto|rasia?**	**miss**æ oan **pahr**rahnahyoakoan**ayn pist**oarahsiah
Can you find me a...?	**Voitteko hankkia minulle...?**	voa'**ttay**koa **hahnkk**iah **minn**oollay
babysitter	**lapsen|vahdin**	**lahps**aynvahhdin
secretary	**sihteerin**	**sihht**ayrin
typewriter	**kirjoidiskone**	**keer**yoa'**diskoan**ay
May I have a/an/ some...?	**Voisinko saada...**	voa'**sink**oa **saad**ah
ashtray	**tuhka|kupin**	**toohk**ah**koop**in
bath towel	**kylpy|pyyhkeen**	**kewl**pewp_ewh_**kayn**
(extra) blanket	**(lisä-) peiton**	(**lees**æ-) **pay**'toan
envelopes	**kirje|kuoria**	**keer**yayk°°**oar**iah
(more) hangers	**(lisää) vaate|ripustimia**	(**lees**æ) **vaat**ayrip**poost**immiah

BREAKFAST, see page 40

hot-water bottle	**kuuma|vesi|pullon**	koomahvayssipoolloan
ice/ice cubes	**jäitä/jää|kuutioita**	yæʰtæ/yækootioaʰtah
needle and thread	**neulan ja lankaa**	nayᵒᵒlahn ya lahnkaa
(extra) pillow	**(lisä-) tyynyn**	(leesæ-) tēwnewn
reading lamp	**luku|lampun**	lookoolahmpoon
soap	**saippuaa**	sahʹppooaa
writing paper	**kirjoitus|paperia**	keeryoaʹtoospahpayriah
Where's the...?	**Missä on...?**	missæ oan
bathroom	**kylpy|huone**	kewlpewhᵒᵒoanay
dining-room	**ruoka|sali**	rᵒᵒoakahsahli
emergency exit	**hätä|ulos|käynti**	hætæooloaskæᵉʷnti
hairdresser's	**kampaaja**	kahmpaayah
lift (elevator)	**hissi**	hissi
Where are the toilets?	**Missä ovat WC:t?**	missæ oavaht vāysāyt

Telephone—Post (Mail) *Puhelin—Posti*

Can you get me Kuusamo 123-45-67?	**Saanko Kuusamo 123-45-67.**	saankoa koosahmoa 123-45-67
Do you have any stamps?	**Onko teillä posti|merkkejä?**	oankoa tayʹllæ poastimayrkkayyæ
Would you post this for me, please?	**Voisitteko postittaa tämän?**	voaʹsittaykoa poastittaa tæmæn
Are there any letters for me?	**Onko minulle kirjeitä?**	oankoa minnoollay keeryayʹttæ
Are there any messages for me?	**Onko minulle viestejä?**	oankoa minnoollay vʹaystayyæ
How much is my telephone bill?	**Kuinka suuri on puhelin|laskuni?**	kooinkah soori oan poohaylinlahskooni

Difficulties *Vaikeuksia*

The... doesn't work.	**... ei toimi.**	ayʹ toaʹmi
air conditioning	**ilmastointi**	ilmahstoaʹnti
bidet	**bidet**	biddāy
fan	**tuuletin**	tōolaytin
heating	**lämmitys**	læmmittewss
light	**valo**	vahloa
radio	**radio**	rahdioa
television	**televisio**	taylayvissioa
The tap (faucet) is dripping.	**Vesi|hana tippuu.**	vayssihahnah tippoo
There's no hot water.	**Ei tule kuumaa vettä.**	ay toolay kōomaa vayttæ

POST OFFICE AND TELEPHONE, see page 132

The washbasin is blocked.	Pesu|allas on tukossa.	**payss**ooahllahs oan tookoassah
The window is jammed.	**Ikkuna** on juuttunut kiinni.	ikkoonah oan jōottoonoot keenni
The curtains are stuck.	**Verho** on juuttunut kiinni.	vayrhoa oan jōottoonoot keenni
The bulb is burned out.	**Lamppu** on palanut.	lahmppoo oan pahlahnoot
My bed hasn't been made up.	**Vuodettani** ei ole sijattu.	v°°oadayttahni ay¹ oalay siyyahttoo
The... is broken.	**... on rikki.**	oan rikki
blind	**kaihdin**	kah¹hdin
lamp	**lamppu**	lahmppoo
plug (electricity)	**pistoke**	pistoakay
plug (water)	**tulppa**	toolppah
shutter	**ikkuna|luukku**	ikkoonahlookkoo
switch	**katkaisija**	kahtkah¹siyah
Can you get it repaired?	**Voitteko korjata sen?**	voa¹ttaykoa koaryahtah sayn

Laundry—Dry cleaner's *Pesula*

I'd like these clothes...	**Haluaisin nämä vaatteet...**	hahlooah¹sin næmæ vaattayt
cleaned	**puhdistukseen**	poohdistōoksäyn
dry-cleaned	**kuiva|pesuun**	koo¹vahpaysōon
ironed	**silitykseen**	sillittewksäyn
pressed	**prässäykseen**	præssæ°ʷksäyn
washed	**pesuun**	paysoon
When will they be ready?	**Milloin ne ovat valmiit?**	milloa¹n nay oavaht vahlmeet
I need them...	**Tarvitsen ne...**	tahrvitsayn nay
today	**tänään**	tænǣn
tonight	**tänä iltana**	tænæ iltahnah
tomorrow	**huomenna**	h°°oamaynnah
before Friday	**ennen perjantaita**	aynnayn payryahntah¹tah
Can you... this?	**Voitteko... tämän?**	voa¹ttaykoa... tæmæn
mend	**korjata**	koaryahtah
patch	**paikata**	pah¹kahtah
stitch	**ommella**	oammayllah
Can you sew on this button?	**Voitteko ommella tämän napin kiinni?**	voa¹ttaykoa oammayllah tæmæn nahpin keenni
Can you get this stain out?	**Voitteko poistaa tämän tahran?**	voa¹ttaykoa poa¹staa tæmæn tahhrahn

Hotelli

Is my laundry ready?	**Onko pyykkini valmis?**	oankoa pewkkini vahlmiss
This isn't mine.	**Tämä ei ole minun.**	tæmæ ay¹ oalay minnoon
There's something missing.	**Jotain puuttuu.**	yatah'n pōōttōō
There's a hole in this.	**Tässä on reikä.**	tæssæ oan ray¹kæ

Hairdresser—Barber *Kampaaja—Parturi*

Is there a hairdresser/ beauty salon in the hotel?	**Onko hotellissa kampaajaa/kauneushoitolaa?**	oankoa hoatayllissah kahmpaajaa/ kah°°nayooshoa¹toalaa
Can I make an appointment for Thursday?	**Voinko varata ajan torstaiksi?**	voa¹nkoa vahrahtah ahyahn toarstah¹ksi
I'd like a cut and blow dry.	**Haluaisin leikkauksen ja föönauksen.**	hahlooah¹sin lay¹kkah°°ksayn yah fūrnah°°ksayn
I'd like a haircut, please.	**Saisinko tukanleikkuun?**	sah¹sinkoa tookahnlay¹kkōōn
blow-dry	**föönaus**	furnah°°ss
colour rinse	**väri|huuhtelu**	værihōōhtayloo
dye	**värjäys**	væryæ°°ss
face pack	**kasvo|naamio**	kahsvoanaammioa
hair gel	**hius|geeli**	hi°°sghāyli
highlights	**raidat**	rah¹daht
manicure	**käsien hoito/manikyyri**	kæs¹ayn hoa¹toa/ mahnikkēwri
perm(anent)	**permanentti**	payrmahnayntti
setting lotion	**kampaus|neste**	kahmpah°°snaystay
shampoo and set	**pesu ja kampaus**	paysoo yah kahmpah°°ss
with a fringe (bangs)	**otsa|tukka**	oatsahtookkah
I'd like a shampoo for... hair.	**Haluaisin shampoon... hiuksille.**	hahlooah¹sin shahmpōan...h¹ooksille
normal/dry/greasy (oily)	**normaaleille/kuiville/rasvaisille**	noarmaalay¹llay/koo¹villay/ rahsvah¹sillay
Do you have a colour chart?	**Onko teillä väri|karttaa?**	oankoa tay¹llæ værikahrttaa
Don't cut it too short.	**Älkää leikatko liian lyhyeksi.**	ælkææ lay¹kahtkoa leeahn lewh°°ayksi
A little more off the...	**Vähän lyhyemmäksi...**	væhæn lewh°°aymmæksi
back	**takaa**	tahkaa
neck	**niskasta**	niskahstah

DAYS OF THE WEEK, see page 151

sides	sivuilta	sivvoo'ltah
top	päältä	pæltæ
I don't want any hairspray.	En halua mitään hius|lakkaa.	ayn hahl°°ah mittæn hi°°uslahkkaa
I'd like a shave.	Haluaisin parran|ajon.	hahlooah'sin pahrrahnahyoan
Would you trim my..., please?	Voisitteko siistiä....	voa'sittaykoa seestiæ
beard	parta|ni	pahrtahni
moustache	viiksiä|ni	veeksiæni
sideboards (sideburns)	pulisonki|ni	poolissoankinni

Checking out *Lähtö*

May I have my bill, please?	Saisinko lasku?	sah'sinkoa lahskoo
I'm leaving early in the morning.	Lähden aikaisin aamulla.	læhdayn ah'kah'sin aamoollah
Please have my bill ready.	Kirjoittaisitteko laskuni valmiiksi.	keeryoa'ttah'sittaykoa lahskooni vahlmeeksi
We'll be checking out around noon.	Lähdemme puolen|päivän aikoihin.	læhdaymmay p°°oalaynpæivæn ah'koa'hin
I must leave at once.	Minun täytyy lähteä heti.	minnoon tæ°wtew læhtayæ hayti
Is everything included?	Sisältyykö siihen kaikki?	sissæltewkur seehhayn kah'kki
Can I pay by credit card?	Voinko maksaa luotto|kortilla?	voa'nkoa mahksaa l°°oattoakoartilla
I think there's a mistake in the bill.	Tässä laskussa taitaa olla virhe.	tæssæ lahskoossah tah'taa oallah virhay
Can you get us a taxi?	Voitteko hankkia meille taksin?	voa'ttaykoa hahnkkiah may'llay tahksin
Could you have our luggage brought down?	Voisitteko toimittaa matka|tavara|mme alas?	voa'sittaykoa toa'mittaa mahtkahtahvahrahmmay ahlahs
Here's the forwarding address.	Tässä on seuraava osoittee|ni.	tæssæ oan say°°raavah oasoa'ttæyni
You have my home address.	Teillä on koti|osoittee|ni.	tay'llæ oan koatioasoa'ttæyni
It's been a very enjoyable stay.	Olen viihtynyt erinomaisesti.	oalayn veehtewnewt ayrinoamah'saysti

TIPPING, see inside back-cover

Camping *Leirintä*

There are more than 350 camp sites, 200 of which belong to the Finnish Travel Association (*Suomen Matkailuliitto*). Sites are graded by stars from one to three, the best offering riding, water-skiing, rowing and fishing. The Finnish camping season starts around the end of May in the south and lasts into September. An international or Finnish camping card is required - obtainable at the sites. It is forbidden to light fires in the countryside so bring a camping stove if you intend to cook.

Is there a camp site near here?	**Onko lähellä leirintä|aluetta?**	oankoa læhayllæ lay'rintæahlooayttah
Can we camp here?	**Voimmeko leiriytyä tässä?**	voa'mmaykoa lay'riewtewæ tæssæ
Do you have room for a tent/caravan (trailer)?	**Onko teillä tilaa teltalle/asunto|vaunulle**	oankoa tay'llæ tillaa tayltahllay/ ahsoontoavah°°noollay
What's the charge...?	**Mitä on maksu...?**	mittæ oan mahksoo
per day	**päivältä**	pæ'væltæ
per person	**hengeltä**	hayngayltæ
for a car	**autosta**	ah°°toastah
for a tent	**teltasta**	tayltahstah
for a caravan (trailer)	**asuntovaunusta**	ahsoontoavah°°noostah
Is tourist tax included?	**Sisältyykö matkailija|vero hintaan?**	sissæltewkur mahtkah'liyahvayroa hintaan
Is there/Are there (a)...?	**Onko...?**	oankoa
drinking water	**juoma|vettä**	y°°oamahvayttæ
electricity	**sähköä**	sæhkuræ
playground	**leikki|kenttää**	lay'kkikayntt̄æ
restaurant	**ravintolaa**	rahvintoalaa
shopping facilities	**myymälää**	mēwmælǣ
swimming pool	**uima|allasta**	oo'mahahllahstah
Where are the showers/toilets?	**Missä ovat suihkut/vessat?**	missæ oavaht soo'hkoot/ vayssaht
Where can I get butane gas?	**Mistä voin saada butaania/ neste|kaasua?**	mistæ voa'n saadah bootaaniah/ naystaykaassooah
Is there a youth hostel near here?	**Onko lähellä retkeily|majaa?**	oankoa læhayllæ raytkay'lewmahyaa

CAMPING EQUIPMENT, see page 106

Eating out

Eating places in Finland range from the basic to the very smart; the list below will help you decide where to choose. However, remember that restaurants are not allowed to serve alcoholic drinks before 11 a.m.

Baari
(**baa**ri)

A 'snack-bar', unlicensed as a rule, although some serve beer, so don't head for one of these if what you want is a stiff drink! Actually the ones which do not offer any alcoholic beverages at all generally have a more pleasant atmosphere. You will see the sign *Baari* everywhere in Finland. The menu usually consists of snacks, simple meals, pastries and ice cream. They will be happy to serve just a cup of coffee or tea; there is no obligation to order a full meal. However, some of these may close quite early in the evening.

Grilli
(**grilli**)

A small informal restaurant, sometimes licensed to serve beer and wine. More popular for luncheons than for dinner.

Kahvio, Kahvila
(**kahh**vioa **kahh**villah)

Kahvila is a cafe or a snack-bar usually specializing in pastries and cakes. Light meals may also be available. *Kahvio* is just a self-service cafeteria, for example in a department store or a service station.

Krouvi
(kroa°°vi)

A small restaurant offering a hearty menu and usually licensed to serve beer and wine. Very similar in style to the restaurants called *Grilli*.

Pub
(**poo**b)

An imitation of an English pub, although sometimes only in name. Many pubs in Finland serve meals and have waitress service as in a restaurant.

Ravintola
(**rah**vintoalah)

The general name for a restaurant. This can cover anything from a small intimate eating place to a grand establishment with live music and a dance floor. A *ravintola* may be either licensed or unlicensed.

Yö|kerho
(ᵉʷ**ur**kayrhoa)

A night-club, always licensed, mostly to be found in big hotels. Open until 2 - 3 a.m.

Eating habits *Ruoka|tavat*

The Finns are coffee drinkers and most of them start their day with a cup of black coffee. A healthy breakfast may then consist of oat porridge or muesli and some black rye bread. In Finland tea is served extremely weak and never with milk.

Most workplaces have subsidized canteens where the employees may have a two or three course lunch which is often their main meal of the day. Nowadays in many families a full dinner is cooked at home only at weekends as the parents have their main meal at work and the children are given theirs at school or at a creche.

In general Finnish food is hearty and homely. Pork, beef and chicken casseroles are common, while lamb and veal are less popular. Cold milk is the typical drink at meal times, wine only being served on special occasions or when entertaining.

Meal times *Ateria-ajat*

In Finland, lunch and dinner are eaten earlier than in most other European countries. Lunch (*lounas*—**loa**^{oo}nahss) at 11 a.m. is not unusual and when at home most families eat dinner (*päivällinen*—**pæ**^{i}vællinnayn) around 5 p.m. However, restaurants continue serving evening meals until late and it is possible to have dinner in a restaurant quite late in the evening, for example after a visit to the theatre or cinema.

Finnish cuisine *Suomalainen keittiö*

Finnish cuisine is a mixture of Scandinavian, European and Russian cooking. The staple diet consists of various potato and meat dishes. Milk is the traditional drink with meals and there are many Finnish dishes in which milk is a prominent ingredient. Pickled and smoked fish is a speciality and there are numerous types of these. Finnish bread is delicious and there is an endless variety. Very dark, sour rye bread is very popular in Finland.

Wild mushrooms and fresh wild berries are widely used. Try *sienisalaatti* (sⁱ**aynisah**laatti), a salad of wild mushrooms in sour cream. A bright red jam, *puolukkahillo* (**poa**lookka**hill**oa), made of uncooked lingonberries which grow wild in the Finnish forests, is a regular accompaniment to meat dishes.

Savoury pasties are another Finnish delicacy. Try *kaalipiirakka* (**kaali**pee**rahkah) made with cabbage and minced meat, or *karjalanpiirakka* (**kahr**yahlahn**pee**rahkkah) which is a traditional Carelian delicacy often served with chopped cooked egg mixed with a knob of butter. Smoked reindeer meat, which resembles venison but is slightly stronger, is a speciality from Lapland.

Mitä saisi olla?	What would you like?
Suosittelen tätä.	I recommend this.
Mitä haluaisitte juoda?	What would you like to drink?
Meillä ei ole...	We don't have...
Ottaisitteko...?	Would you like...?

Hungry? *Nälkäinen?*

I'm hungry/I'm thirsty.	**Olen nälkäinen/ Olen janoinen.**	oalayn nælkæinayn/oalayn yahnoaⁱnayn
Can you recommend a good restaurant?	**Voitteko suositella hyvää ravintolaa?**	voaⁱsittaykoa s^{oo}sittayllah hewvǣ rahvintoalaa
Are there any inexpensive restaurants around here?	**Onko täällä|päin edullista ravintolaa?**	oankoa tǣllæpæin aydoollistah rahvintoalaa

If you want to be sure of getting a table in a well-known restaurant, it may be better to book in advance.

I'd like to reserve a table for 4.	**Varaisin pöydän neljälle.**	vahrahisin p^{ur}ewdæn nayljællay
We'll come at 8.	**Tulemme kello 8.**	toolaymmay kaylloa kahhdayksahn

Could we have a table...?	Voimmeko saada...?	voa'mmaykoa saadah
in the corner	nurkka|pöydän	noorkkahp'ewdæn
by the window	ikkuna|pöydän	ikkoonahp'ewdæn
outside	pöydän ulkoa	p'ewdæn oolkoaah
on the terrace	pöydän terassilta	p'ewdæn tayrahssiltah
in a non-smoking area	pöydän savuttomalta alueelta	p'ewdæn sahvoottoamahltah ahlooāyltah

Asking and ordering *Kysyminen ja tilaaminen*

Waiter/Waitress!	Tarjoilija!	tahryoa'liyah
I'd like something to eat/drink.	Haluaisin jotain syötävää/juotavaa.	hahlooah'sin yoatahin sew'''tævæ/y''oatavaa
May I have the menu, please?	Saisinko ruoka|listan.	sah'sinkoa r''oakahlistahn
Do you have a set menu/local dishes?	Onko teillä vakio|listaa/paikallisia erikoisuuksia?	oankoa tay'llæ vahkioalistaa/ pah'kahllissiah ayrikoa'sōōksiah
What do you recommend?	Mitä suosittelisitte?	mittæ s''oasittaylissittay
Do you have anything ready quickly?	Onko teillä jotakin nopeasti valmista?	oankoa taillæ yoatahkin noapayahsti vahlmisstah
I'm in a hurry.	Minulla on kiire.	minnoollah oan keeray
I'd like...	Saisinko...	sah'sinkoa
Could we have a/an..., please?	Voisimmeko saada...?	voa'simmaykoa saadah
ashtray	tuhka|kupin	toohhkahkoopin
cup	kupin	koopin
fork	haarukan	haarookahn
glass	lasin	lahsin
knife	veitsen	vay'tsayn
napkin (serviette)	lautas|liinan	lah''tahsleenahn
plate	lautasen	lah''tahsayn
spoon	lusikan	loossikkahn
May I have some...?	Voisinko saada...?	voa'sinkoa saadah
bread	leipää	lay'pǣ
butter	voita	voa'tah
lemon	sitruunaa	sitrōōnaa
oil	öljyä	urlyewæ

pepper	**pippuria**	**pip**pooriah
salt	**suolaa**	s°°oalaa
seasoning	**mausteita**	mah°°stay'tah
sugar	**sokeria**	soakayriah
vinegar	**viini|etikkaa**	veeniayttikkaa

Special diet *Erikois\|ruoka\|valio*

Some useful expressions for those with special requirements:

I'm on a diet.	**Olen dieetillä.**	oalayn d'aytillæ
I'm a vegetarian.	**Olen kasvis|syöjä**	oalayn kahsvissew'''yæ
I don't drink alcohol.	**En juo alkoholia.**	ayn y°°oa ahlkoahoaliah
I don't eat meat.	**En syö lihaa.**	ayn sew'' lihaa
I mustn't eat food containing...	**En voi syödä ruo-kaa, jossa on...**	ayn voa' sew''dæ r°°oakaa yoassah oan
flour/fat	**jauhoa/rasvaa**	yah°°hoaah/rahsvaa
salt/sugar	**suolaa/sokeria**	s°°oalaa/soakayriah
Do you have... for diabetics?	**Onko teillä... dia-beetikoille?**	oankoa tay'llæ...diahbātikkoa'llay
cakes	**kakkuja**	kahkkooyah
fruit juice	**hedelmä|mehua**	haydaylmæmayhooah
a special menu	**erikois|ruoka|listaa**	ayrikkoa'sr°°oakahlistah
Do you have any vegetarian dishes?	**Onko teillä kasvis|syöjän annoksia?**	oankoa tay'llæ kahsvissew'''yæn ahnnoaksiah
Could I have... instead of dessert?	**Voisinko saada...-a jälki|ruoan asemasta?**	voa'sinkoa saadah...-a yælkirr°°aahn asaymahstah
Can I have an artificial sweetener?	**Voinko saada makeutus|ainetta?**	voa'nkoa saadah mahkayootoosah'nayttah

And...

I'd like some more.	**Saisinko vähän lisää.**	sah'sinkoa væhæn lissǣ
Can I have more..., please?	**Saisinko lisää...-a, kiitos.**	sah'sinkoa lissǣ...-a keetoass
Just a small portion.	**Vain pieni annos.**	vah'n p'ayni ahnnoass
Nothing more, thanks.	**Kiitos, riittää.**	keetoass riittǣ
Where are the toilets?	**Missä ovat WC:t?**	missæ oavaht vāysāyt

What's on the menu? *Mitä on (ruoka)|listalla?*

During the summer many restaurants offer a tourist menu. Known as the *Finland Menu*, it features a selection of typical dishes. There are three price categories which vary according to the establishment.

Under the headings below you'll find alphabetical lists of dishes that might be offered on a Finnish menu with their English equivalents. You can simply show the book to the waiter. If you want some fruit for example, let *him* point to what's available on the appropriate list. Use pages 36 and 37 for ordering in general.

Reading the menu *Ruoka|listan luku*

Talon erikoisuudet	Specialities of the house
Paikkakunnan erikoisuuksia	Local specialities
Päivän tarjous/annos	Dish of the day
... tapaan	... style
Kotitekoista	Home-made
Valintanne mukaan	Of your choice
Vuodenajan erikoisuudet	In season

alku|paloja	**ahl**koo**pah**loayah	appetizers
hampurilaisia	**hahm**poorillah'sia	burgers
hedelmiä	**hay**daylmiæ	fruit
juomat	y°°amaht	beverages
jälkiruokia	**yæl**kirr°°oakiah	desserts
jäätelöä	**yæ**tayl'ʳæ	ice cream
kalaa	**kah**laa	fish
kanaa	**kah**naa	chicken
keittoja	**kay**'ttoayah	soups
lintua	**lint**°°ah	poultry
muna|ruokia	**moo**nahr°°oakiah	egg dishes
olut	**oa**loot	beer
pasta	**pah**stah	pasta
riistaa	**rees**taa	game
salaatteja	**sah**laattayyah	salads
vihanneksia	**vi**hahnnayksiah	vegetables
viinit	**vee**nit	wine
väli|palaa	**væ**lipahlaa	snacks
väli|ruokia	**væ**lirr°°oakiah	entrees
äyriäisiä	**æ**ᵉʷriæissiæ	seafood

Breakfast *Aamiainen*

A Finnish breakfast is a hearty meal usually consisting of coffee or tea with bread, butter and cheese, cold meats and sometimes eggs or perhaps porridge. Most hotels can also provide an English or American breakfast.

I'd like breakfast, please.	**Saisinko aamiaisen.**	sah'sinkoa aamiah'ssayn
I'll have a/an/some...	**Ottaisin...**	oattah'sin.
bacon and eggs	**pekonia ja munia**	paykoaniah yah mooniah
boiled egg	**keitetyn munan**	kay'taytewn moonahn
soft/hard	**kovaksi/peh-meäksi**	koavahksi/payhmayæksi
cereal	**hiutaleita**	hi^{oo}tahlay'tah
eggs	**munia**	mooniah
fried eggs	**paistettuja munia**	pah'stayttooyah mooniah
scrambled eggs	**muna|kokkelia**	moonahkoakkayliah
poached eggs	**hyydytettyjä munia**	hēwdewtayttewyæ mooniah
fruit juice	**hedelmä|mehua**	haydaylmæmayhoo
grapefruit	**greippi|mehua**	grayppimayhoo
orange	**appelsiini|mehua**	appaylseenimayhoo
ham and eggs	**kinkkua ja munia**	kinkkooah yah mooniah
jam	**hilloa**	hilloah
marmalade	**marmelaadia**	mahrmaylaadiah
toast	**paahto|leipää**	paahhtoalay'pǣ
yoghurt	**jogurttia**	yoagoorttiah
May I have some...?	**Voinko saada vähän...**	voa'nkoa saadah væhæn
bread	**leipää**	lay'pǣ
butter	**voita**	voa'tah
(hot) chocolate	**kaakaota**	kaakahoatah
coffee	**kahvia**	kahhviah
decaffeinated	**kafeiinitonta**	kahfayeenitoantah
black/with milk	**mustana/maidon kanssa**	moostahnah/mah'doan kanssah
honey	**hunajaa**	hoonahjaa
milk	**maitoa**	mah'toa
cold/hot	**kylmää/kuumaa**	kewlmǣ/koomaa
pepper	**pippuria**	pippooriah
rolls	**sämpylöitä**	sæampewlur'tæ

salt	**suolaa**	s°°oalaa
tea	**teetä**	tāytæ
with milk	**maidon kanssa**	mah¹doan kahnssah
with lemon	**sitruunan kanssa**	sitrōōnahn kahnssah
(hot) water	**(kuumaa) vettä**	kōōmaa vayttæ

Seisova pöytä

Finland also has its own variation of the Swedish *smörgåsbord* known as *seisova pöytä*. This is a sumptuous do-it-yourself stand-up cold buffet. Also common in Finland is *voi|leipä|pöytä* which literally means 'bread and butter table'.

This buffet can consist of 50 or more different dishes! You can choose it either as a first course or as a fixed-price complete meal, in which case the only limit on the number of trips you make to the serving table is your own capacity.

The meal is often divided into three phases. The first plateful consists of fish, the second of cold meats and the third of hot foods such as meatballs and casseroles. In addition there are salads, cheese, fruit, several types of bread, milk or buttermilk and beer, all included in the price.

Starters (Appetizers) *Alkuruokia*

Pickled or smoked fish, smoked fish roe, smoked reindeer meat and wild mushrooms are the starters which give a regional flavour to a Finnish meal.

I'd like an appetizer.	**Ottaisin jotain alku|ruokaa.**	oattah¹sin yoatah¹n ahlkoor°°oakaa
What would you recommend?	**Mitä suositteli-sitte?**	mittæ s°°oasittaylissittay
anjovista	ahnyoavisstah	anchovies
katka|rapua	kahtkahrahpooah	shrimp
kaviaaria	kahv¹aariah	caviar
keittoja	kay¹ttoayah	soup
kinkkua	kinkkooah	ham
leikkeleitä	lay¹kkaylaytæ	cold meats

lohta	loahtah	salmon
makkaraa	mahkkahraa	sausage
mätiä	mætiæ	roe
parsaa	pahrsaa	asparagus
poron|kieltä	poaroank'ayltæ	reindeer tongue
poron|lihaa	poaroanlihaa	reindeer meat
rapuja	rahpooyah	crayfish
salaattia	sahlaattiah	salad
sardiineja	sahrdeenayyæ	sardines
silakoita	sillahkoa'tah	Baltic herring
savu|silakoita	sahvoosillahkoa'tah	smoked Baltic herring
silliä	silliæ	salted herring

Soups and stews *Keittoja ja muhennoksia*

A steaming hot bowl of soup is a perfect dish in winter, particularly after skiing or skating, as it warms up the whole body. Thick pea soup with cubed fatty pork *hernekeitto* (**hayr**nay**kay'**ttoa) is traditionally served on Shrove Tuesday. *Kesäkeitto* (**kay**ssae**kay'**ttoa) - 'summer soup' is another Finnish speciality which is most often served in summertime, as its name indicates. This soup is made of fresh summer vegetables stewed in milk, the main ingredient being cauliflower.

I'd like some soup.	**Haluaisin (jotain) keittoa.**	hahlooah'sin (yoatah'n) kay'ttoah
artisokka|keitto	ahrtisoakkahkay'ttoa	artichoke soup
(herkku|)sieni|keitto	(hayrkkoo) s'aynikay'ttoa	mushroom soup
herne|keitto	hayrnaykay'ttoa	pea soup
härän|häntä|liemi	hærænhæntæl'aymi	oxtail soup
juusto|keitto	yōostoakay'ttoa	cheese soup
kaali|keitto	kaalikay'ttoa	cabbage soup
kala|keitto	kahlahkay'ttoa	fish soup
kana|keitto	kahnahkay'ttoa	chicken soup
kukka|kaali|keitto	kookkahkaalikay'ttoa	cauliflower soup
liha|keitto	lihhahkay'ttoa	meat stew
mustikka|keitto	mustikkahkay'ttoa	whortleberry soup
parsa|keitto	pahrsahkay'ttoa	asparagus soup
pinaatti|keitto	pinnaattikay'ttoa	spinach soup
raparperi|keitto	rahpahrpayrikay'ttoa	rhubarb soup
tomaatti|keitto	toamaattikay'ttoa	tomato soup
vihanes|keitto	vihahnnayskay'ttoa	vegetable soup

Salads *Salaatteja*

hapan|kaali|salaatti	**hah**pahnkaali**sah**laatti	sauerkraut salad
kaali-puolukka| salaatti	**kaalip**°°**oa**lookkah **sah**laatti	cabbage and lingonberry salad
rosolli	**roa**soalli	beetroot salad with salt herring
savu|silakka|salaatti	**sah**voosilahkkah **sah**laatti	salad with smoked Baltic herring

Egg dishes *Muna\|ruokia*

I'd like an omelet.	**Haluaisin munakkaan.**	hah**looah**¦sin **moo**nahkkaan
hyydytetty muna	he̅wdewtayttew **moo**nah	poached egg
keitetty muna	**kay**¦tayttew **moo**nah	boiled egg
kovaksi	**koa**vahksi	hard
pehmeäksi	**payh**mayæksi	soft
munakas	**moo**nahkahs	omelet
hillo|munakas	**hillooamoo**nahkahs	cheese omelet
juusto-munakas	**yoo**stoa**moo**nahkahs	ham omelet
kinkku|munakas	**kinkkoomoo**nahkahs	bacon omelet
pekoni|munakas	**pay**koani**moo**nahkas	jam omelet
peruna|munakas	**pay**roonah**moo**nahkahs	potato omelet
sieni|munakas	s¦**ay**ni**moo**nahkahs	mushroom omelet
muna|kokkeli	**moo**nah**koak**kayli	scrambled eggs
paistettu muna	**pah**¦stayttoo **moo**nah	fried egg

Fish and seafood *Kalaa ja äyriäisiä*

With all its lakes, and the Baltic, you'd think Finland would be a land of fish fanciers. Surprisingly, the average Finn eats little fish except for Baltic herring. Restaurants, though, nearly always offer interesting dishes like smoked whitefish or salmon. An excellent lake fish is *muikku*, mainly eaten in the province of Savo.

| I'd like some fish. | **Haluaisin (jotain) kalaa.** | halooah'sin (yoatah'n) kahlaa |
| What kind of seafood do you have? | **Mitä äyriäisiä teillä on?** | mittæ æ^{ew}riæ'ssiæ tay'llæ oan |

ahven	ahhvayn	perch
anjovis	ahnyoavis	anchovies
ankerias	ahnkayriahss	eel
hauki	ha°°ki	pike
hummeri	hoommayri	lobster
kampela	kahmpaylah	flounder
katka|rapu	kahtkahrahpoo	shrimp
kaviaari	kahviaari	caviar
kilo|haili	killoahah'li	sprats
kirjo|lohi	kiryoaloahi	rainbow trout
kolja	koalyah	haddock
kuha	koohah	pike perch
lahna	lahhnah	bream
lohi	loahi	salmon
made	mahday	burbot
makrilli	mahkrilli	mackerel
meri|antura	mayriahntoorah	sole
muikku	moo'kkoo	vendace
muste|kala	moostaykahlah	cuttlefish
mäti	mæti	roe
nahkiainen	nahhkiah'nayn	lamprey
osterit	oastayri	oysters
pikku|silli	pikkoosilli	whitebait
puna|kampela	poonahkahmpaylah	plaice
rapu	rahpoo	crayfish
sampi	sahmpi	sturgeon
sardiinit	sahrdeenit	sardines
siika	seekah	whitefish
silakka	sillahkkah	Baltic herring
silli	silli	herring
sini|simpukat	sinnisimpookaht	mussels
särki	særki	roach
taimen	tah'mayn	trout
tonni|kala	toannikahlah	tuna
turska	toorskah	cod

baked	**uunissa paistettu**	ōōnissah pah'stayttoo
fried	**paistettu**	pah'stayttoo
grilled	**grillattu**	grillahttoo
marinated	**marinoitu**	mahrinoa'too
poached	**keitetty**	kay'tayttew
sautéed	**ruskistettu/käristetty**	rooskistayttoo/ kæristayttew
smoked	**savustettu**	sahvoostayttoo
steamed	**höyryssä keitetty**	hur^{ew}rewssæ kay'tayttew

Fish dishes *Kala|ruokia*

Janssonin kiusaus
(yahnssoanin
ki°°sah°°ss)

'Jansson's temptation'; sliced potatoes, onions and anchovies in cream sauce, baked in the oven

kala|kukko
(kahlahkookkoa)

'fish loaf'; sort of loaf of dark bread with *muikku* (sometimes perch) and pork inside and baked in the oven; speciality of the province of Savo

kulibjaka
(koolibyahkah)

a savoury pie filled with salmon, rice, hard-boiled eggs and dill, served in slices with melted butter

lasi|mestarin silli
(lahsimaystahrin silli)

'glass master's herring'; pickled herring with spices, vinegar, carrot and onion

lipeä|kala
(lippayækahlah)

a Christmas speciality; codfish soaked in lye solution, boiled and served with a white sauce

lohi|laatiko
(loahilaatikkoa)

a potato and salmon casserole, baked in the oven

**mateen|mäti ,
muikun|mäti**
(mahtäÿnmæti
moo'koonmæti)

roe from burbot or whitefish, seasoned with onion; often accompanies *bliny* (small pancakes)

silaaka|laatikko
(sillahkkahlaatikkoa)

casserole made of alternating layers of potato slices, onion and Baltic herring, with an egg and milk sauce, baked in the oven

suutarin|lohi
(sōōtahrinloahi)

'cobbler's salmon'; marinated Baltic herring in vinegar with onion and peppers

venäläinen silli
(vaynælæ'nayn silli)

'Russian herring'; herring fillets with mayonnaise, mustard, vinegar, beetroot, gherkins and onion

Meat *Liha|ruokia*

You'll find most of the familiar meat dishes in Finland, with pork predominating. You'll also meet some exciting novelties: roast elk or reindeer from Lapland, or even bear (mostly imported from Russia).

What kind of meat do you have?	**Mitä liha|ruokia teilä on?**	mittæ lihahr°°oakiah tay¹llæ oan
beef	**naudan|lihaa**	nah°°dahnlihaa
lamb	**lammasta**	lahmmahstah
pork	**porsaan|lihaa**	poarsaanlihaa
veal	**vasikan|lihaa**	vahsikkahnlihaa
filee	filāy	fillet
hirven|liha	hirvaynlihah	elk
härän|häntä	hæ̈rænhæntæ	oxtail
jauheliha|pihvi	yah°°haylihahpihvi	beefburger
kani	kahni	rabbit
karhun|paisti	kahrhoonpah¹sti	bear steak
kieli	k¹ayli	tongue
kinkku	kinkkoo	gammon
kyljys/kotletti	kewlyews/koatlaytti	chop/cutlet
lammasta	lahmmahstah	mutton
(lampaan) jalka	(lahmpaan) yahlkah	leg (of lamb)
leike	lay¹kay	escalope
liha|pyörykät	lihahpew⁻rewkæt	meatballs
makkara	mahkkahrah	sausage
maksa	mahksah	liver
munuaiset	moonooah¹sayt	kidneys
nakit	nahkit	frankfurters
paisti	pah¹sti	sirloin
pekoni	paykoani	bacon
pihvi	pihvi	steak
poron|liha	poaroanlihah	reindeer meat
(savustettu) kinkku	(sahvoostayttoo) kinkkoo	(smoked) ham

baked	**uunissa paistettu**	**ōōnissah pah¹stayttoo**
barbecued	**pariloitu**	**pahriloa¹too**
boiled	**keitetty**	**kay¹tayttew**
braised	**haudutettu**	**hah°°dootayttoo**
fried	**paistettu**	**pah¹stayttoo**
grilled	**grillattu**	**grill**ahttoo
roast	**paahdettu**	**paah**dayttoo
sautéed	**ruskistettu/käristetty**	**rooos**kistayttoo/ **kæristayttew**
stewed	**muhennokseksi**	**moohaynnoaksayksi**
	keitetty	**kay¹tayttew**
very rare	**vain vähän paistettu**	vah¹n **væhæn pah¹stayttoo**
underdone (rare)	**puoli|kypsä**	**p°°oalikewpsæ**
medium	**keski-kypsä**	**kay**ski-**kewpsæ**
well-done	**hyvin/kypsäksi**	**hew**vin/**kewpsæksi**
	paistettu	**pah¹stayttoo**

Meat specialities *Liha|erikoisuuksia*

joulu\|kinkku
(yoa°°lookinkkoo)

Christmas ham; whole ham served as the traditional Finnish Christmas dish with various stews, e.g. *lanttulaatikko*, rutabaga casserole or *porkkanalaatikko*, carrot casserole, peas, plums, etc.

kaali\|kääryleet
(kaalikǣrewlāyt)

cabbage rolls; cabbage leaves stuffed with minced meat and rice

kaali\|piirakka
(kaalipeerahkkah)

pie made with cabbage and minced meat

karjalan\|paisti
(kahryahlahnpah¹sti)

'Carelian stew'; beef, pork and sometimes mutton with allspice

lammas\|kaali
(lahmmahskaali)

stew or soup made with mutton and cabbage

Lindströmin pihvi
(lindsturmin pihvi)

beefburger made with beetroot, served with fried onions and a piquant cream sauce

maksa|laatikko (**mahk**sah**laa**tikkoa)	baked liver purée made with rice and raisins	

meri|mies|pihvi (**may**rim'ays**pih**vi)	'seaman's beef'; casserole of alternate layers of potato slices and meat patties (or minced meat), baked in the oven

pala|paisti (**pah**lah**pah**'sti)	beef ragout

pipar|juuri|liha (**pi**ppah**yoo**ri**li**hah)	boiled beef with horseradish sauce

poron|käristys (**poa**ron**kæ**ristewss)	sautéed reindeer stew, a Lapp speciality

veri|ohukaiset (**vay**rioahookah'sayt)	thin pancakes made with blood, eaten with lingonberry jam

wienin|leike (**vee**ninlay'kay)	veal cutlet, breaded and fried (wiener schnitzel)

Game and Poultry *Riistaa ja lintua*

Finland is noted for its game birds but you may consider the prices high.

ankka	**ahn**kkah	duck
fasaani	fah**saa**hni	pheasant
hanhi	**hahn**hi	goose
hirvi	**hir**vi	venison
jänis	**yæ**nia	hare
kalkkuna	**kahlk**koonah	turkey
kana	**kah**nah	chicken
rinta/koipi/siipi	**rin**tah/**koa**'pi/**see**pi	breast/leg/wing
grillattu kana	**grill**ahttoo **kah**nah	barbecued chicken
pelto|pyy	**payl**toapew	partridge
teeri	**tay**ri	grouse
villi|sika	**villi**sikah	wild boar

Vegetables *Vihanneksia*

artisokka	**ahr**tisoakkah	artichokes
avokado	**ah**voakahdoa	avocado
endive	**ayn**divay	endive (chicory)
espanjan|pippuri	**ays**pahnyahn**pip**poori	chili
herneet	**hayr**nāyt	peas
kaali	**kaa**li	cabbage
kastanja	**kahs**tahnyah	chestnuts
kesäkurpitsa	**kays**sækoorpitsah	courgette (zucchini)
kukka|kaali	**kook**kahkaali	cauliflower
kurkku	**koork**koo	cucumber
kurpitsa	**koor**pitsah	pumpkin (squash)
lanttu	**lahnt**too	swede (rutabaga)
lehti|salaatti	**lay**htisahlaatti	lettuce
linssit	**lins**sit	lentils
maissi	**mah**'ssi	(sweet) corn
muna|koiso	**moo**nahkoa'soa	aubergine (eggplant)
nauriit	**nah**°°reet	turnips
parsa	**pahr**sah	asparagus (tips)
parsa|kaali	**pahr**sakaali	broccoli
pavut	**pah**voot	beans
perunat	**pay**roonaht	potatoes
pinaatti	**pin**naatti	spinach
pippuri	**pip**poori	(sweet) peppers
vihreä/punainen	**vih**rayæ/ **poo**nah'nayn	green/red
porkkanat	**poark**kahnaht	carrots
puna|juuri	**poo**nahyōōri	beetroot
purjo(|sipuli)	(**poor**yoa(sippooli)	leeks
retiisit	**ray**teesit	radishes
ruusu|kaali	**rōō**sookaali	Brussels sprouts
(saksan|)kumina	(**sahk**sahn)**koo**minah	fennel
seka|vihanneket	**say**kahvihahnaykayt	mixed vegetables
selleri	**sayl**layri	celery
sieni	**s**'ayni	mushrooms
sipulit	**sip**poolit	onions
tomaatit	**toa**maatit	tomatoes

lanttu|laatikko (lahnttoolaatikkoa)		swede casserole; a Christmas speciality - mashed swede baked in the oven, served with Christmas ham
porkkana|laatikko (poarkkahnahlaatikkoa)		carrot casserole; mashed carrots and rice baked in the oven
peruna|laatikko (payroonahlaatikkoa)		potato bake
makaroni|laatikko (mahkahroanilaatikkoa)		macaroni bake with milk and egg sauce
pinaatti|ohukaiset (pinnaattioahookah'sayt)		spinach pancakes
porkkana|ohukaiset (poarkkahnahoa hookah'sayt)		carrot pancakes
kesä|keitto (kayssaekayttoa)		cauliflower and milk soup

Sauces *Kastikkeita*

etika	aytikkah	vinegar
herkku|sieni|kastike	hayrkkoos'ayni-kahstikkay	mushroom sauce
juusto|kastike	yo͞ostoakahstikkay	cheese sauce
kastike	kahstikkay	sauce
liemi	l'aymi	broth
majoneesi	mahyoanāyssi	mayonnaise
ranskalainen saalatti|kastike	rahnskahlah'nayn sahlaattikahstikkay	French dressing
ruskea kastike	rooskayah kahstikkay	brown sauce
sian|liha|kastike	siahnlihahkahstikkay	gravy prepared wth sliced pork
tomaatti|kastike	toamaattikahstikkay	tomato sauce
valko|kastike	vahlkoakahstikkay	white sauce
öljy|kastike	urlyewkahstikkay	oil sauce

Herbs and spices *Yrttejä ja mausteita*

anis	**ah**nis	aniseed
basilika	**bah**silikah	basil
inkivääri	**inkivāā**ri	ginger
kaneli	**kah**nayli	cinnamon
kumina	**koo**minah	caraway
laakerin lehti	**laah**kayrin**layh**ti	bay leaf
meirami	**may**'rahmi	marjoram
minttu	**minn**ttoo	mint
muskotti	**moos**koatti	nutmeg
oregano	**oa**raygahnoa	oregano
paprika	**pap**rikah	paprika
persilja	**payr**silyah	parsley
pipar|juuri	**pipah**ry**oo**ri	horseradish
pippuri	**pip**poori	pepper
rakuuna	**rah**k**oo**nah	tarragon
ros|mariini	**ross**mahreeni	rosemary
ruoho|laukka	**r°°oa**hoalah**°°**kkah	chives
salvia	**sahl**viah	sage
sinappi	**sin**ahppi	mustard
suola	**s°°oa**lah	salt
tilli	**til**li	dill
tinjami	**tin**yahmi	thyme
valko|sipuli	**vahl**koasipooli	garlic
yrtti|sekoitus	**ewrt**tisaykoa'toos	mixed herbs

To follow... *Jatko...*

Cheese *Juustoa*

Most Finns eat cheese at breakfast, cut in thin slices, or with the main course, not as a dessert. However, the custom of eating cheese after a meal is spreading. The fine cheeses of Finland are comparable to French or Swiss cheese, which they often resemble. Try some:

Aura
(ah°°rah)

blue veined, strong cheese of the Roquefort type

Hovi
(hoavi)

mild, soft cheese, similar to petit-suisse

Emmental
(aymmmayntahl)

Finnish emmental (*tahko\|juusto*) reminiscent of the Swiss cheese, in mild and strong varieties

Edam (aydahm)	the most common cheese in Finland, not unlike Dutch Edam
Juhla (yoohlah)	hard cheese with a strong flavour, along the lines of Cheddar
Kappeli (kahppayli)	soft, creamy cheese with a strong flavour
Kartano (kahrtahnoa)	cheese resembling Gouda, though milder
Kesti (kaysti)	strong carraway-flavoured cheese
Kreivi (kray'vi)	strong cheese of the Tilsit type
Luostari (l°°oastahri)	soft cheese with a delicate flavour, in the syle of Port-Salut
Turunmaa (tooroonmaa)	mild, creamy cheese

Fruit and nuts *Hedelmiä ja pähkinöitä*

| Do you have any fresh fruit? | **Onko teillä tuoreita hedelmiä?** | oankoa tay'llæ t°°oarayitah haydaylmiæ |
| I'd like a (fresh) fruit cocktail. | **Haluaisin (tuore\|) hedelmä\|cocktailin.** | hahlooah'sin (t°°oaray) haydaylmækoaktah'lin |

ananas	ahnahnahss	pineapple
appelsiini	ahppaylseeni	orange
aprikoosi	ahprikkōassi	apricots
banaani	bahnaani	banana
greippi	gray'ppi	grapefruit
hassel-pähkinät	hahssaylpæhkinæt	hazelnuts
karviais|marjat	kahrviah'smahryaht	gooseberries
kastanjat	kahstahnyaht	chestnuts
kirsikat	keersikkaht	cherries
kookos|pähkinä	kōakoaspæhkinæ	coconut
kuivatut hedelmät	koo'vahttoot haydaylmæt	dried fruit
kuivatut luumut	koo'vahttoot lōomoot	prunes
limetti	limaytti	lime
luumut	lōomoot	plums
maa|pähkinät	maahpæhkinnæt	peanuts
mandariini	mahndahreeni	tangerine
mansikat	mahnsikkaht	strawberries

mantelit	**mahn**taylit	almonds
meloni	**may**loani	melon
musta viini|marjat	**moo**stah veenimahryaht	blackcurrants
nektariini	**nayk**tahreeni	nectarine
omena	**oa**maynah	apple
persikka	**payr**sikkah	peach
päärynä	**pǣ**rewnæ	pear
raparperi	**rah**pahrpayri	rhubarb
rusinat	**roo**ssinaht	raisins
saksan|pähkinät	**sahk**sahnpæhkinæt	walnuts
sitruuna	**sit**rōōnah	lemon
sulttaani-rusinat	**soolt**taaniroosinaht	sultanas
taatelit	**taa**taylit	dates
vadelmat	**vah**daylmaht	raspberries
vesi|meloni	**vay**ssimayloani	water melon
viikunat	**vee**koonaht	figs
viini|rypäleet	**vee**nirewpælāyt	grapes

Finns are keen on berries. A few species are found nowhere else; others are more common berries, widely appreciated.

lakka (**lahk**kah)	Arctic cloudberry; yellow berry growing on the marshes in northern Finland, regarded as the 'queen of berries' in Finland, used in desserts and for making *Lakka* liqueur
karpalo (**kahr**pahloa)	cranberry; also used for making *Polar* liqueur
mesi|marja (**may**ssimahryah)	Arctic bramble; *Mesimarja* liqueur is well known
mustikka (**moos**tikkah)	bilberry, or whortleberry; one of the commonest berries in Finland, used for a variety of desserts and pastries
puolukka (p°°a**look**kah)	lingonberry; used for many desserts and often served as jam or jelly with meat dishes

Desserts—Pastries *Jälki|ruokia—Leivonnaisia*

The most popular Finnish desserts are fruit soups (*kiisseli—* keessayli), pancakes, and ice-cream. Pies and pastries are usually eaten at coffee time, not as dessert. And as for puddings, Finns just don't care for them.

I'd like a dessert, please.	**Haluaisin jälkiruokaa.**	hahlooah'sin yælkir°°oakaa
What do you recommend?	**Mitä suosittelette?**	mittæ s°°oassittaylayttay
Something light, please.	**Jotain kevyttä, kiitos.**	yoatah'n kayvewttæ keetoass
Just a small portion.	**Vain pieni annos.**	vah'n p'ayni ahnnoass

jäätelö	yǣtaylur	ice-cream
mansikka	mahnsikkah	strawberry
suklaa	sooklaa	chocolate
vadelma	vahdaylmah	raspberry
vanilja	vahnilyah	vanilla
kakku	kahkkoo	cake
hedelmä|kakku	haydaylmækahkkoo	fruit cake
sokeri|kakku	soakayrikahkkoo	sponge cake
suklaa|kakku	sooklaakahkkoo	chocolate cake
täyte|kakku	tæ'ᵂtaykahkkoo	layer cake
kerma|vaahto	kayrmahvaahtoa	whipped cream
kohokas	koahoakahss	soufflé
leivos	lay'voass	pastry
marengit	mahrayngit	meringues
ohukaiset	oahookah'sayt	small pancakes
omena|piirakka	oamaynahpeerahkah	apple pie
omena|torttu	oamaynahtoarttoo	apple tart
suklaa|kastike	sooklaakahstikkay	chocolate sauce
torttu	toarttoo	tart
vaahto	vaahtoa	mousse
vanilja|kastike	vahnilyahkahstikkay	custard
vanukas	vahnookahss	pudding
vohvelit	voahvaylit	waffles

kiisseli (**kees**sayli)	dish made of any fruit or berries and their juice, thickened with potato flour, usually served cold, often with sugar and/or cream and milk
köyhät ritarit (**kur**ᵉʷhæt **rit**tahrit)	'poor knights'; dough soaked in milk and then fried, served with jam, berries and whipped cream
luumu|keitto (**loo**mookay**t**toa)	prune soup; dessert soup made with prunes and thickened with potato flour, served cold or hot
mustikka|keitto (**moos**tikkah**kay**ttoa)	bilberry soup
mustikka|piirakka (**moos**tikkah**pee**rahkkah)	bilberry pie
mämmi (**mæm**mi)	an Easter speciality; made of rye-malt, rye meal, treacle, sugar and orange peel, served cold with sugar and cream
piimä|piirakka (**pee**mæ**pee**rahkkah)	a pie made with curdled milk, eggs, vanilla and raisins
puolukka|puuro (p°°oalookkah**poo**roa)	porridge made with semolina and lingonberries, served cold with milk
seka|hedelmä|keitto (**say**kahhaydaylmæ **kay**ttoa)	dessert soup made with prunes and raisins, thickened and served hot or cold

Drinks *Juomia*

Beer *Olut*

Beer has been a part of Finnish culture in some form or another for over 1,000 years. Indeed, Finland's national epic covered the creation of the world in 200 verses but it took 400 verses to describe the invention of beer.

The niceties of Finland's beer classification system may be too complicated for the less enthusiastic drinker. Briefly, category 'A' (Export) beer, often more than five per cent alcohol, is only obtainable at a liquor store or in a licensed restaurant. Weaker beers called I and III are sold at supermarkets. Many foreign lagers, ales and stouts are available at both state liquor stores and supermarkets.

A-olut	ah-**oa**loot	export beer
keskiolut	**kays**kioaloot	medium-strong beer
portteri	**poart**tayri	porter
tumma olut	**toom**maa oaloot	dark beer
vehnäolut	**vayh**næoaloot	wheat beer
I'd like a beer.	**Haluaisin oluen.**	**hah**looah'sin **oa**looayn
a dark beer	**tumma olut**	**toom**mah **oa**loot
a light beer	**vaalea olut**	**vaa**layah **oa**loot
a bottle of beer	**pullo olutta**	**pool**loa **oa**loottah
a draught beer	**tynnyri|olut**	**tewn**newri**oa**loot
half a litre of beer	**puoli litraa olutta**	p°°**oa**li **li**traa **oa**loottah
I'll have another.	**Saisinko toisen.**	**sah**'sinkoa **toa**'sayn

> **KIPPIS**
> (**kip**piss)
> CHEERS

Wine *Viini*

Surprisingly, Finland has a wine industry. Most of the home-grown product is dessert wine. Some cheaper imported wines are bottled in Finland as well. You'll also find a good selection of French, Italian, German, Spanish and other known wines but these are very expensive and only available at the state-run *Alko* stores.

May I please have the wine list?	**Saisinko viini|lis-tan?**	**sah**'sinkoa **vee**nilistahn

I would like a bottle of white/red wine.	**Voisinko saada pullon valko|viiniä/ puna|viiniä.**	voa'sinkoa **saadah** **pooll**oan **vahl**koaveeniæ/ **poon**ahveeniæ
I'd like a glass of...	**Saisinko lasilli- sen...**	**sah'**sinkoa **lahs**illissayn
Waiter/waitress, bring me another..., please.	**Tarjoilija, toisitteko minulle toisen..., kiitos.**	tahryoa'liyah **toa**'sittekoa minnoollay toa'sayn... **keet**toass

red	**puna**	**poon**ah
white	**valko**	**vahl**koa
rosé	**rose**	roassāy
sparkling	**kuohu**	kᵒᵒoahoo
dry	**kuiva**	koo'vah
sweet	**makea**	**mah**kayah

musta|herukka|viini	**moost**ahhayrookkah veeni	blackcurrant wine
puna|herukka|viini	**poon**ahhayrookkah veeni	redcurrant wine
omena|viini	oamaynahveeni	apple wine

Schnapps *Snapsi*

This strong colourless spirit, sometimes flavoured, is the traditional accompaniment to appetizers, especially herring. This traditional Scandinavian firewater comes in several varieties:

akvaviitti (**ahk**vahveetti)	aquavit, flavoured with caraway seed; originally Danish, now also made in Finland
Kosken|korva (**koas**kaynkoarvah)	grain-based unflavoured spirit; fierce and fiery and inexpensive
Pöytä|viina (purᵉʷtæveenah)	perhaps the most popular of the cheaper varieties; distilled from grain
vodka (**voad**kah)	competing with Russian and Polish vodka, the Finns make *Dry Vodka* and, in a special bottle, *Finlandia Vodka*

Liqueurs *Likööri*

Karpi
(kahrpi)

red liqueur made of different berries and fruit

Lakka
(lahkkah)

cloudberry liqueur, dark yellow, full-bodied

Mesi|marja
(mayssimahryah)

made of Arctic bramble, deep red, rather sweet

Polar
(poalahr)

cranberry liqueur, red, with slightly pungent flavour

Other alcoholic drinks *Muita alkoholi|juomia*

glögi
(glurgi)

a heated Christmas and winter drink of berry juice, red wine, almonds, raisins and spices

pontikka
(poantikkah)

illicitly distilled spirit, mountain dew

sahti
(sahhti)

a beer-like home brew with a bitter taste sold legally in certain parts of the province of Häme

I'd like a/an ...	Saisinko ...	sah'sinkoa
aperitif	**aperitiivin**	**ah**payritteevin
cognac	**konjakin**	**koan**yahkin
gin	**ginin**	**gin**nin
liqueur	**liköörin**	**lik**kūrrin
rum	**rommin**	**roam**min
vermouth	**vermutin**	**vayr**mootin
vodka	**vodkan**	**voad**kahn
whisky	**viskin**	**vis**kin
neat (straight)	**sekoittamattomana**	**say**koa'ttah-mahttoamahnah
on the rocks	**jäillä**	**yæ**illæ
with a little water	**ja hieman vettä**	yah h'aymahn **vayt**tæ
Give me a gin and tonic, please.	**Saisinko gin|tonicin, kiitos.**	sah'sinkoa **gin**toanikin **kee**toass
Just a dash of soda, please.	**Vain tilkka soodaa, kiitos.**	vah'n **tilk**kah **sōa**daa **kee**toass

Nonalcoholic drinks *Alkoholittomia juomia*

At mealtimes most Finns prefer to drink milk. Buttermilk (*piimä*—**pee**mæ) is also popular. Beer and mineral water are common too.

Finland is a nation of coffee-drinkers. At any time of day you're likely to see the pot boiling. Coffee (*kahvi*—**kahh**vi) is what is served when Finns invite friends home; coffee parties rather than dinner parties are the rule.

In many restaurants you can also get stronger *espresso* coffee, though it's not necessarily authentic. A glass of iced water is often served with coffee in restaurants.

Tea is also popular but not nearly so fanatically consumed as coffee.

apple juice	**omena|mehu**	**oa**maynah**may**hoo
fruit juice	**hedelmä|mehu**	**hay**daylmæ**may**hoo
grapefruit juice	**greippi|mehu**	**gray**'ppi**may**hoo
herb tea	**yrtti|tee**	**urt**titay
lemon juice	**sitruuna|mehu**	**sir**oonah**may**hoo
lemonade	**limonaadi**	**lim**moanaadi
milk	**maito**	**mah**'to
milkshake	**pirtelö**	**peer**taylur
mineral water	**mineraali|vesi**	**min**nayraali**vay**si
fizzy (carbonated)	**hiili|happo**	**hee**lihah**po**a
still	**hiili|hapoton**	**hee**lihah**po**atoan
orange juice	**appelsiini|mehu**	**ahp**paylseeni**may**hoo
orangeade	**appelsiini|limonaa-** **di**	**ahp**paylseenili- **mmoa**naadi
tomato juice	**tomaatti|mehua**	**toa**maatti**may**hooah
tonic water	**tonic-vesi**	**toa**nik**vay**si

sima (**sim**mah)	a usually non-alcoholic home-made or commercially brewed sparkling drink made with brown sugar, lemon, honey (sometimes), hops and yeast; popular around May Day

Ravintolat

Hot beverages *Kuumia juomia*

(hot) chocolate	**kaakao**	**kaah**kahoa
coffee	**kahvi**	**kahh**vi
black	**mustana**	**moos**tahnah
with cream	**kerman kanssa**	**kayr**mahn **kahns**sah
with milk	**maidon kanssa**	**mah**'doan **kahns**sah
caffeine-free	**kaffeiinitonta**	**kahff**ayeenitoantah
espresso coffee	**espresso-kahvi**	**ays**prayssoa-**kahh**vi
tea	**tee**	tāȳ
cup of tea	**kuppi teetä**	**koop**pi **tāȳ**tæ
with milk/lemon	**maidon/sitruu-nan kanssa**	**mah**'doan/**sit**rōōnahn **kahns**sah
iced tea	**jää|teetä**	**yāȳ**tāȳtæ

Complaints *Valituksia*

There's a plate/glass missing.	**Yksi lautanen/lasi uupuu.**	**ewk**si **lah**°°tahnayn **ōō**pōō
I don't have a knife/fork/spoon.	**Minulla ei ole veistä/haarukkaa/lusikkaa.**	**mi**noollah ay' **oa**lay **vay**'stæ/**haah**rookkaa
That's not what I ordered.	**Tämä ei ole sitä, mitä tilasin.**	**tæ**mæ ay' **oa**lay **sit**tæ **mit**tæ **til**lahsin
I asked for ...	**Pyysin ...**	**pēw**sin
There must be some mistake.	**On sattunut joku erehdys.**	oan **saht**toonoot **yoa**koo **ay**rayhdewss
May I change this?	**Voinko vaihtaa tämän?**	**voa**'nkoa **vah**'taa **tæ**mæn
I asked for a small portion (for the child).	**Pyysin pientä (lasten) annosta.**	**pēw**sin p'**ay**nayn (**lahs**tayn) **ahn**noastah
The meat is ...	**Liha on ...**	**li**hah oan
overdone	**yli|kypsää**	**ew**likewpsǣ
underdone	**puoli|kypsää**	**p**°°**oa**likewpsǣ
too rare	**(liian) raakaa**	(**lee**ahn) **raa**kaa
too tough	**(liian) sitkeää**	(**lee**ahn) **sit**kayǣ

This is too...	**Tämä on liian ...**	tæmæ oan leeahn
bitter/salty/sweet	**kitkerää/suolaista/ makeaa**	kitkayrǣ/s°°alahˈstah/ mahkayaa
I don't like this.	**En pidä tästä.**	ayn piddæ tæstæ
The food is cold.	**Ruoka on kylmää.**	r°°oakah oan kewlmǣ
This isn't fresh.	**Tämä ei ole tuo- retta.**	tæmæ ayˈ oalay t°°aorayttah
What's taking you so long?	**Miksi tämä kestää näin kauan?**	miksi tæmæ kaystǣ næin kah°°ahn
Have you forgotten our drinks?	**Oletteko unohtanut juomamme?**	oalayttaykoa oonoahtahnoot y°°oamahmmay
The wine doesn't taste right.	**Viinissä ei ole oikea maku.**	veenissæ ayˈ oalay oaˈkayah mahkoo
This isn't clean.	**Tämä ei ole puh- das.**	tæmæ ayˈ oalay poohdass
Would you ask the head waiter to come over?	**Pyytäisittekö hovimestarin tänne.**	pēwtæisittaykur haovimaystahrin tænnay

The bill (check) *Lasku*

I'd like to pay.	**Haluaisin maksaa.**	hahlooahˈsin mahksaa
We'd like to pay separately.	**Haluaisimme mak- saa kukin erikseen.**	hahlooahˈmmay mahksaa kookin ayriksāyn
I think there's a mistake in this bill.	**Tässä laskussa taitaa olla virhe.**	tæssæ lahskoossah tahˈtaa oallah veerhay
What's this amount for?	**Mihin tämä summa liittyy?**	mihin tæmæ soommah leettēw
Is service included?	**Sisältyykö tar- joilu|palkkio tähän?**	sissæltēwkur tahryoaˈloopahlkkioa tæhæn
Is everything included?	**Sisältyykö siihen kaikki?**	sissæltēwkur seehayn kahˈkki
Do you accept traveller's cheques?	**Otatteko matka|sekkejä?**	oatattaykoa mahtkahshaykkayyæ
Can I pay with this credit card?	**Voinko maksaa tällä luotto|kortilla?**	voaˈnkoa mahksaa tællæ l°°attoakoartillah

TIPPING, see inside back-cover

Please round it up to...	**Pyöristäkää se...-n.**	p^{ew}urristækææ say...-n
Keep the change.	**Pitäkää vaihto|raha.**	pittækææ vah'htoarahhah
That was delicious.	**Se oli herkullista.**	say oali hayrkoollistah
We enjoyed it, thank you.	**Kiitos, pidimme siitä kovasti.**	keetoass piddimmay seetæ koavahsti

---

> **TARJOILU(\|PALKKIO) SISÄLTYY HINTOIHIN**
> SERVICE INCLUDED

Snacks—Picnic *Väli\|palat—Piknik*

Open sandwiches are found in all bars, cafés and restaurants. Hot sandwiches are also a popular light snack.

Give me two of these and one of those.	**Saisinko kaksi tällaista ja yhden tuollaisen.**	sah'sinkoa kahksi tællah'stah yah ewhdayn t^{oo}oallah'sayn
to the left/right	**vasemmalle/ oikealle**	vahsaymmahllay/ oakayahllay
above/below	**ylä|puolella/ ala|puolella**	ewlæp^{oo}oalayllah/ ahlahp^{oo}oalayllah
It's to take away.	**Se tulee mukaan.**	say toolay mookaan
I'd like a/some...	**Saisinko...**	sah'sinkoa
chicken	**kanaa**	kahnaa
half a roasted chicken	**puolikkaan grillattua kanaa**	p^{oo}oalikkaan grillahttooah kahnaa
chips (french fries)	**ranskalaisia (perunoita)**	rahnskahlah'siah (payroonoa'tah)
frankfurters	**nakkeja**	nahkkayyah
fried sausage	**paistetun makkaran**	pah'staytoon mahkkahrahn
omelet	**munakkaan**	moonahkkaan

open sandwich	**voi|leivän**	voa'lay'væn
with ham	**kinkku|voi|leivän**	kinkkoo voa'lay'væn
with cheese	**juusto|voi|leivän**	yōostoavoa'lay'væn
piece of cake	**palan kakkua**	pahlahn kahkkooah
potato salad	**peruna|salaattia**	payroonahsahlaattiah
sandwich	**voi|leivän**	voa'lay'væn
scrambled eggs	**muna|kokkelia**	moonahkoakkayliah
sweetcorn	**maissia**	mah'ssiah
toasted sandwich	**lämpimän voi|leivän**	læmpimæn voa'lay'væn

kappeli|voi|leipä (kahppaylivoa'-lay'pæ)	'chapel sandwich': fried French bread, bacon, topped with a fried egg
ooppera|voi|leipä (ōāpayrahvoa'-lay'pæ)	'opera sandwich': fried French bread, hamburger patty, egg
muna-anjovis|leipä (moonah-ahnyoavis-lay'pæ)	dark bread, slices of hard-boiled egg, anchovy fillets, tomato
silli|voi|leipä (sillivoa'lay'pæ)	herring sandwich: dark bread, and herring, often egg and tomato

Here's a basic list of food and drink that might come in useful when shopping for a picnic.

I'd like a/an/some…	**Saisinko**	sah'sinkoa
apples	**omenia**	oamayniah
bananas	**banaaneja**	bahnaanayyah
biscuits (Br.)	**keksejä**	kayksayyæ
beer	**olutta**	oaloottah
bread	**leipää**	lay'pǣ

butter	**voita**	voaᵗtah
cheese	**juustoa**	yōostoah
chips (Am.)	**peruna|lastuja**	payroonah**lahs**tooyah
chocolate bar	**suklaa|patukan**	sooklaapah**took**ahn
coffee	**kahvia**	kahhviah
cold cuts	**leikkeleitä**	layᵗkkaylayᵗtæ
cookies	**keksejä**	kayksayyæ
crackers	**voi|leipä|keksejä**	voaᵗlayᵗpækayksayyæ
eggs	**munia**	mooniah
gherkins (pickles)	**suola|kurkkua**	sᵒᵒoalah**koork**kooah
grapes	**viini|rypäleitä**	veenirewpælayᵗtæ
ice-cream	**jäätelöä**	yǣtayluræ
milk	**maitoa**	mahᵗtoah
mustard	**sinappia**	sinnahppiah
oranges	**appelsiineja**	ahppaylseenayya
pepper	**pippuria**	pippooriah
rolls	**sämpylöitä**	sæmpewlurᵗtæ
salt	**suolaa**	sᵒᵒoalaa
sausage	**makkaraa**	mahkkahraa
soft drink	**(alkoholittomia) juomia**	(ahlkoahoalittoamiah) yᵒᵒoamiah
sugar	**sokeria**	soakayriah
tea	**teetä**	tāytæ
yoghurt	**jogurttia**	yoakoorttiah

Travelling around

Plane *Lento*

Is there a flight to Ivalo?	**Onko lentoa Ivaloon?**	oankoa **layn**toah ivvahl**oa**n
Is it a direct flight?	**Onko se suora lento?**	oankoa say s°°oarah **layn**toa
When's the next flight to Jyväskylä?	**Milloin on seuraava lento Jyväskylään?**	milloa'n oan say°°raahvah **layn**toa yewvæskewlæn
Is there a connection to Kajaani?	**Onko yhteyttä Kajaaniin?**	oankoa ewhhtay^ewttæ **kah**yaahneen
I'd like to book a ticket to Oulu.	**Varaisin lipun Ouluun.**	vahrah'sin lippoon oa°°l**oa**n
single (one-way)	**meno|lippu**	maynoa**lip**poo
return (round trip)	**meno|paluu**	maynoapahl**oo**
business class	**business-luokka**	bisnis-l°°oakkah
aisle seat	**käytävä-paikka**	kæ^ewtævæ-pah'kkah
window seat	**ikkuna-paikka**	ik**koo**nahpah'kkah
What time do we take off?	**Mihin aikaan kone lähtee?**	mihin ah'kaahn **koa**nay læht**ay**
What time should I check in?	**Mihin aikaan minun on ilmoittauduttava?**	mihin ah'kaahn oan ilmoa'ttah°°**doot**tahvah
Is there a bus to the airport?	**Onko lentoasemalle bussia?**	oankoa **layn**toaahsaymahllah **boos**siah
What's the flight number?	**Mikä on lennon numero?**	mikkæ oan **layn**noan **noo**mayroa
What time do we arrive?	**Mihin aikaan olemme perillä?**	mihin ah'kaahn oalaymmay **payr**illæ
I'd like to... my reservation.	**Haluaisin... varaukseni.**	hahlooa'siin... vahrahooksayn
cancel	**peruuttaa**	payr**oo**ttaa
change	**muuttaa**	m**oo**ttaa
confirm	**vahvistaa**	**vahh**vistaa

SAAPUVAT	LÄHTEVÄT
ARRIVAL	DEPARTURE

Train *Juna*

Trains in Finland are operated by Finnish State Railways. Most long-distance trains are modern diesel trains. Electric trains make only certain short-distance runs from Helsinki.

Train travel is fast, comfortable and cheap. Long-distance trains usually have dining-cars and also sleeping-cars when necessary. First- and second-class seats may be reserved for a small extra charge; seat reservations are obligatory for special fast trains marked EP or IC. Children aged 6-17 travel half-price, under 6 free. The *Finnrail Pass* entitles to you to unlimited travel for periods of 8, 15 or 22 days.

kiito|juna (**kee**toa**yoo**nah)	long-distance express train between larger cities, stops only at main stations; luxury coaches; seat reservations required
pika|juna (**pik**kah**yoo**nah)	long-distance train, stops at larger stations
paikallis|juna (**kah**ᵗkahllis**yoo**nah)	local train, stops at all stations
kisko|bussi (**kis**koa**boos**si)	small diesel train used on short runs
sähkö|juna (**sæh**kur**yoo**nah)	electric train, used on short runs
makuu|vaunu (mah**koo**vah°°noo)	sleeping car with individual compartments
lepo|vaunu (**lay**poavah°°noo)	berths with blankets and pillows
ravintola|vaunu (**rah**vintoalahvah°°noo)	dining-car
kahvila|vaunu (**kah**villahvah°°noo)	buffet car
junailijan|vaunu (**yoo**nahᵗliyahnvah°°noo)	guard's van or baggage car; only registered luggage permitted

To the railway station *Rauta\|tie\|asemalle*

Where's the railway station?	**Missä on rauta|tie|asema?**	**mis**sæ oan rah°°**tah**tiaya**ah**saymah
Taxi!	**Taksi!**	**tahk**si
Take me to the...	**Viekää minut...**	v'ay**kæ** minnoot
railway station	**rauta|tie|asemalle**	rah°°**tah**tiaa**ah**saymahllay

What's the fare?	**Mitä maksaa?**	mittæ mahksaa

SISÄÄN	ENTRANCE	
ULOS	EXIT	
LAITUREILLE	TO THE PLATFORMS	
NEUVONTA	INFORMATION	

Where's the...? *Missä on...?*

Where is/are (the)...?	**Missä on/ovat...?**	missæ oan/oavaht
bar	**baari**	baari
booking office	**lipun|myynti**	lippoonmēwnti
currency exchange office	**valuutan|vaihto**	vahlōōtahnvah'htoa
left-luggage office (baggage check)	**matka|tavara|säily-tys**	mahtkahtahvahrah sæilewtewss
lost property (lost and found) office	**löytö|tavara|toi-misto**	lur°wturtahvahrahtoa'-mistoa
luggage lockers	**säilytys|lokerot**	sæ'lewtewsloakayroat
newsstand	**lehti|kioski**	layhtikioaski
platform 7	**laituri 7**	lah'toori say'tsaymæn
reservations office	**paikan|varaus**	pah'kahnvahrah°°s
restaurant	**ravintola**	rahvintoal
snack bar	**pika|baari**	pikkahbaari
ticket office	**lippu|toimisto**	lippootoa'mistoa
waiting room	**odotus|huone**	oadoatoosh°°oanay
Where are the toilets?	**Missä ovat WC:t?**	missæ oavaht vāyssäyt

Inquiries *Tiedusteluja*

When is the... train to Tampere?	**Milloin Tampe-reelle lähtee... juna?**	milloa'n tampayrāyllay læhtāy... yoonah
first/last/next	**ensimmäinen/viimeinen/seuraava**	aynsimmæ'nayn/veemay'nayn/say°°raavah
What time does the train to Turku leave?	**Mihin aikaan Tur-kuun lähtee juna?**	mihin ah'kaan toorkōōn læhtāy yoonah
What's the fare to Savonlinna?	**Mitä maksaa lippu Savonlinnaan?**	mittæ mahksaa lippoo sahvoanlinnaan
Is it a through train?	**Onko se suora yhteys?**	oankoa say s°°oarah ewhtay°wss
Is there a connection to...?	**Onko yhteyttä... -n/...-lle?**	oankoa ewhtay°wttæ...-n/ ...-llay

TAXI, see page 21

Do I have to change trains?	**Onko minun vaihdettava junaa?**	oankoa minnoon vah'hdayttahvah yoonaa
Is there enough time to change?	**Onko junan|vaihtoon tarpeeksi aikaa?**	oankoa yoonahnvah'hto͞an tahrpa̅yksi ah'kaa
Is the train running on time?	**Onko juna aika|taulussa?**	oankoa yoonah ah'kahtah°°loossah
What time does the train arrive in Mikkeli?	**Mihin aikaan juna saapuu Mikkeliin?**	mihin ah'kaan yoonah saapoͦͦ mikkayleen
Is there a dining car/ sleeping car on the train?	**Onko junassa ravintola|vaunua/ makuu|vaunua?**	oankoa yoonassah rahvintoalahvah°°nooah/ mahkoͦͦvah°°nooah
Does the train stop in Kouvola?	**Pysähtyykö juna Kouvolassa?**	pewsæht°ʷkur yoonah koa°°voalahssah
Which platform does the train to Lahti leave from?	**Miltä laiturilta juna Lahteen lähtee?**	miltæ lah'tooriltah yoonah lahhta̅yn læhta̅y
Which platform does the train from Vaasa arrive at?	**Mille laiturille juna Vaasasta saapuu?**	millay lah'toorillay yoonah vaassahstah saapoͦͦ
I'd like a time-table.	**Saisinko aika|taulun.**	sah'sinkoa ah'kahtah°°loon

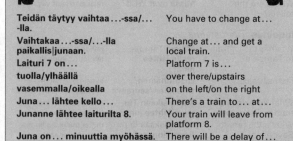

Teidän täytyy vaihtaa...-ssa/...-lla.	You have to change at...
Vaihtakaa...-ssa/...-lla paikallis|junaan.	Change at... and get a local train.
Laituri 7 on...	Platform 7 is...
tuolla/ylhäällä	over there/upstairs
vasemmalla/oikealla	on the left/on the right
Juna... lähtee kello...	There's a train to... at...
Junanne lähtee laiturilta 8.	Your train will leave from platform 8.
Juna on... minuuttia myöhässä.	There will be a delay of... minutes.
Ensimmäinen luokka on edessä/ keskellä/takana.	First class at the front/in the middle/at the rear.

Tickets *Liput*

I'd like a ticket to Pori.	**Saisinko lipun Poriin.**	**sah**'sinkoa **lippoon poa**reen
single (one-way)	**meno|lippu**	**may**noa**lip**poon
return (round trip)	**meno|paluu**	**may**noa**pah**l$\overline{oo}$
first/second class	**ensimmäinen/ toinen luokka**	**ayn**simmæ'**nayn/toa**nayn l^{oo}**oakkah**
for a child	**lasten lippu**	**lah**stayn **lip**poo

Reservation *Varaus*

I'd like to reserve a...	**Haluaisin varata...**	**hah**looah'sin **vah**rahtah
seat (by the window)	**(ikkuna|)paikan**	**(ik**koonah)**pah**'kahn
berth	**makuu|paikan**	**mah**k$\overline{oo}$**pah**'kahn
upper	**ylä|vuoteessa**	**ew**læv^{oo}**oatæes**sah
middle	**keski|vuoteessa**	**kays**kiv^{oo}**oat**æ**ys**sah
lower	**ala|vuoteessa**	**ah**lahv^{oo}**oat**æ**ys**sah
berth in the sleeping car	**makuu|paikan makuu|vaunussa**	**mah**k$\overline{oo}$**pah**'kahn **mah**k$\overline{oo}$**vah**°**noos**sah

All aboard *Kaikki vaunuihin*

Is this the right platform for the train to Pori?	**Onkohan tämä oikea laituri? Määrä|asema|ni on Pori.**	**oan**koa **tæ**mæ **oa**'kayah **lah**'toori mæræ**ahs**aymahni oan **poa**ri
Is this the right train to Tampere?	**Onko tämä Tampereen juna?**	**oan**koa **tæ**mæ **tahm**payr$\overline{ay}$n **yoo**nah
Excuse me. Could I get past?	**Anteeksi. Pääsisinkö ohi?**	**ahn**t$\overline{ay}$ksi **pææ**sissinkur **oa**hi
Is this seat taken?	**Onko tämä paikka varattu?**	**oan**koa **tæ**mæ **pah**'kkah **vah**rahttoo

TUPAKOITSIJOILLE	TUPAKOINTI KIELLETTY
SMOKER	NONSMOKER

I think that's my seat.	**Tämä taitaa olla minun paikka|ni.**	**tæ**mæ **tah**'taa **oal**lah **min**noon **pah**'kahni
Would you let me know before we get to Lahti?	**Ilmoittaisitteko minulle kun tulemme Lahteen.**	**il**moa'ttah'sittaykoa **min**noollay koon **too**laymmay **lahh**t$\overline{ay}$n
What station is this?	**Mikä asema tämä on?**	**mik**kæ **ah**saymah **tæ**mæ oan

| How long does the train stop here? | Kuinka kauan juna seisoo täällä? | koo'nkah ka°°ahn yoonah say'sōa tǣllæ |
| When do we arrive in Vaasa? | Milloin saavumme Vaasaan? | milloa'n saavoommay vaassaan |

Sleeping *Nukkua*

Are there any free compartments in the sleeping car?	Onko makuu|vaunussa vapaita paikkoja?	oankoa mahkōōvah°°noossah vahpah'tah pah'kkoayah
Where's the sleeping car?	Missä on makuu|vaunu?	missæ oan mahkōōvah°°noo
Where's my berth?	Missä on minun vuode|paikka|ni?	missæ oan minnoon v°°oadaypah'kkahni
I'd like a lower berth.	Voisinko saada ala|petin?	voa'sinkoa saadah ahlahpaytin
Would you make up our berths?	Laittaisitteko vuoteemme kuntoon?	lah'ttah'sittaykoa v°°oataȳmmay koontōan
Would you wake me at 7 o'clock?	Herättäisittekö minut kello 7?	hayrættæ'sittaykur minnoot kaylloa say'tsaymæn

Eating *Ruokailu*

If you want a full meal in the dining-car (*ravintola\|vaunu*— **rah**vintoalah**vah**°°noo), you may have to get a ticket from the attendant who'll come to your compartment.

| Where's the dining-car? | Missä on ravintola\|vaunu? | missæ oan rahvintoalah**vah**°°noo |

Baggage—Porters *Matkatavarat—Kantajat*

Porter!	Kantaja!	kahntahyah
Can you help me with my luggage?	Voitteko auttaa kantamisessa?	voa'ttaykoa ah°°ttaa kahntahmisayssah
Where are the luggage trolleys (carts)?	Missä on työntö|kärryjä?	missæ oan tew'''nturkærrewyæ
Where are the luggage lockers?	Missä on säilytys|lokeroita?	missæ oan sæ'lewtewsloakayroa'tah
Where's the left-luggage office (baggage check)?	Missä on matka|tavaran säilytys?	missæ oan mahtkahtahvahrahn sæ'lewtews
I'd like to leave my luggage, please.	Jättäisin matka|tavara|ni säilöön.	yættæ'sin mahtkahtahvahrahni sæ'lürn

| I'd like to register (check) my luggage. | **Lähettäisin matka\|tavara\|ni.** | læhhayttæ'sin **maht**kahtahvahrahni |

LÄHTEVÄ MATKA\|TAVARA
REGISTERING (CHECKING) BAGGAGE

Underground (subway) *Metro*

Helsinki is the only city in Finland with an underground service. The network is fairly limited with the trains running from the city centre to some of the eastern suburbs of Helsinki. The underground service is called the Metro and the city centre metro station may be entered from the main railway station.

Where's the nearest underground station?	**Missä on lähin metro|asema?**	missæ oan læhin maytroaahsaymah
Does this train go to…?	**Meneekö tämä juna…-n/…-lle?**	maynāykur tæmæ yoonah…-n/…-llay
Is the next station…?	**Onko seuraava asema…?**	oankoa say°°raavah ahsaymah

Coach (long-distance bus) *Linja-auto*

Finland's extensve coach network is especially important in northern regions where there are no railways. Modern, comfortable coaches run frequent, fast services. The fares are higher than for trains. Information on routes and timetables are available during office hours from travel information desks at coach stations.

When's the next coach to…?	**Milloin lähtee seuraava bussi…-n/…-lle?**	milloa'n læhtāy say°°raavah boossi…-n/…-llay
Does this coach stop at…?	**Pysähtyykö tämä auto…-ssa/…-lla?**	pewsæhtēwkur tæmæ ah°°toa…ssah/…llah
How long does the journey (trip) take?	**Kuinka kauan matka kestää?**	koo'nkah kah°°ahn mahtkah kaystǣ

Note: Most of the phrases on the previous pages can be used or adapted for travelling on local transport.

PORTERS, see also page 18

Bus—Tram (streetcar) *Bussi—Raitiovaunu*

There are local bus services in all cities and towns, and trams run in the major cities.

In Helsinki local buses serve the city centre and the various suburbs, but the trams operate only in the central area. Both bus and tram tickets may be purchased from the driver, and passengers must stamp their ticket after purchase in a special machine provided in the bus or tram. A ticket inspector may levy an instant fine on a passenger who has not stamped a ticket for the journey. A single ticket or a multiple journey card may be obtained from the driver. A single ticket is valid for an hour and it can be used within this time limit for an unrestricted number of journeys. The tickets are valid for both buses and trams.

Buses should always be boarded at the front. However you may enter the trams through any door - front, back or middle - if you have a ticket ready, but use the front door if you need to buy a ticket.

Taking a round-trip on a tram in Helsinki is a good way to see the city.

I'd like a booklet of tickets for Helsinki.	**Saisinko kymmenen matkan lipun Helsinkiä varten.**	sah'sinkoa **kewm**maynayn **maht**kahn lippoon haylsinkiæ **vahr**tayn
Which tram (streetcar) goes to the town centre?	**Mikä raitiovaunu menee kaupungin keskustaan?**	mikkæ rah'tioavah°°noo maynāy kah°°poongin kayskoostaan
Where can I get a bus/a tram (streetcar) to the opera?	**Missä pääsen bussiin/raitiovaunuun, joka menee oopperan luo?**	missæ pǣsayn **boos**seen/rah'tioavah°°nōōn, yoakah maynāy ōāppayrahn looah
Which bus do I take to Tapiola?	**Millä bussilla pääsen Tapiolaan?**	millæ **boos**sillah pǣsayn **tahp**ioalaan
Where's the bus stop?	**Missä on bussi⏐pysäkki?**	missæ oan **boos**sipewssækki
When is the... bus to Otaniemi?	**Milloin lähtee... bussi Otaniemeen?**	milloa'n **læh**tāȳ ... **boos**si oatahn'ay**mā**yn
first/last/next	**ensimmäinen/ viimeinen/seuraava**	**ayn**simmæ'nayn/ **vee**may'nayn/**say**°°raavah

How much is the fare to...?	**Mitä on maksu... -n/...-lle?**	mittæ oan **mahk**soo...-n/ ...-llay
Do I have to change buses?	**Täytyykö minun vaihtaa bussia?**	tæ^{ew}kur minnoon vah'htaa **boos**siah
How many bus stops are there to...?	**Montako pysäkkiä on...-n/...-lle?**	moantahkoa **pews**ækkiæ oan...-n/...-llay
Will you tell me when to get off?	**Sanoisitteko, kun minun täytyy nousta pois?**	sahnoa'sittaykoa koon minnoon tæ^{ew}tew noa^{oo}stah poais
I want to get off at Finlandia Hall.	**Haluaisin pois Finlandia|talon koh-dalla.**	hahlooah'sin poais finlahndiah**tah**loan **koah**dahllah

PYSÄKKI	BUS STOP

Boat service *Vesi\|liikenne*

There are superb car-ferry services all year round between Germany, Sweden and Finland. These car-ferries are like floating luxury hotels and tax-free shopping centres combined, and in addition they have first class restaurants and night-clubs, swimming-pools and saunas. There are also day-cruises from Helsinki to Tallin, Estonia.

Inland, Finland is a country of thousands of lakes and during the summer both modern pleasure boats and old-fashioned steamers sail them.

When does the next boat for... leave?	**Milloin lähtee seu-raava lautta...-n/...-lle?**	milloa'n læhtāy say^{oo}raavah lah^{oo}ttah...-n/...-llay
Where's the embarkation point?	**Missä noustaan laivaan?**	mistæ noa^{oo}staan lah'vaan
How long does the crossing take?	**Kauanko ylitys kestää?**	kah^{oo}ahnkoa ewlittews kaystæ
Which port(s) do we stop at?	**Mihin satamiin poikkeamme?**	mihin **sat**tahmeen poa'**kka**yahmmay
I'd like to take a cruise/tour of the harbour.	**Haluaisin risteilylle/satama|risteilylle.**	hahlooah'sin ristay'lewllay/ sah**tah**mahristay'lewllay
boat (small)/(large)	**vene/alus**	**vay**nay/**ah**loos

cabin	**hytti**	hewtti
single/double	**yhden hengen/**	ewhdayn/kahhdayn
	kahden hengen	hayngayn
deck	**kansi**	kahnsi
ferry	**lautta**	lah°°ttah
hydrofoil	**kanto|siipi|alus**	kahntoaseepiahloos
life belt/boat	**pelastus|liivit/**	paylahstoosleevit/
	pelastus|vene	paylahstoosvaynay
port	**satama**	sahtahmah
river cruise	**joki|risteily**	yoakiristay'lew
ship	**laiva**	lah'vah
steamer	**höyry|laiva**	hur^{ew}rewlah'vah
reclining seat	**lepo|tuoli**	laypoat°°oali

Other means of transport *Muita kulku\|välineitä*

The land area of Finland is large and the total population is small. You will find plenty of quiet country roads where cycling and walking is enjoyable. In addition, most cities and towns have special paths reserved for cyclists. During the winter long-distance skiing treks are organised.

There are no legal restrictions on hitchhiking, but like everywhere else in the world, it carries its own risks.

helicopter	**helikopteri**	haylikoaptayri
moped	**mopo**	moapoa
motorbike/scooter	**moottori|pyörä/**	mōattoaripew^{ur}ræ/
	skooteri	skōatayri

Or perhaps you prefer:

to hitchhike	**mennä peukalokyy-**	maynnæ
	dillä/liftata	pay°kahloakew̄dillæ/
		liftahtah
to walk	**kävellä**	kævayllæ

Bicycle hire *Pyörän vuokraus*

I'd like to hire a...	**Haluaisin vuok-**	hahlooah'sin
bicycle.	**rata...-pyörän**	v°°oakrahtah...-pew^{ur}ræn
5-gear	**vaihde|**	vah^hday
mountain	**maasto|**	maastoa

Car *Auto*

Cars drive on the right in Finland. Outside built-up areas all vehicles must have dipped headlights switched on at all times, even in broad daylight. Main roads are good throughout the country, but many secondary roads are unsurfaced. The use of both front and rear seat belts is compulsory.

Where's the nearest (self-service) filling station?	Missä on lähin (itse|palvelu)|bensi-ini|asema?	missæ oan læhin (itsaypahlvayloo) baynseeniahsaymah
Fill it up, please.	Tankki täyteen, kiitos.	tahnkki tæ*wtäyn keetoass
Give me... litres of petrol (gasoline).	Saanko... litraa bensiiniä.	saankoa... litraa baynseeniæ
super (premium)/ regular/unleaded/ diesel	Korkea|oktaanista/ matala|oktaanista/ lyijytöntä/die-sel|öljyä	koarkayahoaktaahnistah/ mahtahlahoaktaahnistah/ lew'yewturntæ/ d'aysaylurlyewæ
Please check the...	... Voisitteko tar-kistaa sen.	voa'sittaykoa tahrkistaa sayn
anti-freeze	jäähdytys|neste	yǣhdewtewsnaystay
battery	akku	ahkkoo
brake fluid	jarru|neste	yarroonaystay
oil/coolant/ windscreen water	öljy/jäähdy-tys|neste/ tuuli|lasin|pesu|neste	urlyew/ yǣadewtewsnnaystay/ tōōlilahsinpay soonaystay
Would you check the tyre pressures?	Tarkistaisitteko ilman|paineet?	tahrkistah'sittaykoa ilmahnpah'nāyt
1.6 front, 1.8 rear.	Yksi pilkku kuusi edessä, yksi pilkku kahdeksan takana.	ewksi pilkkoo kōōsi aydayssæ ewksi pilkkoo kahhdayksahn tahkahnah
Please could you check the spare tyre too?	Tarkistaisitteko myös vara|ren-kaan?	tahrkistah'sittaykoa mew""s vahrahraynkaahn
Can you mend this puncture (fix this flat)?	Voitteko korjata tämän renkaan?	voa'ttaykoa koaryahtah tæmæn raynkaahn
Would you change the... please?	Voisitteko vaih-taa ...	voa'sittaykoa vah'htaa
bulb	lampun	lamppoon
fan belt	tuulettimen hihnan	tōōlayttimayn hihnahn
snow chains	lumi|ketjut	loomikaytyoot

CAR HIRE, see page 20

spark(ing) plugs	**sytytys|tulpat**	**sew**tewtews**tool**paht
tyre	**renkaan**	**rayn**kaahn
wipers	**pyyhkijän sulat**	pēwhkiyæn **soo**laht
Would you clean the windscreen (windshield)?	**Puhdistaisitteko tuuli|lasin.**	poohdistah'sittaykoa tōolilahsin

Asking the way—Street directions *Kysyä tietä— Kulku\|ohjeet*

Can you tell me the way to…?	**Voitteko neuvoa tien…-n/…-lle?**	voa'ttaykoa **nay**°°voah tiayn…-n/…- llay
In which direction is…?	**Missä suunnassa on…?**	missæ sōonnahssah oan
How do I get to…?	**Miten pääsen…-n/ …-lle?**	mitayn **pǣ**sayn…-n/… -llay
Are we on the right road for…?	**Viekö tämä tie… -n/…-lle?**	v'**ay**kur tæmæ t'ay…-n/… -llay
How far is the next village?	**Kuinka kaukana on seuraava kylä?**	koo'nkah kah°°kahnah oan say°°raahvah kewlæ
How far is it to… from here?	**Kuinka kaukana täältä on…?**	koo'nkah kah°°kahnah tǣltæ oan
Is there a motorway (expressway)?	**Onko moottori|tietä?**	oankoa mōattoarit'aytæ
How long does it take by car/on foot?	**Kauanko kestää mennä autolla/ jalan?**	ka°°ahnkoa kaystǣ maynnæ ah°°toallah/ yahlahn
Can I drive to the centre of town?	**Voinko ajaa kaupungin keskus- taan?**	voh'nkoa ahyaa kah°°poongin kayskoostaan
Is traffic allowed in the town centre?	**Onko autolla ajo sallittu kaupungin keskustassa?**	oankoa ah°°toallah ahyoa sahllittooah kah°°poongin kayskoostahssah
Can you tell me where… is?	**Voitteko kertoa, missä… on?**	voa'ttaykoa kayrtoah missæ… oan
How can I find this place/address?	**Kuinka löydän tämän paikan/ osoitteen?**	koo'nkah lur**ew**dæn tæmæn pah'kahn/oasoa'ttǣyn
Where's this?	**Missä tämä on?**	missæ tæmæ oan
Can you show me on the map where I am?	**Voitteko näyttää kartalta, missä olen?**	voa'ttaykoa næ**ew**ttǣ kahrtahltah missæ oalayn
Where are the nearest public toilets?	**Missä on lähin yleinen käymälä?**	missæ oan læhin ewlay'nayn kæ**ew**mælæ

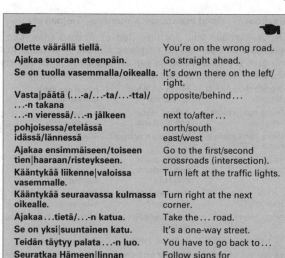

Olette väärällä tiellä.	You're on the wrong road.
Ajakaa suoraan eteenpäin.	Go straight ahead.
Se on tuolla vasemmalla/oikealla.	It's down there on the left/right.
Vasta|päätä (...-a/...-ta/...-tta)/...-n takana	opposite/behind...
...-n vieressä/...-n jälkeen	next to/after...
pohjoisessa/etelässä idässä/lännessä	north/south east/west
Ajakaa ensimmäiseen/toiseen tien|haaraan/risteykseen.	Go to the first/second crossroads (intersection).
Kääntykää liikenne|valoissa vasemmalle.	Turn left at the traffic lights.
Kääntykää seuraavassa kulmassa oikealle.	Turn right at the next corner.
Ajakaa...tietä/...-n katua.	Take the... road.
Se on yksi|suuntainen katu.	It's a one-way street.
Teidän täytyy palata...-n luo.	You have to go back to...
Seuratkaa Hämeen|linnan viittoja/merkkejä.	Follow signs for Hämeen|linna.

Parking *Pysäköinti*

Park in the direction of moving traffic, on the right side of the road. Obey the posted parking restrictions. You may be fined for parking less than three metres from a pedestrian crossing.

Where can I park?	Minne voin pysä-köidä?	minay voa'n pewsækur'dæ
Is there a car park nearby?	Onko lähellä pysä-köinti|aluetta?	oankoa læhayllæ pewsækur'ntiahloo^ay'ttah
May I park here?	Voinko pysäköidä tähän?	voa'nkoa pewsækur'dæ tæhæn
How long can I park here?	Kuinka kauan voin pysäköidä tässä?	koo'nkah kah°°vahn voa'n pewsækur'dæ tæssæ
What's the charge per hour?	Mitä maksu on tunnilta?	mittæ oan mahksoo toonniltah
Do you have some change for the parking meter?	Olisiko teillä koli-koita pysä-köinti|mittariin?	oalisikoa tay'llæ koalikkoa'tah pewsækur'ntimittahreen

Breakdown—Road assistance *Konerikko—Tie|palvelu*

The Automobile and Touring Club of Finland (*Auto-liitto*) operates a 24-hour service telephone number in Helsinki that will give you information on garages anywhere in the country which can come out to your vehicle in case of breakdown.

Where's the nearest garage?	**Missä on lähin korjaamo?**	missæ oan læhin koaryaamoa
My car has broken down.	**Autoni meni epä|kuntoon.**	a⁰⁰toani mayni aypækoontōᾱn
Where can I make a phone call?	**Mistä voin soittaa?**	mistæ voaᶦn soaᶦttaa
I've had a break-down at...	**Autoni meni epä|kuntoon ...n kohdalla.**	a⁰⁰toani mayni aypækoontōᾱn ...-n koahdahllah
Can you send a mechanic?	**Voitteko lähettää korjaajan?**	voaᶦttaykoa læhayttǣ koaryaayahn
My car won't start.	**Autoni ei käyn-nisty.**	ah⁰⁰toani ayᶦ kæᵉᵂnnistew
The battery is dead.	**Akku on tyhjä.**	ahkkoo oan tewhyæ
I've run out of petrol (gasoline)/diesel.	**Minulta on bensa/ dieselöljy lopussa.**	minnooltah oan baynsah/ deessaylurlyew loapoossah
I have a flat tyre.	**Minulla on rengas tyhjänä.**	minoollah oan rayngahs tewhyænæ
The engine is over-heating.	**Moottori yli|kuu-menee.**	mōᾱttoari ewlikōōmaynāy
There's something wrong with the...	**... ei toimi kun-nolla.**	ayᶦ toami koonnoallah
brakes	**jarrut**	yarroot
carburettor	**kaasutin**	kaasootin
exhaust pipe	**pako|putki**	pahkoapootki
radiator	**jäähdyttäjä**	yǣhdewttæyæ
wheel	**pyörä**	pewᵘʳræ
Can you send a breakdown van (tow truck)?	**Voitteko lähettää hinaus|auton?**	voaᶦttaykoa læhayttǣ hinnah⁰⁰sah⁰⁰toan
How long will you be?	**Kuinka pian voitte olla täällä?**	kooᶦnkah pᶦahn voaᶦttay oallah tǣllæ
Can you give me an estimate?	**Voitteko antaa arvion?**	voaᶦttaykoa ahntaa ahrvᶦoan

Accident—Police *Onnettomuus—Poliisi*

Please call the police.	**Kutsukaa poliisi.**	kootsookaa poaleessi
There's been an accident. It's about 2 km. from Tampere.	**On sattunut onnettomuus. Se on noin 2km Tampereelta.**	oan sahttoonoot oannayttoamōōss say oan noain 2km tahmpayrāyltah
Where's there a telephone?	**Missä on puhelin?**	missæ oan poohaylin
Call a doctor/an ambulance quickly.	**Kutsukaa nopeasti lääkäri/ambulanssi.**	kootsookaa noapayahsti lǣkæri/ahmboolahnssi
There are people injured.	**Ihmisiä on loukkaantunut.**	ihmissiæ oan loa°°kkaantoonoot
Here's my driving licence.	**Tässä on ajo|kortti.**	tæssæ oan ahyoakoarttini
What's your name and address?	**Mikä on nimenne ja osoitteenne?**	mikkæ oan nimmaynnay yah oassoa'ttāynnay
What's your insurance company?	**Mikä on vakuutus|yhtiönne?**	mikæ oan vahkōōtoosewht'urnnay

Road signs *Liikenne\|merkkejä*

AJA HITAASTI	Drive slowly
AJO SALLITTU OMALLA VASTUULLA	Drive at own risk
AJO SALLITTU TONTEILLE	Access to residents only
ALUE|RAJOITUS	Local speed limit
HEIKKO TIEN|REUNA	Soft shoulders
IRTO|KIVIÄ	Loose stones
KAPEA SILTA	Narrow bridge
KELI|RIKKO	Frost damage
KOKEILE JARRUJA	Test your brakes
KOULU	School
LINJA-AUTO|KAISTA	Bus has priority
LIUKAS TIE	Slippery road
LOSSI	Ferry
NOPEUS|RAJOITUS	Speed limit... km
NÄHTÄVYYS	Lookout point
PYSÄKÖINTI|PAIKKA	Parking
PYÖRÄILIJÄ	Cycle path
RYHMITYS|MERKKI	Get in lane
SUOSITELTU NOPEUS|RAJOITUS	Recommended speed limit
TIE SAVETTU	Newly-surfaced road
TIE|TYÖ	Road works
TULLI	Customs
YKSITYIS|TIE	Private road

Sightseeing

Where's the tourist office?	**Missä on matka-|toimisto?**	missæ oan mahtkah-toa'mistoa
What are the main points of interest?	**Mitä nähtävyyksiä täällä on?**	mittæ næhtævew̄ksiæ tǣllæ oan
We're here for...	**Olemme täällä ....**	oalaymmay tǣllæ
only a few hours	**vain muutaman tunnin**	vah'n mōōtahmahn toonnin
a day	**päivän**	pæ'væn
a week	**viikon**	veekoan
Can you recommend a sightseeing tour/an excursion?	**Voitteko suositella nähtävyys|kier-rosta/retkeä?**	voa'ttaykoa s°°assittayllah næhtævew̄sk'ayrroastah/raytkayæ
Where do we leave from?	**Mistä on lähtö?**	mistæ oan læhtur
Will the bus pick us up at the hotel?	**Hakeeko bussi meidät hotellilta?**	hahkāykoa boossi maydæt hoatayllilta
How much does the tour cost?	**Paljonko kierros maksaa?**	pahlyoankoa k'ayrroass mahksaa
What time does the tour start?	**Mihin aikaan kier-ros alkaa?**	mihin ah'kaan k'ayrroass ahlkaa
Is lunch included?	**Sisältyykö lounas hintaan?**	sissæltew̄kur loa°°nahs hintaan
What time do we get back?	**Mihin aikaan olemme takaisin?**	mihin ah'kaan oalaymmay tahkah'sin
Do we have free time in...?	**Onko meillä varan aikaa...?**	oankoa may'llæ vahrahn ah'kaa
Is there an English-speaking guide?	**Onko siellä englan-tia puhuva opas?**	oankoa s'ayllæ aynglahntiah poohoovah oapahss
I'd like to hire a private guide for...	**Haluaisin palkata yksityisen oppaan...**	hahlooah'ssin pahlkahtah ewkssittew'sayn oappaann
half a day	**puoleksi päiväksi**	p°°oalayksi pæ'væksi
a day	**päiväksi**	pæ'væksi
Where is/Where are the...?	**Missä on/Missä ovat...?**	missæ oan/missæ oavaht
abbey	**luostari**	l°°oastahri
art gallery	**taide|galleria**	tah'daygahllayriah
botanical gardens	**kasvi|tieteellinen puutarha**	kahsvit'aytǣylinnayn pōōtahrhah

building	**rakennus**	rahkaynnooss
business district	**liike|keskus**	leekaykayskooss
castle	**linna**	linnah
cathedral	**tuomio|kirkko**	t°°amioakeerkkoa
cemetery	**hautaus|maa**	hah°°tah°°smaa
city centre	**(kaupungin) kes-**	(kah°°poongin)
	kusta	kayskkoostah
chapel	**kappeli**	kahppayli
church	**kirkko**	keerkkoa
concert hall	**konsertti|sali/|talo**	koansayrttisahli/tahloa
convent	**nunna|luostari**	noonnahlŌŌoastahri
court house	**oikeus|talo**	oaˈkay°°stahloa
downtown area	**keskusta**	kayskoostah
embankment	**ranta|penger**	rahntahpayngayr
exhibition	**näyttely**	næᵉᵛᵛttaylew
factory	**tehdas**	tayhdahss
fair	**messut/markkinat**	mayssoot/mahrkkinnaht
flea market	**kirppu|tori**	keerppootoari
fortress	**linnoitus**	linnoaˈtooss
fountain	**(suihku)lähde**	(soo'hkoo)læhday
gardens	**puu|tarha**	pōōtahrah
harbour	**satama**	sahtahmah
lake	**järvi**	yærvi
library	**kirjasto**	keeryahstoa
market	**(kauppa|)tori**	(kah°°ppah)toari
memorial	**muisto|merkki**	mooˈstoamayrkki
monastery	**munkki|luostari**	moonkkil°°oastahri
monument	**monumentti**	moanoomayntti
museum	**museo**	moossayoa
old town	**vanha kaupunki**	vahnhah kah°°poonki
opera house	**ooppera|talo**	ŌŌppayrah
palace	**palatsi**	pahlahtsi
park	**puisto**	pooˈstoa
parliament building	**edus|kunta|talo**	aydooskoontahtahloa
planetarium	**planetaario**	plahnaytahrioa
presidential palace	**presidentin|linna**	prayssidayntinlinnah
ruins	**rauniot**	rah°°nˈoat
shopping area	**ostos|keskus**	oastoaskayskooss
square	**tori**	toari
stadium	**stadion**	stahdˈoan
statue	**patsas**	pahtsahs
stock exchange	**pörssi**	purssi
theatre	**teatteri**	tayahttayri
theme park	**tiede|puisto/|kes-**	tˈaydaypooˈstoa/kayskooss
	kus	
tomb	**hauta**	hah°°tah
tower	**torni**	toarni

town hall	**kaupungin|talo/ raati|huone**	kah°°poongintahloa/ raattih°°oanay
university	**yli|opisto**	ewlioapistoa
zoo	**eläin|tarha**	aylæ¹ntahrhah

Admission *Sisään\|pääsy*

Is... open on Sundays?	**Onko... avoinna sunnuntaisin?**	oankoa... ahvoa¹nnah soon¹noontah¹sin
What are the opening hours?	**Mitkä ovat auki|olo|ajat?**	mitkæ oavaht ah°°kioaloaahyaht
When does it close?	**Milloin se suljetaan?**	milloa¹n say soolyaytaan
How much is the entrance fee?	**Mikä on pääsy|maksu?**	mikkæ oan pææsewmahksoo
Is there any reduction for (the)...?	**Onko heille alennuksia...?**	oankoa hay¹llay ahlaynnooksiah
children	**lapsille**	lahpsillay
disabled	**vammaisille**	vahmmah¹ssillay
groups	**ryhmille**	rewhmillay
pensioners	**eläkeläisille**	aylækaylæ¹ssillay
students	**opiskelijoille**	oapiskayliyoa¹llay
Do you have a guide-book (in English)?	**Onko teillä opas|kirjaa (englanniksi)?**	oankoa tay¹llæ oapahskeeryaa
Can I buy a catalogue?	**Voinko ostaa luettelon?**	voa¹nkoa oastaa looayttayloan
Is it all right to take pictures?	**Saako valo|kuvata?**	saakoa vahloakoovahtah

| Is there easy access for the disabled? | **Onko vammaisille omaa sisään\|käyntiä?** | oankoa vahmmah¹ssillay oamaa sissāēnkæ⁻ᵛntiæ |
| Are there facilities/ activities for children? | **Onko lapsille omia tiloja/omaa toimintaa?** | oankoa lahpsillay oamiah tiloayah/oamaa toa¹mintaa |

Who—What—When? *Kuka—Mikä—Milloin?*

| What's that building? | **Mikä tuo rakennus on?** | mikkæ t°°oa rahkaynnooss |
| Who was the...? | **Kuka oli...** | kookah oali |

architect	arkkitehti	ahrkkitayhti
artist	taiteilija	tah'tay'liyah
painter	taide|maalari	tah'daymaalahri
sculptor	kuvan|veistäjä	koovahnvay'stæyæ
Who built it?	Kenen rakentama se on?	kaynayn rahkayntahmah say oan
Who painted that picture?	Kenen maalaama tuo taulu on?	kaynayn maalaamah t°°oa tah°°loo oan
When did he live?	Milloin hän eli?	milloa'n hæn ayli
When was it built?	Milloin se on rakennettu?	milloa'n say oan rahkaynnayttoo
Where's the house where... lived?	Missä on talo, jossa ... asui?	missæ oan tahloa yoassah ... ahsoo'
We're interested in...	Meitä kiinnostaa/ kiinnostavat...	may'tæ keennoastaa/ keennoastahvaht
antiques	antiikki	ahnteekki
archaeology	arkeologia	ahrkayoaloagiah
art	taide	tah'day
botany	kasvi|tiede	kahsvit'ayday
ceramics	keramiikka	kayrahmeekkah
coins	(metalli|)rahat	(maytahlli)rahhaht
fine arts	taide-esineet	tah'dayaysinnäyt
furniture	huone|kalut	h°°oanaykahloot
geology	geologia	g°'oaloagiah
handicrafts	käsi|työ(|tuotteet)	kæsitew°'t°°oattäyt
history	historia	histoariah
medicine	lääke|tiede	lækayt'ayday
music	musiikki	mooseekki
natural history	luonnon|historia	l°°oannoanhistoariah
ornithology	lintu|tiede	lintoot'ayday
painting	maalaus(|taide)	maalah°°s(tah'day)
pottery	saven|valanta	sahvaynvahlahntah
religion	uskonto	ooskoantoa
sculpture	kuvan|veisto (|taide)	koovahnvay'stoa(tah'day)
zoology	eläin|tiede	aylæ'nt'ayday
Where's the... department?	Missä on ...osasto?	missæ oan ... oassahstoa
It's...	Se on...	say oan
amazing	hämmästyttävä	hæmmæstewttævā
awful	kaamea	kaamayah
beautiful	kaunis	kah°°niss
gloomy	synkkä	sewnkkæ
impressive	vaikuttava	vah'koottavah
interesting	mielen|kiintoinen	m'aylaynkeentoa'nayn

magnificent	**komea**	koamayah
pretty	**sievä**	s'ayvæ
strange	**outo**	oa°°toa
superb	**erinomainen**	ayrinoamah'nayn
terrifying	**pelottava**	payloattahvah
tremendous	**valtava**	vahltahvah
ugly	**ruma**	roomah

Churches—Religious services *Jumalan│palvelus*

The vast majority of Finns are Protestants (Evangelical Lutheran). Churches are usually open for visiting. In Helsinki there are also two Roman Catholic churches, a Greek Orthodox cathedral, an Anglican church, American (Protestant) services and a synagogue.

Is there a... near here?	**Onko täällä ...?**	oankoa tǣllæ
Catholic church	**katolista kirkkoa**	kahtoallistah keerkkoaah
Protestant church	**protestanttista kirkkoa**	proataystahnttistah keerkkkoaah
mosque	**moskeijaa**	moaskay'yaa
synagogue	**synagoogaa**	sewnahgōāgaa
What time is...?	**Mihin aikaan on...?**	mihin ah'kaan oan
mass/the service	**messu/jumalan-│palvelus**	mayssoo/yoomahlahnpahlvayllooss
Where can I find a... who speaks English?	**Mistä löytyisi..., joka puhuu englantia?**	mistæ lur^{ew}tew'si... yoakah poohōō aynglahntiah
priest/minister/rabbi	**katolinen pappi/ (protestanttinen) pappi/rabbi**	kahtoallinayn pahppi (proataystahnttinayn) pahppi/rahbbi
I'd like to visit the church.	**Haluaisin käydä kirkossa.**	hahlooah'sin kæewdæ keerkoassah
I'd like to go to confession.	**Haluaisin mennä ripittäytymään.**	hahlooah'sin maynnæ rippittæ^{ew}tewmǣn

In the countryside *Maaseudulla*

| Is there a scenic route to...? | **Onko kaunista reittiä ...?** | oankoa kah°°nistah ray'ttiæ |
| How far is it to...? | **Kuinka kaukana on...?** | koo'nkah kah°°kahnah oan |

Can we walk there?	**Voiko sinne kävellä?**	voaⁱkoa sinnay kævayllæ
How high is that mountain?	**Kuinka korkea tuo vuori on?**	koo'nnkah koarkayah t°°oa v°°oari oan
What kind of... is that?	**Minkä lajin ... tuo on?**	minkæ lahyin ... t°°oa oan
animal	**eläin**	aylæin
bird	**lintu**	lintoo
flower	**kukka**	kookkah
tree	**puu**	pōō

Landmarks Maa|merkkejä

bridge	**silta**	siltah
cliff	**jyrkänne**	yewrkænnay
farm	**maa|talo**	maatahloa
field	**pelto**	payltoa
fjord	**vuono**	v°°oanoa
footpath	**polku**	poalkoo
forest	**metsä**	maytsæ
garden	**puu|tarha**	pōōtahrhah
glacier	**jäätikkö**	yǣtikkur
hill	**mäki**	mæki
house	**talo**	tahloa
island	**saari**	saari
lake	**järvi**	yærvi
meadow	**niitty**	neettew
mountain	**vuori**	v°°oari
(mountain) pass	**sola**	soalah
path	**polku**	poalkoo
peak	**huippu**	hoo'ppoo
pond	**lampi**	lahmpi
river	**joki**	yoaki
road	**tie**	t'ay
sea	**meri**	mayri
spring	**lähde**	læhday
valley	**laakso**	laaksoa
village	**kylä**	kewlæ
vineyard	**viini|tarha**	veenitahrhah
wall	**muuri**	mōōri
waterfall	**vesi|putous**	vaysipootoa^{uu}ss
wood	**metsä**	maytsæ

ASKING THE WAY, see page 76

Relaxing

Cinema (movies)—Theatre *Elo|kuvat—Teatteri*

All films are shown in the original version with Finnish and Swedish subtitles. There are ususally two showings at 7 and 9 p.m. You can buy tickets in advance.

In theatres curtain time is normally 7.30 p.m. Advance booking is advisable.

The newspapers list the day's stage and screen schedules.

What's on at the cinema tonight?	**Mitä elo|kuvissa on tänä iltana?**	mittæ ayloakoovissah oan tænæ iltahnah
What's playing at the... Theatre?	**Mitä... -teatterissa esitetään?**	mittæ... tayahttayrissah ayssittaytǣn
What sort of play is it?	**Millainen näytelmä se on?**	millah'nayn næ⁰ʷtaylmæ say oan
Who's it by?	**Kenen kirjoittama se on?**	kaynayn keeryoattahmah say oan
Can you recommend a good...?	**Mikä olisi hyvä...?**	mikkæ oalissi hewvæ
film	**filmi**	filmi
comedy	**komedia**	koamayd'ah
musical	**musikaali**	moossikkaali
Where's that new film directed by... being shown?	**Missä esitetään sitä uutta filmiä, jonka on ohjan-nut...?**	missæ ayssitaytǣn sittæ ōōttah filmiæ yonkah oan oahyahnnoot
Who's in it?	**Kuka siinä näytte-lee?**	kookah seenæ næ⁰ʷttaylāy
Who's playing the lead?	**Kuka on pää|osassa?**	kookah oan pǣoassahssah
Who's the director?	**Kuka on ohjaaja?**	kookah oan oahyaayah
At which theatre is that new play by... being performed?	**Missä teatterissa esitetään sitä uutta näytelmää, jonka on kirjoittanut...?**	missæ tayahttayrissah ayssittaytǣn sittæ ōōttah næ⁰ʷtaylmæ yoankah oan keeryoattahnoot
What time does it begin?	**Mihin aikaan se alkaa?**	mihin ah'kaan say ahlkaa
Are there any seats for tonight?	**Onko täksi illaksi paikkoja?**	oankoa tæksi illahksi pah'kkoayah
How much are the seats?	**Paljonko liput mak-savat?**	pahlyoankoa lippoot mahksahvaht

I'd like to reserve 2 seats for the show on Friday evening.	**Haluaisin varata 2 paikkaa perjantai-illan näytökseen.**	hahlooah'sin **vah**rahtah kahksi pah'kkaa payryahntai illahn næ⁰ʷturksāyn
Can I have a ticket for the matinée on Tuesday?	**Saisinko lipun tiis-tain varhais|näy-täntöön.**	sah'sinkoa lippoon teestah'n vahrhah'snæ⁰ʷtæntūrn
I'd like a seat in the stalls (orchestra).	**Haluaisin paikan etu|permannolta.**	hahlooah'sin pah'kahn aytoopayrmannoaltah
Not too far back.	**Ei liian takaa.**	ay' leeahntahkaa
Somewhere in the middle.	**Jostain keskeltä.**	yoastah'n kayskayltæ
How much are the seats in the circle (mezzanine)?	**Paljonko maksavat parveke|paikat?**	pahlyoankoa **mahks**ahvaht pahrvaykaypah'kaht
May I have a programme, please?	**Saisinko ohjelman.**	sah'sinkoa oahyaylmahn
Where's the cloakroom?	**Missä on vaate|säilö?**	missæ oan vaataysæ'liur

---

Valitettavasti näytös on loppuun|myyty.	I'm sorry, we're sold out.
Jäljellä on vain muutamia paikkoja parvekkeella.	There are only a few seats left in the circle (mezzanine).
Saanko nähdä lippunne?	May I see your ticket?
Tässä on paikkanne.	This is your seat.

Opera—Ballet—Concert *Ooppera—Baletti—Konsertti*

Finland is a country of music and architecture and both of these forms of art are combined in the new ultra modern opera house in the centre of Helsinki. Nearby there is also a large concert hall, Finlandia House, designed by Alvar Aalto, one of Finland's foremost architects.

Can you recommend a good...?	**Mikä olisi hyvä...?**	mikkæ oalisi hewvæ
ballet	**baletti**	bahlaytti
concert	**konsertti**	koansayrtti

DAYS OF THE WEEK, see page 151

opera	**ooppera**	ōāppayrah
operetta	**operetti**	oapayrayrti
Where's the opera house/the concert hall?	**Missä on ooppera|talo/kon-sertti|sali?**	missæ oan ōāppayrahtahloa/koansayrttisahli
What's on at the opera tonight?	**Mitä ooperassa on tänä iltana?**	mittæ ōāppayrahssah oan tænæ iltahnah
Who's singing/dancing?	**Kuka laulaa/tans-sii?**	kookah lah°°laa/tahnssee
Which orchestra is playing?	**Mikä orkesteri soit-taa?**	mikkæ oarkaystayri soaˈttaa
What are they playing?	**Mitä he esittävät?**	mittæ hay ayssittævæt
Who's the conductor/soloist?	**Kuka on kapelli|mestari/solisti?**	kookah oan kahpayllimaystahri

Nightclubs—Discos *Yö\|kerho—Disko*

In the larger towns there are nightclubs and discotheques. Some restaurants provide cabaret-type entertainment and most large restaurants have a dance-floor. Men are usually required to wear a jacket and tie.

During the summer open air dances are very popular. These are held on large, purpose-built covered platforms called *tanssilava* (**tahn**ssila**vah**), which are usually situated in a picturesque setting near a lake or in a forest clearing.

Can you recommend a good nightclub?	**Voitteko suositella hyvää yö|kerhoa?**	voaˈttaykoa s°°asittayllah hewvæ ewˈˈkayrhoaah
Is there a floor show?	**Onko siellä ohjel-maa?**	oankoa sˈayllæ oahyaylmaa
What time does the show start?	**Mihin aikaan ohjelma alkaa?**	mihin ahˈkaan oahyaylmah ahlkaa
Is evening dress required?	**Vaaditaanko ilta|puku?**	vaadittaankoa iltahpookoo
Where can we go dancing?	**Minne voimme mennä tanssi-maan?**	minnay voaˈmmay maynnæ tahnssimmaan
Is there a disco-theque in town?	**Onko tässä kau-pungissa diskoa?**	oankoa tæssæ kah°°poongissah diskoaah
Would you like to dance?	**Haluaisitteko tans-sia?**	hahlooaiˈsittaykoa tahnssiah

Sports *Urheilu*

Is there a football (soccer) match anywhere this Saturday?	**Onko jossain jalka|pallo-ottelua tänä lauantaina?**	oankoa yoassah'n yalkahpahlloa-oattaylooah tænæ lah°°ahntah'nah
Which teams are playing?	**Mitkä joukkueet pelaavat?**	mitkæ yoa°°kkooāyt paylaavaht
Can you get me a ticket?	**Voitteko hankkia minulle lipun?**	voa'ttaykoa hahnkkiah minnoollay lippoon

basketball	**kori|pallo**	koaripahlloa
boxing	**nyrkkeily**	newrkkaylew
car racing	**kilpa-ajot**	kilpahahyoat
cycling	**pyöräily**	pew⁖ræilew
cycle racing	**pyörä|kilpailut**	pew⁖rækilpah'loot
football (soccer)	**jalka|pallo**	yahlkahpahlloa
ice hockey	**jää|hockey**	yæhoakkay'
(horse-back) riding	**ratsastus**	rahtsahstooss
mountaineering	**vuoristo|kiipeily**	v°°oaristoakeepay'lew
speed skating	**pika|luistelu**	pikkahloo'stayloo
ski jumping	**mäki|hyppy**	mækihewppew
skiing	**hiihto**	heehtoa
swimming	**uinti**	oo'nti
tennis	**tennis**	taynnis
trotting race	**ravi|kilpailut**	rahvikilpah'loot
volleyball	**lento|pallo**	layntoapahlloa

I'd like to see a boxing match.	**Haluaisin nähdä nyrkkeily|ottelun.**	hahlooah'sin næhdæ newrkkaylewoattayloon
What's the admission charge?	**Mitä on pääsy|maksu?**	mikkæ oan pæsewmahksoo
Where's the nearest golf course?	**Missä on lähin golf-rata?**	missæ oan læhin golf-rahtah
Where are the tennis courts?	**Missä on tennis-kenttiä?**	missæ oan taynniskaynttiæ
What's the charge per ...?	**Mitä on maksu ...?**	mikkæ oan mahksoo
day/round/hour	**päivältä/kierrok-selta/tunnilta**	pæ'væltæ/k'ayrroaksayltah/toonniltah
Can I hire (rent) rackets?	**Voinko vuokrata mailat?**	voa'nkoa v°°oakrahtah mah'laht
Where's the race course (track)?	**Missä on kilpa|rata?**	missæ oan kilpahrahtah

Is there any good fishing/hunting around here?	Onko t="ällä hyviä kalastus	/metsästys	paikkoja?	oankoa tællæ hewviæ kahlahstoos/maytsæstewspah'kkoayah
Do I need a permit?	Tarvitsenko luvan?	tahrvitsaynkoa loovahn
Where can I get one?	Mistä voin saada sellaisen?	mistæ voa'n saadah sayllah'sayn
Can one swim in the lake/river?	Voiko tuossa järvessä/joessa uida?	voa'koa t°°oassah yærvayssæ/yoa"ssæ oo'dah
Is there a swimming pool here?	Onko täällä uima-allasta?	oankoa tællæ oo'mahahllahstah
Is it open-air or indoor?	Onko se ulko	allas vai sisä	allas?	oankoa say oolkoaahllahs vah' sissæahllahs
Is it heated?	Lämmitetäänkö sitä?	læmmittaytæænkur sittæ
What's the temperature of the water?	Mikä on veden lämpö	tila?	mikkæ oan vaydayn læmpurtillah
Is there a sandy beach?	Onko hiekka	rantaa?	oankoa h'aykkahrahntaa

On the beach Rannalla

Is it safe to swim here?	Onko täällä turvallista uida?	oankoa tællæ toorvahllistah oo'dah
Is there a lifeguard?	Onko täällä hengen|pelastajaa?	oankoa tællæ hayngaynpaylahstahyaa
Is it safe for children?	Onko se turvallinen lapsille?	oankoa say toorvahllinayn lahpsillay
The sea is very calm.	Meri on hyvin tyyni.	mayri oan hewvin tēwni
There are some big waves.	Suuria aaltoja on jonkin verran.	sōōriah aaltoayah oan yoankin vayrrahn
Are there any dangerous currents?	Onko täällä vaarallisia virtoja?	oankoa tællæ vaarahllissiah virtoayah
I want to hire (rent) a/an/ some ...	Olisiko ... vuokrattavissa?	oalissikkoa ... v°°oakrahttahvissah
bathing hut (cabana)	uima|koppia	oo'mahkoappiah
deck chair	kansi|tuolia/lepoa|tuolia	kahnsit°°oaliah/laypoat°°oaliah
motorboat	moottori|venettä	mōōttoarivaynayttæ
rowing-boat	soutu|venettä	soa°°toovaynayttæ
sailing boat	purje|venettä	pooryayvaynayttæ
skin-diving equipment	sukellus|varusteita	sookaylloosvahroostay'tah
sunshade (umbrella)	aurinko|varjoa	ah°°rinkoavahryoaah

surfboard	laine|lautaa	lah'naylah°°taa
water-skis	vesi|suksia	vayssisooksiah
windsurfer	purje|lautaa	pooryaylah°°taa

| **YKSITYINEN RANTA** | PRIVATE BEACH |
| **UIMINEN KIELLETTY** | NO SWIMMING |

Winter sports *Talvi\|Urheilu*

Cross-country skiing is the number-one winter sport in Finland.
Every child learns to ski at the age of 3 or 4, and continues to
ski very often for the rest of his or her life. Slalom has also
become fashionable during the last few years, although Finnish
slopes are modest compared to the Alpine region, for instance.
The skiing season lasts from January to March in the southern
parts of the country, but in Lapland the best skiing period is in
April. Skating is also popular among younger people, and all
boys of school age play ice-hockey.

Is there a skating rink near here?	Onko täällä lähellä luistin|rataa?	oankoa tæællæ læhayllæ loo'stinrahtaa
I'd like to ski.	Haluaisin hiihtää.	hahlooah'sin heehtææ
downhill/cross-country skiing	laskettelu/murto|maa|hiihto	lahskayttayloo/moortoamaaheehtoa
Are there any ski runs for...?	Onko rinnettä ...?	oankoa rinnayttæ
beginners	aloittelijoille	ahloa'ttayliyoa'llay
average skiers	tavallisille hiihtäjille	tahvahllisillay heehtæyillay
good skiers	hyville hiihtäjille	hewvillay heehtæyillay
Can I take skiing lessons?	Voinko saada hiihto|tunteja?	voa'nkoa saadah heehtoatoontayyah
Are there any ski lifts?	Onko hiihto|his-sejä?	oankoa heehtoahissayyæ
Are there floodlit ski runs?	Onko valaistuja hiihtomäkiä?	oankoa vahlah'stooyah heehtoamækiæ
I want to hire...	Voinko vuok-rata...?	voa'nkoa v°°oakrahtah
poles	sauvat	sah°°vaht
skates	luistimet	loo'stimmayt
ski boots	hiihto|kengät	heehtoakayngæt
skiing equipment	hiihto|varusteet	heehtoavahroostāyt
skis	sukset	sooksayt

Making friends

Introductions *Esittely*

May I introduce...?	**Saanko esitellä...?**	**saan**koa **ayss**ittayllæ
Esko, this is...	**Esko, tässä on...**	**ays**koa **tæss**æ oan
My name is...	**Nimeni on...**	**nimm**ayni oan
Pleased to meet you!	**Hauska tutustua.**	**hah**ᵒᵒskah **too**toostooah
What's your name?	**Mikä teidän nimenne on?/Mikä sinun nimesi on?**	**mikk**æ **tay**ⁱdæn **nimm**aynnay oan/**mikk**æ **sinn**oon **nimm**ayssi oan
How are you?	**Kuinka voitte?/ Mitä kuuluu?**	**koo**ⁱnkah **voa**ⁱttay/**mitt**æ **koo**loo
Fine, thanks. And you?	**Kiitos, hyvin. Entä te?/Kiitos, hyvää. Entä sinulle?**	**kee**toass **hew**vin **aynt**æ tay/**kee**toass **hew**vᾱ **aynt**æ **sinn**oollay

Follow up *Jatko-osa*

How long have you been here?	**Kauanko olet(te) ollut täällä?**	**kah**ᵒᵒahnkoa **oa**layt(tay) **oall**oot **tæll**æ
We've been here a week.	**Olemme olleet täällä viikon.**	**oa**laymmay **oall**ᾱyt **tæll**æ **vee**koan
Is this your first visit?	**Onko tämä teille/ sinulle ensimmäi-nen käynti?**	**oan**koa **tæm**æ **tay**ⁱllay/**sinn**oollay **ayn**simmæinayn **kæ**ᵉʷⁿti
No, we came here last year.	**Ei, tulimme tänne viime vuonna.**	**ay**ⁱ **too**limmay **tænn**ay **vee**nay **v**ᵒᵒ**oann**ah
Are you enjoying your stay?	**Viihdyt(te)kö täällä?**	**veeh**dewt(tay)kur **tæll**æ
Yes, I like it very much.	**Kyllä, minusta täällä on mukavaa.**	**kewll**æ **minn**oostah **tæll**æ oan **mook**ahvaa
I like the scenery a lot.	**Pidän maisemasta.**	**pidd**æn **mah**ⁱsaymahstah
What do you think of the country/people?	**Mitä pidät(te) maasta/ihmisistä?**	**mitt**æ **pidd**æt(tay) **maas**tah/**ihm**issistæ
Where do you come from?	**Mistä päin tulet (te)?**	**mist**æ **pæ**ⁱn **too**layttay
I'm from...	**Olen...-sta/...-lta**	**oa**layn...-stah/...-ltah

---

Finnish has two words for 'you': *te* and *sinä*, *te* being the polite form. Throughout this section we give the formal version of the phrase followed by the informal where appropriate. See GRAMMAR for more details.

What nationality are you?	**Mitä kansallisuutta olet(te)?**	mittæ **kahn**sallissōottah oalaytay(tay)
I'm...	**Olen...**	oalayn
American	**amerikkalainen**	ah**may**rikkahlah'nayn
British	**britti**	britti
Canadian	**kanadalainen**	kah**nah**dahlah'nayn
English	**englantilainen**	ayng**lahn**tillah'nayn
Irish	**irlantilainen**	eer**lahn**tillah'nayn
Where are you staying?	**Missä asut(te)?**	missæ ah**soott**ay
Are you on your own?	**Olet(te)ko yksin?**	oalayt(tay)koa **ewk**sin
I'm with my...	**Minulla on mukana...**	minnoollah oan **moo**kahnah
wife	**vaimo**	vah'moa
husband	**aviomies**	ah**vioam**'ays
family	**perhe**	payrhay
children	**lapset**	lahpsayt
parents	**vanhemmat**	**vahn**haymmaht
boyfriend/girlfriend	**poika**|**ystävä/ tyttö**|**ystävä**	poa'**kah**ewstævæ/ tewtturewstævæ

father/mother	**isä/äiti**	issæ/**æi**ti
son/daughter	**poika/tytär**	poa'kah/tewtær
brother/sister	**veli/sisko**	**vay**li/**sis**koa
uncle/aunt	**setä/täti**	**sayt**tæ/**tæt**ti
nephew (brother's son)/niece (brother's daughter)	**veljen**|**poika/ veljen**|**tytär**	**vayl**yaynpoa'kah/ **vayl**yayntewtær
nephew (sister's son)/niece (sister's daughter)	**sisaren**|**poika/ sisaren**|**tytär**	**sis**sahraynpoa'kah/ **sis**sahrayntewtær
cousin	**serkku**	**sayrk**koo

Are you married/ single?	**Olet(te)ko naimi- sissa/naimaton?**	oalayt(tay)koa **nah**'mississah/ **nah**'mahtoan
Do you have children?	**Onko teillä/sinulla lapsia?**	oankoa tay'llæ/sinnoollah lahpsiah
What do you do?	**Mitä teet(te) täällä?**	mittæ **tayt**(tay) tællæ
I'm a student.	**Olen opiskelija.**	oalayn oa**pis**kayliyah

COUNTRIES, see page 146

What are you studying?	**Mitä opiskelet(te)?**	mittæ oapiskaylayt(tay)
I'm here on a business trip/on holiday.	**Olen täällä liike|matkalla/ lomalla.**	oalayn tæællæ leekaymahtkahllah/ loamahllah
Do you travel a lot?	**Matkustat(te)ko paljon?**	mahtkoostaht(tay)koa pahlyoan

The weather *Sää*

What a lovely day!	**Ihana päivä!**	ihhahnah pæivæ
What awful weather!	**Kaamea ilma!**	kaamayah ilmah
Isn't it cold/ hot today?	**Eikö olekin kylmä/ kuuma tänään?**	aykur oalaykin kewlmæ/ koomah tænæn
Is it usually as warm as this?	**Onko tavallisesti näin lämmintä?**	oankoa tahvahllissaysti næin læmmintæ
Do you think it's going to... tomorrow?	**Luulet(te)ko, että huomenna...?**	loolayt(tay)koa ayttæ hoooamaynnah
be a nice day	**on kaunis päivä**	oan kahoonis pæivæ
rain	**sataa**	sahtaa
snow	**sataa lunta**	sahtaa loontah
What's the weather forecast?	**Mikä on sää|ennuste?**	mikkæ oan sææaynnoostay

cloud	**pilvi**	pilvi
fog	**sumu**	soomoo
frost	**pakkanen**	pahkkahnayn
hail	**rae**	rahay
ice	**jää**	yææ
lightning	**salama**	sahlahmah
moon	**kuu**	koo
rain	**sade**	sahday
sky	**taivas**	tahivahs
snow	**lumi**	loomi
star	**tähti**	tæhti
sun	**aurinko**	ahoorinkoa
thunder	**ukkonen**	ookkoanayn
thunderstorm	**ukkos|myrsky**	ookkoasmewrskew
wind	**tuuli**	tooli

DAYS OF THE WEEK, see page 151

Invitations *Kutsuja*

Would you like to have dinner with us on...?	Haluaisit(te)ko syödä päivällistä kanssamme...na?	hahlooah'sit(tay)koa s^{ew}urdæ pæ'vællistæ kahnssahmmay...nah
May I invite you to lunch?	Tulisit(te)ko kans-sani lounaalle?	toolissit(tay)koa kahnssahni loa^{oo}naallay
Can you come round for a drink this evening?	Tulisit(te)ko kans-sani drinkille tänä iltana?	toolissit(tay)koa kahnssahni drinkillay tænæ iltahnah
There's a party. Are you coming?	On kutsut. Olet-(te)ko tulossa?	oan kootsoot oalayt(tay)-koa tooloassah
That's very kind of you.	Hyvin ystävällistä.	hewvin ewstævællistæ
Great. I'd love to come.	Hienoa. Tulen mie-lelläni.	h'aynoah toolayn m'aylayllæni
What time shall we come?	Mihin aikaan voimme tulla?	mihin ah'kaan voa'mmay toollah
May I bring a friend?	Voinko tuoda erään ystäväni?	voa'nkoa t^{oo}adah ayræn ewstævæni
I'm afraid we have to leave now.	Nyt meidän täytyy lähteä.	newt may'dæn tæ^{ew}tew læhtayæ
Next time you must come to visit us.	Ensi kerralla tei-dän/sinun täytyy tulla käymään meillä.	aynsi kayrrahllah tay'dæn/sinnoon tæ^{ew}tew toollah kæ^{ew}mæn may'llæ
Thanks for the evening. It was great.	Kiitos illasta. Oli oikein mukavaa.	keetoass illahstah oali oa'kay'n mookahvaa

Dating *Treffit*

Do you mind if I smoke?	Häiritseekö, jos poltan?	hæ'ritsāyk^{ew} yoas poaltahn
Would you like a cigarette?	Haluaisit(te)ko savukkeen?	haahlooah'sit(tay)koa sahvookkāyn
Do you have a light, please?	Saisinko tulta?	sah'sinkoa tooltah
Why are you laughing?	Miksi naurat(te)?	miksi nah^{oo}raht(tay)
Is my Finnish that bad?	Onko suomen|kie-leni niin kehnoa?	oankoa s^{oo}oamaynk'aylayni neen kayhnoah
Do you mind if I sit here?	Häiritseekö, jos istun tähän?	hæ'ritsāyk^{ew} yoas istoon tæhæn
Can I get you a drink?	Saanko tarjota drinkin?	saankoa tahryoatah drinkin

Are you waiting for someone?	Odotat(te)ko jotak-uta?	oadoataht(tay)koa yoatahkootah
Are you free this evening?	Olet(te)ko vapaa tänä iltana?	oalayttaykoa vahpaa tænæ iltahnah
Would you like to go out with me tonight?	Lähtisit(te)kö kans-sani ulos tänä iltana?	læhtissit(tay)kur kahnssahni oolooass tænæ iltahnah
Would you like to go dancing?	Lähtisit(te)kö tans-simaan?	læhtissit(tay)kur tahnssimmaan
I know a good discotheque.	Tiedän hyvän dis-kon.	t'aydæn hewvæn diskoan
Shall we go to the cinema (movies)?	Menisimmekö elo-kuviin?	maynissimmaykur ayloakooveen
Would you like to go for a drive?	Lähtisit(te)kö aje-lulle?	læhtissit(tay)kur ahyayloollay
Where shall we meet?	Missä tapaamme?	missæ tahpaammay
I'll pick you up at your hotel.	Haen teidät/sinut hotellilta.	hahayn tay'dæt/sinnoot hoataylliltah
I'll call for you at 8.	Tulen kello 8.	toolayn kaylloa kahdayksahltah
May I take you home?	Saanko saattaa teidät/sinut kotiin?	saankoa saattaa tay'dæt/sinnoot koateen
Can I see you again tomorrow?	Voimmeko tavata huomenna uudel-leen?	voa'mmaykoa tahvahtah h°°amaynnah ōōdayllāyn
I hope we'll meet again.	Toivon, että tapaamme uudel-leen.	toa'voan ayttæ tahpaammay ōōdayllāyn

... and you might answer:

I'd love to, thank you.	Kiitos, mielelläni.	keetoass m'aylayllæni
Thank you, but I'm busy.	Kiitos, mutta minulle ei sovi.	keetoass moottah minnoollay ay' soavi
No, I'm not inter-ested, thank you.	Ei kiitos. Ei kiin-nosta.	ay' keetoass ay' keennoastah
Leave me alone, please!	Jättäkää minut rauhaan!	yættækāē minnoot rah°°haan
Thank you, it's been a wonderful evening.	Kiitos, on ollut ihana ilta.	keetoass oan oalloot ihhahnah iltah
I've enjoyed myself.	Minulla on ollut hauskaa.	minnoollah oan oalloot hah°°skaa

Shopping Guide

This shopping guide is designed to help you find what you want with ease, accuracy and speed. It features:

1. A list of all major shops, stores and services (p.98).

2. Some general expressions required when shopping to allow you to be specific and selective (p.100).

3. Full details of the shops and services most likely to concern you. Here you'll find advice, alphabetical lists of items and conversion charts listed under the headings below.

LAUNDRY, see page 29/HAIRDRESSER'S, see page 30

Shops, stores and services Myymälät, tavara|talot ja palvelut

Shops are usually open from 9 a.m. to 5 or 6 p.m. on weekdays, closing at 3 p.m. on Saturday and all day Sunday. Some large stores stay open until 8 p.m. one or two nights, usually Mondays and Fridays. During June, July and August, however, shopping hours are somewhat limited.

Where's the nearest...?	**Missä on lähin...?**	missæ oan læhin
antique shop	**antiikki|kauppa**	ahnteekkikah°°uppah
art gallery	**taide|galleria**	tah'daygahllayriah
baker's	**leipomo**	laypoamoa
bank	**pankki**	pahnkki
barber's	**parturi**	pahrtoori
beauty salon	**kauneus|hoitola**	kah°°nay°°shoa'toalah
bookshop	**kirja|kauppa**	keeryuakа°°uppah
butcher's	**liha|kauppa**	lihahkа°°uppah
camera shop	**valo|kuvaus|liike**	vahloakoovah°°usleekay
chemist's	**apteekki**	ahptāykki
dairy	**maito|kauppa**	mah'tokа°°uppah
delicatessen	**herkku|myymälä**	hayrkkoomewmælæ
dentist	**hammas|lääkäri**	hahmmahslǣkæri
department store	**tavara|talo**	tahvahrahtaloa
drugstore	**apteekki**	ahptāykki
dry cleaner's	**pesula**	payssoolah
electrical goods shop	**sähkö|liike**	sæhkurleekay
fishmonger's	**kala|kauppa**	kahlahkа°°uppah
florist's	**kukka|kauppa**	kookkahkа°°uppah
furrier's	**turkis|liike**	toorkisleekay
greengrocer's	**vihannes|myymälä**	vihahnnaysmēwmælæ
grocer's	**seka|tavara|kauppa**	saykahtahvahrahkа°°uppah
hairdresser's (ladies/ men)	**kampaaja/parturi**	kahmpaayah/pahrtoori
hardware store	**kodin|kone|myy-mälä**	koadinkoaneymēwmælæ
health food shop	**luon-tais|tuote|myy-mälä**	l°°oantah'st°°oataymēw mælæ
hospital	**sairaala**	sah'raahlah
ironmonger's	**rauta|kauppa**	rah°°tahkah°°ppah
jeweller's	**kulta|seppä**	kooltahsayppæ
launderette	**itse|palvelu|pesula**	itsaypahlvayloopayssoolah
laundry	**pesula**	payssoolah

library	kirjasto	keeryahstoa
market	tori	toari
newsagent's	lehti|myymälä	layhtimewmælæ
newsstand	lehti|kioski	layhtikioaski
optician	optikko	oaptikkoa
pastry shop	konditoria	koanditoariah
photographer	valo|kuvaamo	vahloakoovaamoa
police station	poliisi|asema	poaleesiahsaymah
post office	posti	poasti
second-hand shop	osto- ja myynti|liike	oasto- yah mewntileekey
shoemaker's (repairs)	suutari	sootahri
shoe shop	kenkä|kauppa	kaynkækah°°ppah
shopping centre	ostos|keskus	oastoaskayskooss
souvenir shop	matka|muisto|myy-mälä	mahtkamoo'stoamew-mælæ
sporting goods shop	urheilu|väline|kauppa	oorhayloovælinaykah°°p-pah
stationer's	paperi|kauppa	pahpayrikah°°ppah
supermarket	valinta|myymälä	vahlintahmewmælæ
sweet shop	makeis|kauppa/karkki|kauppa	mahkayskah°°ppah/kahrkkikah°°ppah
tailor's	räätäli	rætæli
telegraph office	lennätin	laynnætin
tobacconist's	tupakka|kauppa	toopahkkahkah°°ppah
toy shop	lelu|kauppa	laylookah°°ppah
travel agency	matka|toimisto	mahtkahtoa'mistoa
vegetable store	vihannes|kauppa	vihahnnayskah°°ppah
veterinarian	eläin|lääkäri	elæ'nlækæri
watchmaker's	kello|seppä	kaylloasayppæ
wine merchant	alko	ahlkoa

SISÄÄN	ENTRANCE
ULOS	EXIT
HÄTÄ|ULOS|KÄYNTI	EMERGENCY EXIT

General expressions *Yleisiä ilmauksia*

Where? *Missä?*

Where's there a good...?	**Missä on hyvä...?**	missæ oan hewvæ
Where can I find a...?	**Mistä löytyy...?**	mistæ lur^{ew}tew
Where's the main shopping area?	**Missä on tärkein ostos|alue?**	missæ oan tærkay'n oastoasahlooay
Is it far from here?	**Onko se kaukana täältä?**	oankoa say kah°°kahnah tæltæ
How do I get there?	**Miten sinne pääsee?**	mittayn sinnay pæsay

> **ALE/ALENNUS\|MYYNTI**   SALE

Service *Palvelu*

Can you help me?	**Voitteko auttaa minua?**	voa'ttaykoa ah°°ttaa minnooah
I'm just looking.	**Minä vain katselen.**	minnæ vah'n kahtsaylayn
Do you sell...?	**Myyttekö...a?**	mewttaykur...-a
I'd like to buy...	**Ostaisin...-n/-a**	oastah'sin...-n/-a
I'd like...	**Haluaisin...-n/-a**	hahlooah'sin...-n/-a
Can you show me some...?	**Voitteko näyttää minulle...-n/-a?**	voa'ttaykoa næ^{ew}ttæ minnoollay...-n/-a
Do you have any...?	**Onko teillä...-a?**	oankoa tay'llæ...-a
Where's the... department?	**Missä on... -osasto?**	missæ oan...-oasahstoh
Where is the lift (elevator)?	**Missä on hissi?**	missæ oan hissi
Can you show me...?	**Voitteko näyttää minulle...?**	voa'ttaykoa næ^{ew}ttæ minnoollay
this/that	**tätä/tuota**	tætæ/t°°oatah
the one in the window/in the display case	**sitä, joka on ikkunassa/ näytteillä olevaa**	sittæ yoakah oan ikkoonahssah/ næ^{ew}ttay'llæ oalayvaa

Defining the article *Tavaran määrittely*

I'd like a... one.	Minulle saisi olla...	minnullay **sah**¹si oallah
big	**iso**	**is**soa
cheap	**halpa**	**hahl**pah
dark	**tumma**	**toom**mah
good	**hyvä**	**hew**væ
heavy	**painava**	**pah**¹nahvah
large	**suurta kokoa**	**soor**tah **ko**akoah
light (weight)	**kevyt**	**kay**vewt
light (colour)	**vaalea**	**vaa**layah
oval	**soikea**	**soa**¹kayah
rectangular	**suora|kulmainen**	s°°oarah**kool**mah¹nayn
round	**pyöreä**	p°ʷ**ur**rayæ
small	**pieni**	p¹**ay**ni
square	**nelis|kulmainen**	naylis**kool**mah¹nayn
sturdy	**tanakka**	**tah**nahkkah
I don't want any-thing too expensive.	**En halua mitään liian kallista.**	ayn **hah**looah mit**tæn lee**ahn **kahl**listah

Preference *Mieltymykset*

Can you show me some others?	**Voitteko näyttää jotain muita?**	voa¹**ttayk**koa næ°ʷ**ttæ yo**atah¹n **moo**¹tah
Don't you have any-thing...?	**Eikö teillä olisi jotain...?**	**ayk**ur **tay**¹llæ **oa**lissi **yo**atah¹n
cheaper/better	**halvempaa/parem-paa**	**hahl**vaympaa/**pah**raympaa
larger/smaller	**suurempaa/pie-nempää**	**soo**raympaa/p¹**ay**naympæ

How much? *Paljonko?*

How much is this?	**Paljonko tämä maksaa?**	**pahl**yoankoa **tæ**mæ **mahk**saa
How much are they?	**Paljonko nämä maksavat?**	**pahl**yonkoa **næ**mæ **mahk**savaht
I don't understand.	**En ymmärrä.**	ayn **ewm**mærræ
Please write it down.	**Voisitteko kirjoit-taa.**	voa¹**sit**tayko **keer**yoattaa
I don't want to spend more than... marks.	**En halua maksaa enempää kuin... markkaa.**	ayn **hah**looah **mahk**saa **ay**naympæ koo¹n... **mahrk**kaa

COLOURS, see page 112

Decision *Päätös*

It's not quite what I want.	**Se ei ole aivan sitä, mitä haluan.**	say ayⁱ oalay ahⁱvahn sittæ mittæ hahlooahn
No, I don't like it.	**Ei, en pidä siitä.**	ayⁱ ayn piddæ seetæ
I'll take it.	**Otan sen.**	oatahn sayn

Ordering *Tilaaminen*

Can you order it for me?	**Voitteko tilata sen minulle?**	voaⁱttaykoa tillahtah sayn minnoollay
How long will it take?	**Kauanko se kestää?**	kah°°ahnkoa say kaystǣ

Delivery *Toimitus*

I'll take it with me.	**Otan sen mukaan.**	oatahn sayn mookaan
Deliver it to the... Hotel.	**Hotelli.... Toimittakaa se sinne.**	hoataylli... toaⁱmittahkaa say sinnay
Please send it to this address.	**Lähettäisittekö sen tähän osoitteeseen.**	læhayttæⁱsittaykur sayn tæhæn oassoaⁱttæysayn
Will I have any difficulty with the customs?	**Onko minulla vaikeuksia tullissa?**	oankoa minnoollah vahⁱkay°°ksiah toollissah

Paying *Maksaminen*

How much is it?	**Paljonko se maksaa?**	pahlyoankoa say mahksaa
Can I pay by traveller's cheque?	**Voinko maksaa matka|shekillä?**	voaⁱnkoa mahksaa mahtkahshaykillæ
Do you accept dollars/pounds?	**Hyväksyttekö dollareita/puntia?**	hewvæksewttaykur doallahraytah/poontiah
Do you accept credit cards?	**Hyväksyttekö luotto|kortteja?**	hewvæksewttaykur l°°oattoakoarttayyah
Do I have to pay the VAT (sales tax)?	**Täytyykö minun maksaa liike|vaihto|vero?**	tæ^{ew}tēwkur minnoon mahksaa leekayvahⁱhtoavayroa
I think there's a mistake in the bill.	**Laskussa taitaa olla virhe.**	lahskoossah tahⁱtaa oallah veerhay

Anything else? *Saako olla muuta?*

No, thanks, that's all.	Ei, kiitos. Siinä kaikki.	ayⁱ keetoass seenæ kahⁱkki
Yes, I'd like ...	Kyllä. Haluaisin ...	kewllæ hahlooahⁱsin
Can you show me ...?	Voitteko näyttää minulle ...-n/-a?	voaⁱttaykoa næ^{ew}ttæ minnoolle ...-n/-a
May I have a bag, please?	Saisinko kassin, kiitos.	sahⁱsinkoa kahssin keetoass
Could you wrap it up for me, please?	Panisitteko sen pakettiin.	pahnissittaykoa sayn pahkaytteen
May I have a receipt?	Saisinko kuitin.	sahⁱsinkoa kooⁱtin

Dissatisfied? *Tyytymätön?*

Can you exchange this, please?	Voisitteko vaihtaa tämän.	voaⁱsittaykoa vahⁱhtaa tæmæn
I want to return this.	Palauttaisin tämän.	pahlah^{oo}ttahⁱsin tæmæn
I'd like a refund. Here's the receipt.	Saisinko rahat takaisin. Tässä on kuitti.	sahⁱsinkoa rahhaht tahkahⁱsin tæssæ oankooⁱtti

---

Voinko auttaa?	Can I help you?
Mitä saisi olla?	What would you like?
Mitä ... saisi olla?	What ... would you like?
väriä/muotoa/laatua	colour/shape/quality
Valitettavasti meillä ei ole sellaista.	I'm sorry, we don't have any.
Tällä hetkellä meillä ei ole sitä varastossa.	We're out of stock at the moment.
Tilaammeko teille sellaisen?	Shall we order it for you?
Otatteko sen mukaanne vai lähetämmekö sen?	Will you take it with you or shall we send it?
Entä muuta?/Saako olla muuta?	Anything else?
... markkaa, olkaa hyvä.	That's ... marks, please.
Kassa on tuolla.	The cash desk is over there.

Bookshop—Stationer's *Kirja|kauppa—Paperi|kauppa*

In Finland bookshops and stationers' are usually combined, but separate stationers' also exist. Newspapers and magazines are sold at newsstands.

Where's the nearest...?	**Missä on lähin...?**	missæ oan læhin
bookshop	**kirja|kauppa**	keeryahkah°°ppah
stationer's	**paperikauppa**	pahpayrika°°ppah
newsstand	**lehtikioski**	layhtikioaski
Where can I buy an English-language newspaper?	**Mistä voi ostaa englannin|kielisiä sanoma|lehtiä?**	mistæ voa¹ oastaa aynglahnnink¹aylissiæ sahnoamahlayhtiæ
Where's the guide-book section?	**Missä on opas|kirja|osasto?**	missæ oan oapahskeeryahoassahstoa
Where do you keep the English books?	**Missä teillä on englannin|kielisiä kirjoja?**	missæ tay¹llæ oan aynglahnnink¹aylissiæ keeryoayah
Have you any of...'s books in English?	**Onko teillä... kir-joja englanniksi?**	oankoa tay¹llæ keeryoayah aynglahnniksi
Do you have second-hand books?	**Onko teillä antik-variaatti-osastoa?**	oankoa tayllæ ahnteekvahriaatti-oasahstoa
I want to buy a/an/some...	**Saisinko....**	sah¹sinkoa
address book	**osoite|kirjan**	oassoa¹taykeeryahn
adhesive tape	**teippi|rullan**	tay¹ppiroollahn
ball-point pen	**kuula|kärki|kynän**	koolahkærkikewnæn
book	**kirjan**	keeryan
calendar	**kalenterin**	kahlayntayrin
carbon paper	**hiili|(jäljen-nös)|paperia**	heeli(yælyaynnus) pahpayriah
crayons	**väri|kyniä**	værikewniæ
dictionary	**sana|kirjan**	sahnahkeeryan
Finnish-English	**suomi-englanti**	s°°oami-aynglahnti
pocket	**tasku|kokoa**	tahskookoakoah
drawing paper	**piirustus|paperia**	peeroostoospahpayriah
drawing pins	**piirustus|neuloja**	peeroostoosnay°°loayah
envelopes	**kirje|kuoria**	keeryayk°°oariah
eraser	**pyyhe|kumin**	pēwhaykoomin
exercise book	**kirjoitus|vihon**	keeryoa¹toosvihhoan
felt-tip pen	**huopa|kärki|kynän**	h°°oapahkærkikewnæn
fountain pen	**täyte|kynän**	tæᵉʷtaykewnæn
glue	**liimaa**	leemaa

grammar book	kieli|opin	k'aylioapin
guidebook	opas|kirjan	oapahskeeryahn
ink	mustetta	moostayttah
black/red/blue/	mustaa /punaista/sinistä	moostaa /poonnah'stah/ sinnistæ
(adhesive) labels	(itse|liimautuvia) nimi|lappuja	(ittseleemah°°tooviah) nimmilahppooyah
magazine	aika|kaus|lehden	ah'kahkah°°slayhdayn
map	kartan	kahrtahn
street map	kaupungin kartan	ka°°poongin kahrtahn
road map of...	tie|kartan, jossa näkyy...	t'aykahrtahn yoassa nækew
mechanical pencil	lyijy|täyte|kynän	lew'yewtæ°°taykewnæn
newspaper	sanomalehden	sahnoamahlayhdayn
American/English	amerikkalaisen/ englantilaisen	ahmayrikkahlah'sayn/ aynglantillah'sen
notebook	muisti|kirjan	moo'stikeeryahn
note paper	kirjoitus|paperia	keeryoa'toospahpayriah
paintbox	vesi|väri|rasian	vayssiværirahsiahn
paper	paperia	pahpayriah
paperback	tasku|kirjan	tahskookeeryan
paperclips	(paperi|)liittimiä	(pahpayri)leettimmiæ
paper napkins	paperi|lautas|lii- noja	pahpayrilah°°tahslee- noayah
paste	liimaa	leemaa
pen	kynän	kewnæn
pencil	lyijy|kynän	lew'yewkewnæn
pencil sharpener	kynän|teroittimen	kewnæntayroa'ttimmayn
playing cards	peli|kortit	paylikoartit
pocket calculator	tasku|laskimen	tahskoolahskimmayn
postcard	posti|kortin	poastikoartin
propelling pencil	(kierrettävän) lyijy|täyte|kynän	(k'ayrrayttævæn) lew'yewtæ°°taykewnæn
refill (for a pen)	säiliön (kynään)	sæ'liurn (kewnæn)
rubber	pyyhe|kumin	pewhaykoomin
ruler	viivottimen	veevoattimmayn
staples	niittejä	neettayyæ
string	narua	nahrooah
thumbtacks	piirustus|nastoja	peeroostoosnahstoayah
travel guide	matka|oppaan	mahtkahoappaan
typewriter ribbon	kirjoitus|koneen väri|nauhan	keeryoa'tooskoanāyn værinah°°hahn
typing paper	kone|kirjoi- tus|paperia	koanaykeeryoa'toospah- payriah
writing pad	lehtiön	layhtiurn

Camping and sports equipment *Leirintä ja urheilu|varusteita*

I'd like to hire a(n)/some...	**Haluaisin vuok-rata...-n/-a**	hahlooah'sin v°°oakrahtah...-n/-a
air bed (mattress)	**ilma|patjan**	ilmahpahtyahn
butane gas	**nestekaasua (butaania)**	naystaykaassooah (bootaahniah)
campbed	**teltta|sängyn**	taylttahsængewn
(folding) chair	**(kokoon|pantavan) tuolin**	(koakoōnpahntahvahn) t°°oalin
charcoal	**grilli|hiiliä**	grilliheeliæ
compass	**kompassin**	koampahssin
cool box	**kylmä|kassin**	kewlmækahssin
fire lighters	**sytykkeitä**	sewtewkkay'tæ
fishing tackle	**kalastus|välineitä**	kahlahstoosvælinnay'tæ
flashlight	**tasku|lampun**	tahskoolahmpoon
groundsheet	**teltta|patjan**	taylttahpahtyahn
hammock	**riippu|maton**	reeppoomahtoan
ice pack	**jää|pussin**	yæpoossin
insect spray (killer)	**hyönteis|suihkeen**	h°°urntay'ssoo'hkayn
kerosene	**valo|petrolia**	vahloapaytroaliah
lamp	**lampun**	lahmpoon
lantern	**lyhdyn**	lewhdewn
mallet	**nuijan**	noo'yahn
matches	**tuli|tikkuja**	toolitikkooyah
(foam rubber) mattress	**(vaahto|muovi|) patjan**	(vaahtoam°°oavi)pahtyahn
mosquito net	**hyttys|verkkoa**	hewttewsvayrkkoah
paraffin	**valo|petrolia /(lamppu|öljyä)**	vahloapaytroaliah /(lahmppoourlyewæ)
picnic basket	**eväs|korin**	ayvæskoarin
pump	**pumpun**	poompoon
rope	**köyttä**	kur°ew'ttæ
rucksack	**repun**	raypoon
skiing equipment	**hiihto|välineet**	heehtoavælinnāyt
skin-diving equipment	**sukellus|välineet**	sookaylloosvælinnāyt
sleeping bag	**makuu|pussin**	mahkōōpoossin
(folding) table	**(kokoon|taitetta-van) pöydän**	(koakoāntah'tayttahvahn) pur°ew'dæn
tent	**teltan**	tayltahn
tent pegs	**teltta|puikkoja**	taylttahpoo'kkoayah
tent pole	**teltta|seipään**	taylttahsay'ppæn
torch	**tasku|lampun**	tahskoolahmpoon
windsurfer	**purje|laudan**	pooryaylah°°dahn
water flask	**kenttä|pullon**	kaynttæpoolloan

CAMPING, see page 32

Chemist's (drugstore) *Apteekki*

Finnish chemists' don't stock the great range of goods you'll find in Britain or the U.S. They only sell medicines. Because of strict Finnish regulations, it's difficult to buy anything much stronger than aspirin without a prescription. This means that, although what you're looking for may be on the chemist's shelf, you may not be able to obtain it. For perfume, cosmetics etc., you must go to a *kemikaali|kauppa* (**kay**mikkaali-**kah**°°**p**pah).

A notice in the window of any chemist's shop lists the address of the nearest all-night chemist's.

This section has been divided into two parts:

1. Pharmaceutical—medicine, first-aid etc.
2. Toiletry—toilet articles, cosmetics

General *Yleistä*

Where's the nearest (all-night) chemist's?	**Missä on lähin (yö|)apteekki?**	missæ oan læhin (°°ur) ahptäykki
What time does the chemist's open/ close?	**Mihin aikaan apteekki aukeaa/ menee kiinni?**	mihin ah'kaan ahptäykki ah°°kayaa/maynäy keenni

1—Pharmaceutical *Lääkkeitä*

I'd like something for...	**Saisinko jotain ...**	sah'sinkoa yoatah'n
a cold/a cough	**vilustumiseen/ yskään**	viloostoomissäyn/ewskään
hay fever	**heinä|nuhaan**	hay'nænoohaahn
insect bites	**hyönteisen pistok-siin**	h°°urntay'sayn pistoakseen
sunburn	**auringon poltta-maan ihoon**	ah°°ringoan poalttahmaan ihoān
travel/altitude sickness	**matka-/lento-pahoin|vointiin**	mahtkah-/layntoa-pahhoa'nvoa'nteen
an upset stomach	**vatsa|vaivoihin**	vahtsahvah'voa'hin
Can you prepare this prescription for me?	**Saisinko lääkkeen tällä reseptillä.**	sah'sinkoa lǣkkayn tællæ rayssayptillæ
Can I get it without a prescription?	**Saako sen ilman reseptiä?**	saakoa sayn ilmahn rayssayptiæ
Shall I wait?	**Odotanko?/Saako sen odotaessa?**	oadoatahnkoa/saakoa sayn oadoattahayssah

DOCTOR, see page 137

Can I have a/an/some...?	**Saisinko...**	sah'sinkoa
adhesive plaster	**laastaria**	laastahriah
analgesic	**jotain kipua lievittävää**	yottah'n kippooah l'ayvittævǣ
antiseptic cream	**antiseptistä voidetta**	ahntissayptistæ voa'dayttah
aspirin	**aspiriinia**	aahspireeniah
bandage	**siteen**	sittāyn
elastic bandage	**kimmo|siteen/ideaali|siteen**	kimmoasittāyn/iddayaallisittāyn
Band-Aids®	**laastaria**	laastahriah
condoms	**kondomeja**	koandoamayyah
contraceptives	**ehkäisy|välineitä**	ayhkæ'sewvælinnay'tæ
corn plasters	**liika|varvas|laastaria**	leekahvahrvahslaastahriah
cotton wool (absorbent cotton)	**vanua**	vahnooah
cough drops	**yskän|lääkettä**	ewskænlǣkayttæ
disinfectant	**desifiointi|ainetta**	dayssinfioa'ntiah'nayttah
ear drops	**korva|tippoja**	koarvahtippoayah
eye drops	**silmä|tippoja**	silmætippoayah
first-aid kit	**ensi|apu|pakkauksen**	aynsiahpoopahkkah°°ksayn
gauze	**side|harsoa**	siddayhahrsoaah
insect repellent/spray	**hyttys|öljyä/hyönteis|suihketta**	hewttewsurlyewæ/h°°urntay'ssoo'hkayttah
iodine	**jodia**	yoadiah
laxative	**ulostus|lääkettä**	ooloastooslǣkayttæ
mouthwash	**suu|vettä**	soovayttæ
nose drops	**nenä|tippoja**	naynætippoayah
sanitary towels (napkins)	**terveys|siteitä**	tayrvay°ºssittay'tæ
sleeping pills	**uni|tabletteja**	oonitahblayttayyah
suppositories	**perä|puikkoja**	payræpoo'kkoayah
... tablets	**...-tabletteja**	-tahblayttayyah
tampons	**tampooneja**	tahmpoanayyah
thermometer	**lämpö|mittarin**	læmpurmittahrin
throat lozenges	**kurkku|tabletteja**	koorkkootahblayttayyah
tranquillizers	**rauhoittavaa lääkettä**	rah°ohoa'ttahvaa lǣkayttæ
vitamin pills	**vitamiini|pillereitä**	vittahmeenipillayray'tæ

MYRKKYÄ	POISON
VAIN ULKOISEEN KÄYTTÖÖN	FOR EXTERNAL USE ONLY

2—Toiletry *Kosmetiikka*

I'd like a/an/some...	**Saisinko...**	sah'sinkoa
after-shave lotion	**parta|vettä**	pahrtahvayttæ
astringent	**kasvo|vettä**	kahsvoavayttæ
bath salts	**kylpy|suolaa**	kewlpews°°oalaa
blusher (rouge)	**poski|punaa**	poaskipoonaa
bubble bath	**kylpy|vaahtoa**	kewlpewvaahtoah
cream	**voidetta**	voa'dayttah
cleansing cream	**puhdistus|voidetta**	poohdistoosvoa'dayttah
foundation cream	**alus|voidetta**	ahloosvoa'dayttah
moisturizing cream	**kosteus|voidetta**	koastay°°svoa'dayttah
night cream	**yö|voidetta**	°wurvoa'dayttah
cuticle remover	**kynsi|nauha|vettä**	kewnsinah°°hahvayttæ
deodorant	**deodoranttia**	dayoadoarahnttiah
emery board	**hiekka|paperi|viilan**	h'aykkahpahpayriveelahn
eyebrow pencil	**kulma|kynän**	koolmahkewnæn
eyeliner	**silmän|rajaus|väriä/rajaus|kynän**	silmænrahyahoosværiæ/rahyahooskewnæn
eye shadow	**luomi|väriä**	l°°oamiværiæ
face powder	**kasvo|puuteria**	kahsvoapootayriah
foot cream	**jalka|voidetta**	yahlkahvoa'dayttah
hand cream	**käsi|voidetta**	kæsivoa'dayttah
lipsalve	**huuli|rasvaa**	hoolirahsvaa
lipstick	**huuli|punaa**	hoolipoonaa
make-up remover pads	**meikin|poisto|-vanua**	may'kin poa'stoavahnooah
nail brush	**kynsi|harjan**	kewnsihahryahn
nail clippers	**kynsi|leikkurin**	kewnsilay'kkoorin
nail file	**kynsi|viilan**	kewnsiveelahn
nail polish	**kynsi|lakkaa**	kewnsilahkkaa
nail polish remover	**kynsi|lakan|poisto|ainetta**	kewnsilahkahnpoa'stoaah'nayttah
nail scissors	**kynsi|sakset**	kewnsisahksayt
perfume	**haju|vettä**	hahyoovayttæ
powder	**puuteria**	pootayriah
powder puff	**puuteri|huisku**	pootayrihoo'skoo
razor	**parta|kone**	pahrtahkoanay
razor blades	**parta|koneen teriä**	pahrtahkoanayn tayriæ
rouge	**poski|punaa**	poaskipoonaa
safety pins	**haka|neuloja**	hahkahnay°°loayah
shaving brush	**parta|sudin**	pahrtahsoodin
shaving cream	**parta|vaahdoketta**	pahrtahvaahdoakayttah

soap	**saippuaa**	sa'ppooaa
sponge	**pesu|sienen**	payssoos'aynayn
sun-tan cream	**aurinko|voidetta**	ah°°rinkoavoa'dayttah
sun-tan oil	**aurinko|öljyä**	ah°°rinkoaurlyewæ
talcum powder	**talkkia**	talkkiah
tissues	**paperi|pyyhkeitä**	pahpayripewhkay'tæ
toilet paper	**vessa|paperia**	vayssahpahpayriah
toilet water	**eau de toilette**	ur day tooahlayt
toothbrush	**hammas|harjan**	hahmmahshahryahn
toothpaste	**hammas|tahnaa**	hahmmahstahhnaa
towel	**pyyhkeen**	pewhkāyn
tweezers	**pinsetit**	pinsaytit

For your hair *Hiuksia varten*

bobby pins	**hius|neuloja**	hi°°snay°°loayah
colour shampoo	**väri|shampoota**	værishahmpōatah
comb	**kamman**	kahmmahn
curlers	**papiljotteja**	pahpillyoattayyah
dry shampoo	**kuiva|shampoota**	koo'vahshahmpōatah
dye	**hius|väriä**	hi°°sværiæ
hairbrush	**hius|harjan**	hi°°shahryahn
hair gel	**hius|geeliä**	hi°°sghāÿlliæ
hairgrips	**hius|solkia**	hi°°ssoalkiah
hair lotion	**hius|vettä**	hi°°svayttæ
hairpins	**(hius|)pinnejä**	(hi°°s)pinnayyæ
hair slide	**hius|soljen**	hi°°ssoalyayn
hair spray	**hius|lakkaa**	hi°°slahkkaa
setting lotion	**kampaus|nestettä**	kahmpah°°snaystayttæ
shampoo	**shampoota/hius-ten|pesu|ainetta**	shahmpoatah/hi°°staynpaysooah'-nayttah
for dry/greasy (oily) hair	**kuiville/rasvai-sille hiuksille**	koo'villay/rahsvah'sillay hi°°ksillay
tint	**hius|väriä**	hi°°sværiæ
wig	**peruukin**	payrōokin

For the baby *Vauvalle*

baby food	**vauvan|ruokaa**	vah°°vahnr°°ahkaa
dummy (pacifier)	**(huvi|)tutin**	(hoovi)tootin
feeding bottle	**tutti|pullon**	toottipoolloan
nappies (diapers)	**vaippoja**	vah'ppoayah

Clothing *Vaatetus*

If you want to buy something specific, prepare yourself in advance. Look at the list of clothing on page 115. Get some idea of the colour, material and size you want. They're all listed on the next few pages.

General *Yleistä*

Do you have...	**Löytyisikö teiltä...?**	lur*wtew¹sikur tay¹ltæ
Do you have... for a 10-year-old boy/girl?	**Löytyisikö teiltä... 10-vuotiaalle pojalle/tytölle?**	lur*wtew¹sikur tay¹ltæ... kewmmaynv°°oatiaallay poayallay/tewturllay
I'd like something like this.	**Haluaisin jotain tällaista.**	hahlooah¹sin yotah¹n tællah¹stah
I like the one in the window.	**Haluaisin sen joka on ikkunassa.**	hahlooah¹sin sayn joakah oan ikkoonassah
How much is that per metre?	**Mitä tuo maksaa metriltä?**	mitæ t°°oa mahksaa maytriltæ

1 centimetre (cm) = 0.39 in.	1 inch = 2.54 cm	
1 metre (m) = 39.37 in.	1 foot = 30.5 cm	
10 metres = 32.81 ft.	1 yard = 0.91 m.	

Colour *Väri*

I'd like something in...	**Haluaisin jotain...**	hahlooah¹sin yotah¹n
I'd like a darker/lighter shade.	**Haluaisin tummem-paa/vaaleampaa sävyä.**	hahlooah¹sin toommaympaa/ vaalayahmpaa sævewæ
I'd like something to match this.	**Haluaisin jotain tämän kanssa yhteen|sopivaa.**	hahlooah¹sin yotah¹n tæmæn kahnssah ewhht͞aȳnsoapivaa
I don't like the colour.	**En pidä väristä.**	ayn pidæ væristæ

beige	**beigeä**	**bay**shiæ
black	**mustaa**	**moo**staa
blue	**sinistä**	**sin**nistæ
brown	**ruskeata**	**roos**kayahtah
fawn	**vaalean|ruskeaa**	vaalayahan**roo**skayah
golden	**kullan|väristä**	**kool**lahnværistæ
green	**vihreää**	**vih**rayæ
grey	**harmaata**	**hahr**maahtah
mauve	**malvan|väristä**	**mahl**vahnværistæ
	(hailakan|punaista)	(hah¹lahkahn**poo**-
		nah¹stah)
orange	**oranssia**	**oar**ahnssiah
pink	**vaalean|punaista**	vaalayahn**poo**nah¹stah
purple	**sini|punaista**	sinipoonah¹stah
red	**punaista**	**poo**nah¹stah
scarlet	**helakan|punaista**	haylahkahn**poo**nah¹stah
silver	**hopean|väristä**	**hoa**payahnværistæ
turquoise	**turkoosia**	**toor**koassiah (**sini**vih-
	(sini|vihreää)	rayæ)
white	**valkoista**	**vahl**koa¹stah
yellow	**keltaista**	**kayl**tah¹stah
light...	**vaalean|...**	**vaa**layahn
dark...	**tumman|...**	**toom**mahn

yksiväristä (ewksiværistæ)	**ruudullista** (r°°doollistah)	**kuvioitua** (koovioa¹tooa)	**raidallista** (rah¹dahllistah)	**(iso|)pilkullista** ((isoa)pilkoollistah)

Fabric *Kangas*

Do you have anything in ...?	**Onko teillä mitään ...?**	oankoa tay¹llæ mittæn
Is that ...?	**Onko tämä ...?**	oankoa tæmæ
handmade	**käsin|tehtyä**	kæsintayhtewæ
imported	**maahan|tuotua**	maahahnt°°oatooah
made here	**kotimaista**	kottimah¹stah
I'd like something thinner.	**Haluaisin jotain ohuempaa.**	hahlooah¹sin yotah¹n oahooaympaa
Do you have anything of better quality?	**Onko teillä mitään parempi|laatuista?**	oankoa tay¹llæ mittæn pahraympilaatoo¹stah
What's it made of?	**Mistä se on tehty?**	mistæ say oan tayhtew
It's made of ...	**Se on ...**	say oan

cambric	**hienoa palttinaa**	h'aynoah **pahltt**inaa
camel-hair	**kamelin|karvaa**	kahmaylinkahrvaa
chiffon	**shifonkia**	shiffoankiah
corduroy	**vako|samettia**	vahkoasahmayttiah
cotton	**puu|villaa**	poovillaa
crepe	**kreppiä**	krayppiæ
denim	**farkku|kangasta**	fahrkkookahngahstah
felt	**huopaa**	h°°oapaa
flannel	**flanellia**	flahnaylliah
gabardine	**gabardiinia**	gahbahrdeeniah
lace	**pitsiä**	pitsiæ
leather	**nahkaa**	nahhkaa
linen	**pellavaa**	payllahvaa
poplin	**popliinia**	poapleeniah
satin	**satiinia**	sahteeniah
silk	**silkkiä**	silkkiæ
suede	**mokkaa**	moakkaa
towelling	**pyyhe|kangasta**	pewhaykahngahstah
velvet	**samettia**	sahmayttiah
velveteen	**puu|villa|samettia**	poovillahsahmayttiah
wool	**villaa**	villaa
worsted	**kampa|lankaa**	kahmpahlahnkaa

Is it...?	**Onko se...?**	oankoa say
pure cotton/wool	**täyttä (puhdasta)** **puuvillaa/villaa**	tæewttæ **(poohh**dahstah) poovillaa/**villaa**
synthetic	**teko|kuitua**	taykoakoo'tooah
colourfast	**väriä|päästämätön**	væriæpæstæmæturn
crease (wrinkle) resistant	**rypistymätöntä**	rewpistewmæturntæ
Is it hand washable/ machine washable?	**Onko se käsin|pes- tävä/kone|pestävä?**	oanko say kæsinpaystævæ/ koanaypaystævæ
Will it shrink?	**Kutistuuko se?**	kootistookoa say

Size *Koko*

I take size 38.	**Otan kokoa 38.**	oatahn koakoah 38
Could you measure me?	**Voisitteko tarkistaa kokoni?**	voa'sittaykoa tahrkistaa koakoani
I don't know the Finnish sizes.	**En tunne suomalai- sia kokoja.**	ayn toonnay s°°oamahlah'ssiah koakoayah

Women

Sizes can vary somewhat from one manufacturer to another, so be sure to try on shoes and clothing before you buy.

	Dresses/Suits					
American	8	10	12	14	16	18
British	10	12	14	16	18	20
Continental	36	38	40	42	44	46

	Stockings					Shoes			
American } British	8½	9	9½	10	10½	6	7	8	9
						4½	5½	6½	7½
Continental	0	1	2	3	4	5	37	38	40	41

Men

	Suits/overcoats						Shirts			
American } British	36	38	40	42	44	46	15	16	17	18
Continental	46	48	50	52	54	56	38	40	42	44

	Shoes								
American } British	5	6	7	8	8½	9	9½	10	11
Continental	38	39	40	41	42	43	44	44	45

A good fit? *Sopiva?*

Can I try it on?	**Voinko sovittaa sitä?**	voa'nkoa soavittaa sittæ
Where's the fitting room?	**Missä on sovitus|koppi?**	missæ oan soavittooskoappi
Is there a mirror?	**Onko siellä peiliä?**	oankoa s'ayllæ pay'liæ
It fits very well.	**Se istuu oikein hyvin.**	say istoo oa'kayin hewvin
It doesn't fit.	**Se ei istu.**	say ay istoo
It's too ...	**Se on liian ...**	say oan leeahn
short/long	**lyhyt/pitkä**	lewhhewt/pitkæ
tight/loose	**tiukka/väljä**	ti°°kkah/vælyæ
How long will it take to alter?	**Kauanko sen korjaus kestää?**	kah°°ahnkoa sayn koaryaoos kaystǣ

NUMBERS, see page 147

Clothes and accessories *Vaatteita ja asusteita*

I'd like a/an/ some...	**Haluaisin ...**	hahlooah'sin
anorak	**anorakin**	ahnoarahkin
bathing cap	**uima|lakin**	oo'mahlahkin
bathing suit	**uima|puvun**	oo'mahpoovoon
bathrobe	**kylpy|takin**	kewlpewtahkin
blouse	**puseron**	poosayroan
bow tie	**rusetin**	roosaytin
bra	**rinta|liivit**	rintahleevit
braces	**henkselit**	haynksaylit
cap	**lakin**	lahkin
cardigan	**neule|takin/ villa|takin**	nay°°laytahkin/villahtahkin
coat	**takin**	tahkin
dress	**leningin**	layningin
with long sleeves	**pitkä|hihaisen ...**	pitkæhihhah'sayn
with short sleeves	**lyhyt|hihaisen ...**	lewhewthihhah'sayn
sleeveless	**hihattoman ...**	hihhahttoamahn
dressing gown	**aamu|takin**	aamootahkin
evening dress (woman's)	**ilta|puvun**	iltahpoovoon
girdle	**(naisten) liivit**	(nah'stayn) leevit
gloves	**hansikkaat**	hahnsikkaat
handbag	**käsi|laukun**	kæsilah°°koon
handkerchief	**nenä|liinan**	naynæleenahn
hat	**hatun**	hahtoon
jacket	**(lyhyen) takin/ pusakan**	(lewhewayn) tahkin/ poosahkahn
jeans	**farmari|housut/ farkut**	fahrmahrihoa°°soot/ fahrkoot
jersey	**villa|takin**	villahtahkin
jumper (Br.)	**villa|puseron**	villahpoosayroan
kneesocks	**polvi|sukat**	poalvisookaht
nightdress	**yö|paidan**	ᵉʷurpah'dahn
overalls	**haalarit**	haalahrit
pair of...	**parin ...**	pahrin
panties	**pikku|housut**	pikkoohoa°°soot
pants (Am.)	**housut**	hoa°°soot
panty girdle	**housu|liivit**	hoa°°sooleevit
panty hose	**sukka|housut**	sookkahhoa°°soot
parka	**sade|pusakan**	sahdaypoosahkahn
pullover	**villa|paidan**	villahpah'dahn
polo (turtle)-neck	**jossa on poolo- kaulus**	yoassah oan poaloa- kah°°loos
round-neck	**jossa on pyöreä kaula-aukko**	yoassah oan pᵉʷurayæ kah°°lahah°°kkoa

V-neck	**jossa on V-aukko**	yoassah oan V-**ah**°°kkoa
with long/short	**jossa on pitkät/**	yoassah oan **pitkæt/**
sleeves	**lyhyet hihat**	lewhhewayt hihhaht
without sleeves	**joka on hihaton**	yoakah oan hihhahtoan
pyjamas	**pyjaman**	pewyahmahn
raincoat	**sade|takin**	sahdaytahkin
scarf	**huivin**	hoo'vin
shirt	**paidan**	pah'dahn
shorts	**shortsit**	shoartsit
skirt	**hameen**	hahmāyn
slip	**alus|hameen**	ahlooshahmāyn
socks	**(nilkka|)sukat**	(nilkkah)sookaht
stockings	**(naisten) sukat**	(nah'stayn) sookaht
suit (man's)	**puvun**	poovoon
suit (woman's)	**kävely|puvun/**	kævaylewpoovoon/
	jakku|puvun	yahkkoopoovoon
suspenders (Am.)	**henkselit**	haynksaylit
sweater	**neule|puseron/**	nay°°laypoosayroan/
	villa|paidan	villahpah'dahn
sweatshirt	**college-paidan**	koallaygay-pah'dahn
swimming trunks	**uima|housut**	oo'mahhoa°°soot
swimsuit	**uima|puvun**	oo'mahpoovoon
T-shirt	**T-paidan**	tāypah'dahn
tie	**solmion/kravatin**	soalmioan/krahvahtin
tights	**sukka|housut**	sookkahhoa°°soot
tracksuit	**verryttely|puvun**	vayrrewttaylewpoovoon
trousers	**(pitkät) housut**	(pitkæt) hoa°°soot
umbrella	**sateen|varjon**	sahtaynvahryoan
underpants	**(miesten) alus|hou-**	(m'aystayn)
	sut	ahlooshoa°°soot
undershirt	**alus|paidan**	ahloospah'dahn
vest (Am.)	**(miesten) liivit**	(m'aystayn) leevit
vest (Br.)	**alus|paidan**	ahloospah'dahn
waistcoat	**liivin/hihattoman**	leevin/hihhahttoamahn
	(villa|)takin	(villah)tahkin

belt	**vyö**	v°ʷur
buckle	**solki**	soalki
button	**nappi**	nahppi
collar	**kaulus**	kah°°looss
hood	**huppu**	hooppoo
pocket	**tasku**	tahskoo
press stud (snap fastener)	**paino|nappi**	pah'noanahppi
zip (zipper)	**veto|ketju**	vaytoakaytyoo

Shoes Kengät

I'd like a pair of...	Haluaisin...	hahlooah'sin
boots	saappaat	saappaat
moccasins	mokkasiinit	moakkahseenit
plimsolls (sneakers)	kumi|tossut	koomitoassoot
sandals	sandaalit	sahndaalit
shoes	kengät	kayngæt
flat	matala|korkoi-set...	mahtahlahkoarkoa'sayt
with a heel	..., korolliset	koaroallisayt
with leather soles	..., joissa on nahka|pohja	yoa'ssah oan nahhkahpoahyah
with rubber soles	..., joissa on kumi|pohja	yoa'ssah oan koomipoahyah
slippers	tohvelit	toahvaylit
These are too...	Nämä ovat liian...	næmæ oavaht leeahn
narrow/wide	kapeat/leveät	kahpayaht/layvayæt
big/small	isot/pienet	issoat/p'aynayt
Do you have a larger/smaller size?	Onko teillä suurempaa/pienempää kokoa?	oankoa tay'llæ sooraympaa/p'aynaympǣ koakoah
Do you have the same in black?	Onko teillä tätä mustana?	oankoa tay'llæ tætæ moostahnah
cloth	kangasta	kahngahstah
leather	nahkaa	nahhkaa
rubber	kumia	koomiah
suede	mokka|nahkaa	moakkahnahhkaa
Is it real leather?	Onko se aitoa nahkaa?	oankoa say ah'toaah nahhkaa
I need some shoe polish/shoelaces.	Tarvitsen kengän|kiilloketta/kengän|nauhat	tahrvitsayn kayngænkeelloakayttah/kayngænnah°°haht

Repairs Korjaukset

Can you repair these shoes?	Voitteko korjata nämä kengät?	voa'ttaykoa koaryahtah næmæ kayngæt
Can you stitch this?	Voitteko ommella tämän?	voa'ttaykoa oammayllah tæmæn
I want new soles and heels.	Haluaisin uudet pohjat ja korot.	hahlooah'sin ōōdayt poahyat yah koaroat
When will they be ready?	Milloin ne ovat valmiit?	milloa'n nay oavaht vahlmeet

COLOURS, see page 112

Electrical appliances *Sähkö|koneet*

Voltage in Finland is 220 AC 60 cycle. Plugs are of the 2-pin (round hole) type, for which adaptors are available.

What's the voltage?	**Mikä on jännite?**	mikkæ oan yænnittay
Do you have a battery for this?	**Olisiko teillä paristoa tähän?**	oalisikoa tay'llæ pahristoaah tæhæn
This is broken. Can you repair it?	**Tämä on rikki. Voitteko korjata sen?**	tæmæ oan **rikki** voa'ttaykoa **koar**yahtah sayn
Can you show me how it works?	**Voitteko näyttää, miten se toimii?**	voa'ttaykoa næ°ʷttæ mittayn say toa'mee
I'd like to hire/to buy a video cassette.	**Haluaisin vuokrata/ ostaa video|kasetin.**	hahlooah'isin v°°oakrahtah/ oastaa viddayoakahsaytin
I'd like a/an/ some...	**Haluaisin...**	hahlooah'isin
adaptor	**adapterin/sovittimen**	ahdahptayrin/ soavittimmayn
amplifier	**vahvistimen**	vahhvistimmayn
bulb	**(hehku|)lampun**	(hayhkoo)**lahm**poon
CD player	**CD-soittimen**	sāydāy-soa'ttimmayn
clock-radio	**kello|radion**	kaylloarahdioan
electric toothbrush	**sähkö|hammas|harjan**	sæhkurhahmmahshahryahn
extension lead (cord)	**jatko|johdon**	yahtkoayoahdoan
hair dryer	**hiusten|kuivaajan**	hi°°staynkoo'vaayahn
headphones	**kuulokkeet**	kōōloakkāyt
(travelling) iron	**(matka|)silitys|raudan**	(mahtkah) sillittewsra°°dahn
lamp	**lampun**	lahmpoon
plug	**pistokkeen**	pistoakkāyn
portable...	**kannettavan...**	kahnnayttahvahn
radio	**radion**	rahd'oan
car radio	**auto|radion**	ah°°toarahd'oan
(cassette) recorder	**(kasetti|)nauhurin**	(kahsaytti)nah°°hoorin
record player	**levy|soittimen**	layvewsoa'ttimmayn
shaver	**parran|ajo|koneen**	pahrrahnahyoakoanāyn
speakers	**kaiuttimet**	kah'oottimmayt
(colour) television	**(väri|)television**	(værri)taylayvissioan
transformer	**muuntajan**	moontahjan
video-recorder	**video|nauhurin**	vidayoanah°°hoorin

Grocer's *Elin|tarvike|myymälä*

I'd like some bread, please.	**Haluaisin leipää.**	hahlooah'sin lay'pææ
What sort of cheese do you have?	**Mitä eri juusto|laatuja teillä on?**	mittæ ayri yoostoalaatooya tay'llæ oan
A piece of...	**Pala...**	pahlah
that one	**tuota**	t°°oatah
the one on the shelf	**tuota hyllyllä olevaa**	t°°oatah hewllewllæ oalayvaa
I'll have one of those, please.	**Saisinko yhden noita.**	sah'sinkoa ewhdayn noa'tah
May I help myself?	**Voinko ottaa itse?**	voa'nkoa oattaa itsay
I'd like...	**Saisinko...**	sah'sinkoa
a kilo of apples	**kilon omenia**	killoan oamayniah
half a kilo of tomatoes	**puoli kiloa tomaatteja**	p°°oali killoah toamaattayyah
100 grams of butter	**100 grammaa voita**	sahtah grahmmaa voa'tah
a litre of milk	**litran maitoa**	litrahn mah'toah
half a dozen eggs	**puoli tusinaa munia**	p°°oali toosinaa mooniah
4 slices of ham	**4 siivua kinkkua**	naylyæ seevooah kinkkooah
a packet of tea	**paketin teetä**	pahkaytin tāytæ
a jar of jam	**purkin hilloa**	poorkin hilloaah
a tin (can) of peaches	**tölkin persikoita**	turlkin payrsikoa'tah
a tube of mustard	**putkilon sinappia**	pootkiloan sinnahppiah
a box of chocolates	**suklaa|rasia**	sooklaarahsiah

---

1 kilogram or kilo (kg.) = 1000 grams (g.)

100 g. = 3.5 oz.	½ kg. = 1.1 lb.
200 g. = 7.0 oz.	1 kg. = 2.2 lb.

1 oz. = 28.35 g.

1 lb. = 453.60 g.

---

1 litre (l.) = 0.88 imp. quarts = 1.06 U.S. quarts

1 imp. quart = 1.14 l.	1 U.S. quart = 0.95 l.
1 imp. gallon = 4.55 l.	1 U.S. gallon = 3.8 l.

FOOD, see also page 62

Household articles *Talous|tarvikkeita*

aluminium foil	**alumiini|folio**	ahloomeenifoalioa
bottle opener	**pullon|avaaja**	poolloanahvaayah
bucket	**ämpäri**	æmppæri
can opener	**purkin|avaaja**	poorkinahvaayah
candles	**kynttilät**	kewnttilæt
clothes pegs (pins)	**pyykkipojat**	pewkkipoayaht
frying pan	**paistin|pannu**	pah'stinpahnnoo
matches	**tuli|tikut**	toolitikkoot
paper napkins	**paperi|lautas|liinat**	pahpayrilah°°tahslee-naht
paper towel	**paperi|pyyhe**	pahpayripewhay
plastic bags	**muovi|kassi**	m°°oavikahssi
saucepan	**kattila**	kahttilah
tea towel	**astia|pyyhe**	ahstiahpewhay
vacuum flask	**termos|pullo**	tayrmoaspoolloa
washing powder	**pesu|pulveri**	paysoopoolvayri
washing-up liquid	**nestemäinen pesu|aine**	naystaymæinayn paysooah'nay

Tools *Työ|kaluja*

hammer	**vasara**	vahsahrah
nails	**naulat**	nah°°laht
penknife	**kynä|veitsi**	kewnævay'tsi
pliers	**pihdit**	pihhdit
scissors	**sakset**	sahksayt
screws	**ruuveja**	roovayyah
screwdriver	**ruuvi|meisseli**	roovimay'ssayli
(adjustable) spanner	**jako|avain**	yakoaahvah'n

Crockery *Astiat*

cups	**kupit**	koopit
mugs	**mukit**	mookit
plates	**lautaset**	lah°°tahsayt
saucers	**tee|vadit/kahvi|lau-taset**	täyvahdit/ kahhvilah°°tahsayt
tumblers	**(juoma|)lasit**	(y°°oamah)lahsit

Cutlery (flatware) *Ruokailu|välineet*

forks	**haarukat**	haarookat
knives	**veitset**	vay'tsayt
spoons	**lusikat**	loosikkaht
teaspoons	**tee|lusikat**	tayloosikkaht
plastic	**muovista**	m°°oavistah
stainless steel	**ruostumattomasta teräksestä**	r°°oastoomahttoah-mahstah tayræksaystæ

Jeweller's—Watchmaker's *Kulta|seppä—Kello|seppä*

Could I see that, please?	**Saisinko katsoa tuota?**	sah'sinkoa kahtsoah t°°oatah
Do you have anything in gold?	**Onko teillä mitään, joka on kultaa?**	oankoa tay'llæ mittǣn yoakah oan kooltaa
How many carats is this?	**Montako karaattia tässä on?**	moantahkoa kahraattiah tæssæ oan
Is this real silver?	**Onko tämä aitoa hopeaa?**	oankoa tæmmæ ah'toaah hoapayaa
Can you repair this watch?	**Voitteko korjata tämän kellon?**	voa'ttaykoa koaryahtah tæmæn kaylloan
I'd like a/an/some...	**Haluaisin...**	hahlooah'sin
alarm clock	**herätys|kellon**	hayrætewskaylloan
bangle	**ranne|renkaan**	rahnnayraynkaan
battery	**pariston**	pahristoan
bracelet	**ranne|korun**	rahnnaykoaroon
chain bracelet	**ranne|ketjun**	rahnnaykaytyoon
charm bracelet	**amu-letti|ranne|ketju**	ahmoolaytti**rahnnay**kaytyoon
brooch	**rinta|korun**	rintahkoaroon
chain	**ketjun**	kaytyoon
charm	**amuletin**	ahmoolaytin
cigarette case	**savuke|kotelon**	sahvookaykoatayloan
cigarette lighter	**tupakan|sytyttimen**	toopahkahnsew-tewttimmayn
clock	**kellon**	kaylloan
cross	**ristin**	ristin
cuckoo clock	**käki|kellon**	kækikaylloan
cuff links	**kalvosin|napit**	kahlvoassinnahpit
cutlery	**ruokailu|välineet**	r°°oakah'loovælinäyt
earrings	**korva|korut**	koarvahkoaroot
gem	**jalokiven**	yahloakivayn
jewel box	**koru|lippaan**	koaroolippaan
mechanical pencil	**lyijy|täyte|kynän**	lew'yewtæ°°taykewnæn
music box	**soitto|rasian**	soa'ttoarahsiahn
necklace	**kaula|korun**	kah°°lahkoaroon
pendant	**riipuksen**	reepooksayn
pin	**neulan**	nay°°lahn
pocket watch	**tasku|kellon**	tahskookaylloan
powder compact	**puuteri|rasian**	pōōtayrirahsiahn
propelling pencil	**(kierrettävän) lyijy|täyte|kynän**	(k'ayrrayttævæn) lew'yewtæ°°taykewnæn

ring	**sormuksen**	soarmooksayn
engagement ring	**kihla|sormuksen**	kihhlahsoarmooksayn
signet ring	**sinetti|sormuk-sen**	sinnayttisoarmooksayn
wedding ring	**vihki|sormuksen**	vihhkisoarmooksayn
rosary	**rukous|nauhan**	rookoa°°snah°°hahn
silverware	**hopea|esineitä**	hoapayahayssinnay'tæ
tie clip	**solmion pidikkeen**	soalmioan piddikkāyn
tie pin	**solmio|neulan**	soalmioanay°°lahn
watch	**kellon**	kaylloan
automatic	**automaatti|**	ah°°toamaatti
digital	**digitaali|**	diggitaali
quartz	**kvartsi|**	kvahrtsi
with a second hand	**..., jossa on sekunti|viisari**	yoassah oan saykoonttiveesahri
waterproof	**veden|pitävän**	vaydaynpittævæ
watchstrap	**kellon hihnan**	kaylloan hihnahn
wristwatch	**ranne|kellon**	rahnnaykaylloan

amber	**meri|pihka**	mayripihkah
amethyst	**ametisti**	ahmaytisti
chromium	**kromi**	kroami
copper	**kupari**	koopahri
coral	**koralli**	koarahlli
crystal	**kristalli**	kristahlli
cut glass	**hiottu lasi**	hioattoo lahsi
diamond	**timantti**	timmahntti
emerald	**smaragdi**	smahrahgdi
enamel	**emali**	aymahli
gold	**kulta**	kooltah
gold plate	**kullattu**	koollahttoo
ivory	**norsun|luu**	noarsoonloo
jade	**jade**	yahday
onyx	**onyks**	oanewks
pearl	**helmi**	haylmi
pewter	**tina**	tinnah
platinum	**platina**	plahtinnah
ruby	**rubiini**	roobeeni
sapphire	**safiiri**	sahfeeri
silver	**hopea**	hoapayah
silver plate	**hopeoitu**	hoapayoa'too
stainless steel	**ruostumaton teräs**	r°°oastoomahtoan tayræs
topaz	**topaasi**	toapaassi
turquoise	**turkoosi**	toorkōāssi

Optician *Optikko*

I've broken my glasses.	**Silmä|lasini menivät rikki.**	silmælahsinni **may**nivæt rikki
Can you repair them for me?	**Voitteko korjata ne?**	voaⁱttaykoa **koar**yahtah nay
When will they be ready?	**Milloin ne ovat valmiit?**	milloaⁱn nay oavaht **vahl**meet
Can you change the lenses?	**Voitteko vaihtaa linssit?**	voaⁱttaykoa **vah**ⁱhtaa linssit
I'd like tinted lenses.	**Haluaisin värjätyt linssit.**	hahlooahⁱsin **vær**yætewt linssit
The frame is broken.	**Sangat ovat rikki.**	**sahn**gaht oavaht rikki
I'd like a spectacle case.	**Haluaisin silmä|lasi|kotelon.**	hahlooahⁱsin silmælahsikoatayloan
I'd like to have my eyesight checked.	**Haluaisin näkö|tarkastuksen.**	hahlooahⁱsin nækurtahrkahstooksayn
I'm short-sighted/long-sighted.	**Olen liki|näköinen/ kauko|näköinen**	oalayn likkinækurⁱnayn/ kah°°koanækurⁱnayn
I'd like some contact lenses.	**Haluaisin kontakti|linssit**	hahlooahⁱsin koantahktilinssit
I've lost one of my contact lenses.	**Olen hukannut toisen kontakti|linssini.**	oalayn hookahnnoot toaⁱsayn koantahktilinssini
Could you give me another one?	**Voitteko antaa minulle toisen?**	voaⁱttaykoa **ahn**taa minnoollay toaⁱsayn
I have hard/soft lenses.	**Minulla on kovat/pehmeät linssit.**	minnoollah oan **koa**vaht/ **payh**mayæt linssit
Do you have any contact-lens fluid?	**Onko teillä kontakti|linssi|nestettä?.**	oankoa tayⁱllæ koantahktilinssinaystayttæ
I'd like to buy a pair of sunglasses.	**Haluaisin ostaa aurinko|lasit.**	hahlooahⁱsin oastaa ah°°rinkoalahsit
May I look in a mirror?	**Voinko katsoa peiliin?**	voaⁱnkoa **kaht**soah payⁱleen
I'd like to buy a pair of binoculars.	**Haluaisin ostaa kiikarin.**	hahlooahⁱsin oastaa **kee**kahrin

Photography *Valokuvaus*

I'd like a(n)... camera.	Haluaisin ... kameran.	hahlooah'sin... kahmayrahn
automatic	automaatti|	ah°°toamaatti
inexpensive	huokean	h°°oakayahn
simple	yksinkertaisen	ewksinkayrtah'sayn
Can you show me some video cameras please?	Voisitteko näyttää minulle video|kameroita.	voa'sittaykoa næewttæ minnoollay vidayoakahmayroa'tah
I'd like to have some passport photos taken.	Haluaisin passi|kuvaan.	hahlooah'sin pahssikoovahn

Film *Filmi*

I'd like a film for this camera.	Haluaisin filmin tähän kameraan.	hahlooah'sin filmin tæhæn kahmayraan
black and white	musta|valkoista	moostahvahlkoa'stah
colour	värillistä	værillistæ
colour negative	väri|negatiivi	værinaygahteevi
colour slide	väri|dia	væridihah
cartridge	kasetti	kahsaytti
disc film	filmi|kiekko	filmik'aykkoa
roll film	filmi|rulla	filmiroollah
video cassette	video|kasetti	videokahsaytti
24/36 exposures	kahden|kymmenen |neljän/kolmen |kymmenen| kuuden kuvan	kahhdaynkewmmaynay naylyæn/koalmayn kewmmaynayn kōōdayn koovahn
this size	tätä kokoa	tætæ koakoah
this ASA/DIN number	tätä ASA/DIN numeroa	tætæ ASA/DIN noomayroah
artificial light type	keino|valoon sopivaa	kay'noavahlōān soapivaa
daylight type	päivän|valoon sopivaa	pæ'vænvahlōān soapivaa
fast (high-speed)	herkkää (nopeaa)	hayrkkææ (noapayaa)
fine grain	hieno|rakeista	h'aynoarahkay'stah

Processing *Kehitys*

How much do you charge for processing?	**Paljonko kehittämi-nen maksaa?**	pahlyoankoa kayhittæminayn mahksaa
I'd like ... prints of each negative.	**Haluaisin ... kuvaa kustakin negatii-vista.**	hahlooah¹sin ... koovaa koostahkin naygahteevistah
with a matt finish	**matta|pintaisia**	mahttahpintah¹siah
with a glossy finish	**kiiltävä|pintaisia**	keeltævæpintah¹siah
Will you enlarge this, please?	**Suurentaisitteko tämän.**	soorayntah¹sittaykoa tæmæn
When will the photos be ready?	**Milloin kuvat ovat valmiit?**	milloa¹n koovaht oavaht vahlmeet

Accessories and repairs *Lisä\|laitteet ja korjaukset*

I'd like a/an/some ...	**Haluaisin ...**	hahlooah¹sin
battery	**pariston**	pahristoan
cable release	**lanka|laukaisimen**	lahnkahlah°°kah¹simmayn
camera case	**kamera|laukun**	kahmayrahlah°°koon
(electronic) flash	**(electronisen) salama|laitteen**	(aylayktroanissayn) sahlahmahlah¹ttæyn
filter	**suodattimen**	s°°oadahttimayn
for black and white	**musta|valkoiselle**	moostahvahlkoa¹sayllay
for colour	**värille**	værillay
lens	**objektiivin**	oabyaykteevin
telephoto lens	**tele|objektiivin**	taylayoabyaykteevin
wide-angle lens	**laaja|kulma|objek-tiivin**	laayahkoolmahoab-yaykteevin
lens cap	**linssin|suojuksen**	linssis°°oayooksayn
Can you repair this camera?	**Voitteko korjata tämän kameran?**	voa¹ttaykoa koaryahtah tæmæn kahmayrahn
The film is jammed.	**Filmi on juuttunut kiinni.**	fi¹lmi oan yo͞ottoonoot keenni
There's something wrong with the ...	**... ei toimi kun-nolla.**	ay¹ toa¹mi koonnoallah
exposure counter	**kuva|laskuri**	koovahlahskoori
film winder	**filmin|kelaaja**	filminkaylaayah
flash attachment	**salama|laite**	sahlahmahlah¹tay
lens	**objektiivi**	oabyaykteevi
light meter	**valotus|mittari**	vahloatoosmittahri
rangefinder	**etäisyys|mittari**	aytæ¹sewsmittahri
shutter	**suljin**	soolyin

NUMBERS, see page 147

Tobacconist's *Tupakka|kauppa*

A packet of ciga-rettes, please.	**Saisinko rasian savukkeita?**	sah¦sinkoa **rahs**iahn sah**vook**kay¦tah
Do you have any American/English cigarettes?	**Onko teillä amerik-kalaisia/englantilai-sia savukkeita?**	**oan**koa tay¦llæ ahmayrikkahlah¦siah/ aynglahntilah¦siah sah**vook**kay¦tah
I'd like a carton.	**Saisinko kartongin.**	sah¦sinkoa **kahr**toangin
Give me a/some..., please.	**Saisinko...**	sah¦sinkoa
candy	**makeisia**	mahkay¦siah
chewing gum	**puru|kumia**	poorookoomiah
chewing tobacco	**puru|tupakkaa**	poorootoopahkkaa
chocolate	**suklaata**	sooklaatah
cigarette case	**savuke|kotelon**	sah**vook**aykoatayloan
cigarette holder	**imukkeen**	immook**kayn**
cigarettes	**savukkeita**	sah**vook**kay¦tah
filter-tipped/ without filter	**suodatin|.../ ilman filtteriä**	s°°oadahtin|¦lmahn filttayriæ
light/dark tobacco	**vaaleaa/tummaa tupakkaa**	vaalayaa/**toom**maa toopahkkaa
mild/strong	**mietoja/väke-viä...**	m¦aytoayah/**væk**ayviæ
menthol	**mentholi|...**	**mayn**toali
king-size	**king-size-kokoa**	king-size-**koak**oah
cigars	**sikaareja**	sik**kaar**ayyah
lighter	**sytyttimen**	sew**tewt**timmayn
lighter fluid/gas	**besiiniä/kaasua sytyttimeen**	**bayn**seeniæ/**kaas**ooah sew**tewt**timmāyn
matches	**tuli|tikkuja**	**tool**itikkooyah
pipe	**piipun**	**peep**oon
pipe cleaners	**piipun puhdis-timia/piippu|ras-seja**	**peep**oon **pooh**distimmiah/ peeppoo**rahs**sayyah
pipe tobacco	**piippu|tupakkaa**	peeppootoopahkkaa
pipe tool	**piippu|kalun**	peeppookahloon
postcard	**posti|kortin**	**poast**ikoartin
snuff	**nuuskaa**	**noos**kaa
stamps	**posti|merkkejä**	**poast**imayrkkayyæ
sweets	**jotain makeaa**	**joat**ah¦n **mah**kayaa
wick	**sytyttimeen sydä-men**	sew**tewt**timmāyn sew**dæm**mayn

Miscellaneous *Sekalaista*

Souvenirs *Muistoesineitä*

Souvenirs include objects made of wood, *puukko* hunting
knives and reindeer skins and antlers. Lapp crafts are popular
too. Look for carvings made from reindeer bones, felt items and
dolls.

candles	**kyntillät**	kewnttilæt
candlesticks	**kyntillän|jalat**	kewnttilænjahlaht
ceramics	**keramiikka/posliini**	kayrahmeekkah/poasleeni
furs	**turkikset**	toorkiksayt
glass	**lasi**	lahsi
handicrafts	**käsi|työt**	kæsit[ew]urt
jewellery	**korut**	koaroot
reindeer hide	**poron|talja**	poaroantahlyah
table linen	**pöytä|-ja lautas|lii-nat**	pur[ew]tæ-yah lah°otahsleenaht
textiles	**tekstiilit**	tayksteelit
wall rug	**ryijy**	rew'yew
wooden toys	**puu|lelut**	poolayloot

Records—Cassettes *Levyt—Kasetit*

I'd like a...	**Saisinko...**	sah'sinkoa
cassette	**kasetin**	kahsaytin
video cassette	**video|kasetin**	videokahsaytin
compact disc	**CD-levyn**	sāydāy-layvewn

L.P. (33 rpm)	**LP-levyn (kolme|kymmentä| kolme kierrosta minuutissa)**	ælpāy-layvewn (koalmaykewmmayntæ koalmay k'ayrroastah minnootissah)
E.P. (45 rpm)	**EP-levy (neljä|kymmentä| viisi kierrosta minuutissa)**	āypāy-layvew (naylyækewmmayntæ veesi k'ayrroastah minnootissah)
single	**single**	singayl

Do you have any records by ...?	Onko teillä levyjä?	oankoa tay'llæ layvewyæ
Can I listen to this record?	Voinko kuunnella tämän levyn?	voa'nkoa koonnayllah tæmæn layvewn
chamber music	kamari|musiikki	kahmahrimooseekki
classical music	klassinen musiikki	klahssinayn mooseekki
folk music	kansan|musiikki	kahnsahnmooseekki
folk song	kansan|laulu	kahnsahnlah°°loo
instrumental music	soitin|musiikki	soa'tinmooseekki
jazz	jatsi	yahtsi
light music	kevyt musiikki	kayvewt mooseekki
orchestral music	orkesteri|musiikki	oarkaystayrimooseekki
pop music	pop-musiikki	popmooseekki

Toys *Leikki\|kalut*

I'd like a toy/game...	Haluaisin leikki|kalun/pelin	hahlooah'sin lay'kkikahloon/paylin
for a boy	pojalle	poayahllay
for a 5-year-old girl	5-vuotiaalle tytölle	veesi-v°°oatiaallay tewturllay
(beach) ball	(ranta|)pallon	(rahntah)pahlloan
bucket and spade (pail and shovel)	ämpärin ja lapion	æmpærin yah lahpioan
building blocks (bricks)	rakennus|palikoita	rahkaynnoospahlikoa'tah
card game	kortti|pelin	koarttipaylin
chess set	shakki|pelin	shahkkipaylin
doll	nuken	nookayn
electronic game	elektronisen pelin	aylayktroanissayn paylin
roller skates	rulla|luistimet	roollahloo'stimayt
snorkel	snorkkelin	snoarkkaylin

Your money: banks—currency

Banks are open from Monday to Friday, 9.15 a.m. to 4.15 p.m., both summer and winter. There's certain to be someone who speaks English at any large bank. You can also change your money at most hotels, department stores and the larger shops. Though you will normally have to change your money at a bank, there are a few exchange offices in the large towns. Out of hours, try the exchange office at the Helsinki Railway Station. It remains open from 8.30 a.m. to 8 p.m., Monday to Saturday, and on Sundays from 12.30 p.m. to 7 p.m.

Remember to take your passport with you when changing money.

Major credit cards are accepted in most hotels and restaurants, service stations, department stores and shops. Internationally recognized traveller's cheques are easily cashed. Other traveller's cheques can only be cashed in banks or currency exchange offices.

The basic unit of the Finnish monetary system is the mark (*markka*), which is divided into 100 pennies (*penni, penniä*). The abbreviation for mark is *mk* and for penni *p*.

There are coins of 10 and 50 pennies and of 1, 5 and 10 marks. Banknotes are of 10, 50, 100, 500 and 1000 marks.

| Where's the nearest bank? | **Missä on lähin pankki?** | missæ oan læhin pahnkki |
| Where's the nearest currency exchange office? | **Missä on lähin valuu-tan\|vaihto\|paikka?** | missæ oan læhin vahlōōtahnvah'htoa paihkkah |

At the bank *Pankissa*

I want to change some dollars/pounds.	**Haluaisin vaihtaa dollareita/puntia.**	hahlooah'sin vah'htaa doallahray'tah/**poon**tiah
I want to cash a traveller's cheque.	**Haluaisin muuttaa matka|shekin rahaksi.**	hahlooah'sin mōōttaa mahtkahshaykin rahhaahksi
What's the exchange rate?	**Mikä on vaihto|kurssi?**	mikkæ oan vah'htoakoorssi
How much commission do you charge?	**Mikä on väli|tys|palkkionne?**	mikkæ oan vælittewspahlkk'oannay
Can you cash a personal cheque?	**Otatteko vastaan henkilö|kohtaisen shekin?**	oatahttaykoa vahstaan haynkillurkoahtah'sayn shaykin
Can you fax my bank in London?	**Voitteko lähettää faksin pankkiini Lontooseen?**	voa'ttaykoa læhayttæ fahksin pahnkkeeni loantōassāyn
I have a/an/some ...	**Minulla on ...**	minnoollah oan
credit card	**luotto|kortti**	l°°oattoakoartti
Eurocheques	**euroshekkejä**	ayroashaykkayyæ
letter of credit	**remburssi**	raymboorssi
I'm expecting some money from New York. Has it arrived?	**Odotan rahaa New Yorkista. Onko se tullut?**	oadoatahn rahhaa new yoarkistah oankoa say toolllōot
Please give me ... notes (bills) and some small change.	**Saisinko ... sete-leinä ja loput vaihto|rahana.**	sah'sinkoa ... saytaylay'næ yah loapoot vah'htoarahhahnah
Give me ... large notes and the rest in small notes.	**Saisinko ... suurina ja loput pieninä seteleinä.**	sah'sinkoa ... sōōrinnah yah loapoot p'ayninnæ saytaylay'næ

Deposits—Withdrawals *Panot—Otot*

I want to ...	**Haluaisin ...**	hahlooah'sin
open an account	**avata tilin**	ahvahtah tillin
withdraw ... marks	**nostaa ... markkaa.**	noastaa ... mahrkkaa
Where should I sign?	**Mihin alle|kirjoi-tan?**	mihin ahllaykeeryoatahn
I'd like to pay this into my account.	**Tallettaisin tämän tililleni.**	tahllayttah'sin tæmæn tillillayni

NUMBERS, see page 147

Business terms *Liike|termejä*

My name is…	**Nimeni on…**	nimmayni oan
Here's my card.	**Tässä on korttini.**	tæssæ oan koarttini
I have an appointment with…	**Minulla on tarnaminen… kanssa.**	minnoollah oan tahrnahminayn… kahnssah
Can you give me an estimate of the cost?	**Voitteko antaa arvion kustannuksista?**	voa'ttaykoa ahntaa ahrv'oan koostahnnooksistah
What's the rate of inflation?	**Mikä on inflaatiotaso?**	mikkæ oan inflaatioatahsoa
Can you provide me with a(n)…?	**Voitteko järjestää minulle…**	voa'ttaykoa yæryaystæ minnoollay
interpreter	**tulkin**	toolkin
personal computer	**henkilö|kohtaisen tieto|koneen**	haynkillurkoahtah'sayn t'aytoakoanāyn
secretary	**sihteerin**	sihtāyrin
Where can I make photocopies?	**Missä voin ottaa valo|kopioita?**	missæ voa'n oattaa vahloakoapioa'tah

amount	**summa**	soommah
balance	**saldo**	saldoa
capital	**pää|oma**	pæoamah
cheque	**shekki**	shaykki
contract	**sopimus**	soapimmoos
discount	**alennus**	ahlaynnoos
expenses	**kulut**	kooloot
interest	**korko**	koarkoa
investment	**investointi**	invaystoa'nti
invoice	**lasku**	lahskoo
loss	**tappio**	tahppioa
mortgage	**kiinnitys**	keennittews
payment	**maksu**	mahksoo
percentage	**prosentti**	proasayntti
profit	**voitto**	voa'ttoa
purchase	**osto**	oastoa
sale	**myynti**	mēwnti
share	**osake**	oasahkay
transfer	**siirto**	seertoa
value	**arvo**	ahrvoa

At the post office

A symbolic hunting horn and the words *Posti—Post* identify post offices in Finland. Mailboxes are painted yellow. Business hours normally are from 9 a.m. to 5 p.m., Monday to Friday.

Out of hours, a limited-service post office operates at the Helsinki Railway Station. It is open from 7 a.m. to 9 p.m., Monday to Saturday, and on Sundays from 9 a.m. to 9 p.m.

At the Helsinki Airport the post office is open from 7 a.m. to 7 p.m., Monday to Saturday, and on Sundays from 9 am. to 3 p.m.

Where's the nearest post office?	**Missä on lähin posti?**	missæ oan læhin **poasti**
What time does the post office open/close?	**Mihin aikaan posti aukeaa/suljetaan?**	mihin ah'kaan **poasti** ah°°kayaa/**sool**yaytaan
A stamp for this letter/postcard, please.	**Saisinko posti|merkin tähän kirjeeseen/korttiin.**	sah'sinkoa **poasti**mayrkin tæhæn keeryaȳsaȳn/koartteen
A... penni stamp, please.	**Saisinko... pennin posti|merkin.**	sah'sinkoa... paynnin **poasti**mayrkin
What's the postage for a letter to London?	**Mikä on kirje|maksu Lontooseen?**	mikkæ oan keeryaymahksoo loantōasaȳn
What's the postage for a postcard to Los Angeles?	**Mitä maksaa postikortti Los Angelesiin?**	mittæ mahksaa **poasti**koartti loas ahngaylaysseen
Where's the letter box (mailbox)?	**Missä on posti|laatikko?**	missæ oan **poasti**laatikkoa
I want to send this parcel.	**Haluaisin lähettää tämän paketin.**	hahlooah'sin læhayttǣ tæmæn pahkaytin
I'd like to send this (by)...	**Lähettäisin tämän...**	læhayttæisin tæmæn
airmail	**lento|postissa**	layntoapoastissah
express (special delivery)	**pikana**	pikkahnah
registered mail	**kirjattuna**	keeryahttoonah

At which counter can I cash an international money order?	Millä luukulla voin lunastaa kansain|välisen maksu|määräyksen?	millæ lōōkoollah voa'n loonahstaa kahnsah'nvælissayn mahksoomæræ^(ew)ksayn
Where's the poste restante (general delivery)?	Missä on poste restante?	missæ oan poastay raystahntay
Is there any post (mail) for me? My name is...	Onko minulle postia? Nimeni on...	oankoa minnoollay poastiah nimmayni oan

POSTIMERKIT	STAMPS
PAKETIT	PARCELS
MAKSU|ÄÄRÄYKSET	MONEY ORDERS

Telegrams—Telexes—Faxes *Sähkeet—Teleksit—Faksit*

Telegrams are accepted at Helsinki's main post office round the clock.

I'd like to send a telegram/telex.	Haluaisin lähettää sähkeen/teleksin.	hahlooah'sin læhayttǣ sæhkāyn/taylayksin
May I have a form, please?	Saisinko kaavakkeen?	sah'sinkoa kaavahkkāyn
How much is it per word?	Mitä maksu on sanalta?	mittæ mahksoo oan sahnahltah
How long will a cable to Boston take?	Paljonko sähke Bostoniin vie aikaa?	pahlyoankoa sæhkae boastoaneen v'ay ah'kaa
How much will this (tele)fax cost?	Paljonko tämä faksi maksaa?	pahlyoankoa tæmæ fahksi mahksaa

Telephoning *Puhelut*

Finland has automatic telephone service within the country; consult a telephone directory for long-distance codes. Direct dialling also exists to most European networks: dial 990 followed by the code number of the country desired, local area code and subscriber's number. For non-European countries, dial 92022 and the operator will put you through. Street booths can be used for local and domestic long-distance calls.

Where's the telephone?	**Missä on puhelin?**	missæ oan **poo**haylin
Where's the nearest telephone booth?	**Missä on lähin puhelin|kioski?**	missæ oan læhin **poo**haylink'oaski
May I use your phone?	**Voinko käyttää puhelintanne?**	voa'nnkoa kæ^ew'ttǣ **poo**haylintahnnay
Do you have a telephone directory for Helsinki?	**Onko teillä Helsingin puhelin|luetteloa?**	oankoa tayllæ hayl**s**ingin poohaylinl^oo**ayt**tayloah
I'd like to call . . . in England.	**Haluaisin soittaa . . . Englannissa.**	hahlooah'sin soa'ttaa . . . aynglahnnissah
What's the dialling (area) code for Vaasa?	**Mikä on suunta|numero Vaasaan?**	mikkæ oan sōōntah**noo**mayroa
How do I get the international operator?	**Miten pääsen ulkomaan|puhelu|keskukseen?**	mitayn pǣsayn oolkoamaan**poo**hayloo kayskooksāyn

Operator *Keskus*

I'd like Kuopio 234 567.	**Saisinko Kuopio 234567.**	sah'sinkoa k^oo**oa**pioa 234567
Can you help me get this number?	**Auttaisitteko minua soittamaan tähän numeroon?**	ah^oo'ttah'ssittaykoa minnooah soa'ttahmaan tæhæn **noo**mayrōān
I'd like to place a personal (person-to-person) call.	**Saisinko henkilö|puhelun.**	sah'sinkoa haynkillur**poo**hayloon
I'd like to reverse the charges (call collect).	**Saisinko vastaan|ottaja maksaa-puhelun.**	sah'sinkoa vahstaanoattahyah **mahk**saa-poohayloon

NUMBERS, see page 147

Speaking *Puhelimessa*

Hello. This is ...	**Hei. Täällä ...**	hay' **tæ**llæ
I'd like to speak to ...	**Onko ... tavatta-vissa?**	**oan**koa ... tah**vaht**tahvissah
Extension ...	**Saanko (ala|)nume-roon ...**	**saan**koah (**ah**lah) **noo**mayr**ōā**n
Speak louder/more slowly, please.	**Voisitteko puhua kovemmalla äänellä/hitaammin.**	voa'**sit**taykoa poo**hoo**ah koa**vaym**mahllah **ǣ**nayllæ/ hit**taam**min

Bad luck *Huonoa onnea*

Would you try again later, please?	**Yrittäisitteko myö-hemmin uudelleen.**	ewrit**tǣ**'sit**tay**kur m**ew**urhaymmin **ōō**dayll**āy**n
Operator, you gave me the wrong number.	**Keskus, annoitte minulle väärän numeron.**	**kays**kooss ahno'**ttay** minnoollay v**ǣ**ræn **noo**mayroan
Operator, we were cut off.	**Keskus, puhelu meni poikki.**	**kays**koos poo**hay**loo **may**ni poa'kki

Finnish telephone alphabet *Suomalaiset puhelin\|aakkoset*

A	**Anna**	ahnnah	R	**Risto**	ristoa
B	**Bertta**	bayrttah	S	**Sakari**	sahkahri
C	**Cecilia**	saysilliah	T	**Tauno**	tah°°noa
D	**Daavid**	daavid	U	**Urho**	oorhoa
E	**Erkki**	ayerkki	V	**Väinö**	vǣ'nur
F	**Faarao**	faarahoa	W	**kaksin|-kertainen v**	kahksinkayr-tah'nayn vāy
G	**Gabriel**	gahbr'ayl			
H	**Heikki**	hay'kki			
I	**Iivari**	eevahri	X	**Xeres**	ksayrays
J	**Jaakko**	yaakkoa	Y	**Yrjö**	uryur
K	**Kalle**	kahllay	Z	**Zeppelin**	tsayppaylin
L	**Lauri**	lah°°ri	Å	**ruotsalainen o**	r°°oat-sahlah'nayn ōā
M	**Mikko**	mikkoa			
N	**Niilo**	neeloa			
O	**Otto**	oattoa	Ä	**äiti**	ǣiti
P	**Pekka**	paykkah	Ö	**öljy**	urlyew
Q	**Quintus**	kvintoos			

Not there *Ei paikalla*

When will he/she be back?	**Milloin hän palaa?**	milloa¹n hæn pahlaa
Will you tell him/her I called? My name is...	**Kertoisitteko hänelle, että soitin. Nimeni on...**	kayrtoa¹sittaykoa hænayllaay aytt æ soa¹tin nimmayŋi oan
Would you ask him/her to call me?	**Pyytäisittekö häntä soittamaan minulle.**	pēwtæisittaykur hæntæ soa¹ttahmaan minnoollay
Would you take a message, please?	**Voisinko jättää viestin?**	voa¹sinkoa yættǣ v¹aystin

Charges *Maksut*

What was the cost of that call?	**Mitä tämä puhelu maksoi?**	mitæ tæmæ poohayloo mahksoa¹
I want to pay for the call.	**Haluaisin maksaa puhelun.**	hahlooah¹sin mahksaa poohayloon

☞	🕮
Teille on puhelu.	There's a telephone call for you.
Mihin numeroon soitatte?	What number are you calling?
Linja on varattu.	The line's engaged.
Numero ei vastaa.	There's no answer.
Teillä on väärä numero.	You've got the wrong number.
Puhelin on epä|kunnossa.	The phone is out of order.
Hetkinen.	Just a moment.
Hetkinen.	Hold on, please.
Hän on juuri nyt ulkona./Hän ei ole juuri nyt paikalla.	He's/She's out at the moment.

Doctor

You should ensure that your health insurance policy covers the cost of any accident or illness while on holiday. Finland has reciprocal health agreements with the Nordic countries, covering medical care and doctors' fees. There are also similar agreements with Britain. The quality of medical care in Finland is very high. All hospitals have doctors on duty 24 hours a day and many of them speak English.

General *Yleistä*

Can you get me a doctor?	**Voitteko hakea minulle lääkärin.**	voa'ttaykoa hahkayah minnoollay lǣkærin
Is there a doctor here?	**Onko täällä lääkäriä?**	oankoa tǣllæ lǣkæriæ
I need a doctor, quickly.	**Tarvitsen lääkärin, nopeasti.**	tahrvitsayn lǣkærin noapayahsti
Where can I find a doctor who speaks English?	**Mistä löytyisi lääkäri, joka puhuu englantia?**	mistæ lur⁽ᵉʷ⁾tew'si lǣkæri yoakah poohōō aynglahntiah
Where's the surgery (doctor's office)?	**Missä on lääkärin vastaan|otto?**	missæ oan lǣkærin vahstaanoattoa
What are the surgery (office) hours?	**Mitkä ovat vastaan|otto|ajat?**	mitkæ oavaht vahstaanoattoaahyaht
Could the doctor come to see me here?	**Voisiko lääkäri tulla katsomaan minua tänne?**	voa'sikoa lǣkæri toollah kahtsoamaan minnooah tænnay
What time can the doctor come?	**Mihin aikaan lääkäri voi tulla?**	mihin ah'kaan lǣkæri voa' toollah
Can you recommend a/an...?	**Voitteko suositella...**	voa'ttaykoa sᵒᵒoasittayllah
general practitioner	**yleis|lääkäriä**	ewlay'slǣkæriæ
children's doctor	**lasten|lääkäriä**	lahstaynlǣkæriæ
eye specialist	**silmä|lääkäriä**	silmælǣkæriæ
gynaecologist	**gynekologia**	gewnaykoaloagiah
Can I have an appointment...?	**Voinko saada ajan...?**	voa'nkoah saadah ahyahn
tomorrow	**huomenna**	hᵒᵒoamaynnah
as soon as possible	**mahdollisimman pian**	mahhdoallissimmahn p'ahn

CHEMIST'S, see page 107

Parts of the body *Ruumiin|osia*

appendix	**umpi|lisäke**	oompilissækay
arm	**käsi|varsi**	kæsivahrsi
back	**selkä**	saylkæ
bladder	**virtsa|rakko**	virtsahrahkkoa
bone	**luu**	lōō
bowel	**suoli**	s°°oali
breast	**rinta**	rintah
chest	**rinta|kehä**	rintahkayhæ
ear	**korva**	koarvah
eye(s)	**silmä(t)**	silmæ(t)
face	**kasvot**	kahsvoat
finger	**sormi**	soarmi
foot	**jalka**	yahlkah
genitals	**suku|elimet**	sookooaylimmayt
gland	**rauhanen**	rah°°hahnayn
hand	**käsi**	kæsi
head	**pää**	pǣ
heart	**sydän**	sewdæn
jaw	**leuka**	lay°°kah
joint	**nivel**	nivvayl
kidney	**munuainen**	moonooah'nayn
knee	**polvi**	poalvi
leg	**sääri**	sǣri
ligament	**nivel|side**	nivvaylsidday
lip	**huuli**	hōōli
liver	**maksa**	mahksah
lung	**keuhko**	kay°°hkoa
mouth	**suu**	sōō
muscle	**lihas**	lihhahss
(back of the) neck	**kaula (ja niska)**	kah°°lah (yah niskah)
nerve	**hermo**	hayrmoa
nose	**nenä**	naynæ
rib	**kylki|luu**	kewlkillōō
shoulder	**olka|pää**	oalkahpǣ
skin	**iho**	ihhoa
spine	**selkä|ranka**	saylkærahnkah
stomach (inside/ outside)	**maha/vatsa**	mahhah/vahtsah
tendon	**jänne**	yænnay
thigh	**reisi**	ray'si
throat	**kurkku**	koorkkoo
thumb	**peukalo**	pay°°kahloa
toe	**varvas**	vahrvahs
tongue	**kieli**	k'ayli
tonsils	**kita|risat**	kittahrissaht
vein	**suoni**	s°°oani

Accident—Injury *Onnettomuus—Vamma*

There's been an accident.	**On sattunut onnettomuus.**	oan **sahtt**oonoot oan**nayttoam̄ooss**
My child has had a bad fall.	**Lapselleni sattui paha kaatuminen.**	**lahps**ayllayni **sahtt**ooi **pahhah kaatoom**innayn
He/She has hurt his/her head.	**Hän loukkasi päänsä.**	hæn **loa°°kk**ahsi **pæn**sæ
He's/She's unconscious.	**Hän on tajuton.**	hæn oan **tahy**ootoan
He's/She's bleeding (heavily).	**Hän vuotaa verta (runsaasti).**	hæn v°°oataa **vayrt**aa (**roons**aasti)
He's/She's (seriously) injured.	**Hän on (vakavasti) loukkaantunut.**	hæn oan (**vahkahvahsti**) **loa°°kk**aantoonoot
His/Her arm is broken.	**Häneltä on käsi murtunut.**	**hæn**ayltæ oan **kæsi moort**oonoot
His/Her ankle is swollen.	**Hänen nilkkansa on turvoksissa.**	**hæn**ayn **nilkk**ahnsah oan **toorv**oaksissah
I've been stung.	**Olen saanut pistoksen.**	**oa**layn **saan**oot **pist**oaksayn
I've got something in my eye.	**Olen saanut jotain silmääni.**	**oa**layn **saan**oot **yoa**tahⁱn **silm**æni
I've got a/an...	**Minulle on tullut...**	**minn**oollay oan **tooll**oot
blister	**rakko**	**rahkk**oa
boil	**paise**	**pahⁱ**say
bruise	**mustelma**	**moost**aylmah
burn	**palo|haava**	**pahl**oa**haav**ah
cut	**(viilto|)haava**	(**veelt**oa)**haav**ah
graze	**raapaisu/ veri|naarmu**	**raap**ahⁱ**soo**/**vayrin**aar**moo**
insect bite	**hyönteisen purema**	h°°**urnt**aysayn **poor**aymah
lump	**kyhmy**	**kewh**mew
rash	**ihottuma**	**ihh**oatt**oom**ah
sting	**pistos**	**pist**oass
swelling	**turvotusta**	**toorv**oat**oos**tah
wound	**haava**	**haav**ah
Could you have a look at it?	**Voisitteko katsoa sitä?**	voaⁱ**sitt**aykoa **kaht**soah **sitt**æ
I can't move my...	**En voi liikuttaa...**	ayn voaⁱ **leek**oottaa
It hurts.	**Siihen koskee.**	**see**hayn **koask**ēȳ

Ilmoittautuminen	Reception
Seuraava!	Next!
Mihin koskee?	Where does it hurt?
Millaista kipua se on?	What kind of pain is it?
lievää/pistävää/tykyttävää	dull/sharp/throbbing
jatkuvaa/ajoittaista	constant/on and off
Se on...	It's...
murtunut/nyrjähtänyt	broken/sprained
pois sijoiltaan/revähtänyt	dislocated/torn
Täytyy ottaa röntgen|kuva.	I'd like you to have an X-ray.
Se täytyy laittaa kipsiin.	We'll have to put it in plaster.
Se on tulehtunut.	It's infected.
Oletteko saanut jäykkä|kouristus|rokotuksen?	Have you been vaccinated against tetanus?
Annan teille särky|lääkettä.	I'll give you a painkiller.

Illness *Tauti*

I'm not feeling well.	**En voi hyvin.**	ayn voa^i **hew**vin
I'm ill.	**Olen sairas.**	**oa**layn sah^{i}rahs
I feel...	**Minulla on...**	**min**noollah oan
dizzy	**huimausta**	hoo^{i}mah^{oo}stah
nauseous	**pahoin|vointia**	**pah**hoa^{i}nvoa^{i}ntiah
shivery	**puistatuksia**	**poo^{i}s**tahtooksiah
I have a temperature (fever).	**Minulla on kuu-metta.**	**min**noollah oan **kōō**mayttah
My temperature is 38 degrees.	**Minulla on 38 astetta kuumetta.**	**min**noollah oan 38 **ahs**tayttah **kōō**mayttah
I've been vomiting.	**Olen oksentanut.**	**oa**layn **oak**sayntahnoot
I'm constipated/ I've got diarrhoea.	**Minulla on umme-tusta/ripuli.**	**min**noollah oan **oom**maytoostah/**rip**pooli
My... hurt(s).	**...-ni on kipeä.**	-ni oan **kip**payæ
I've got (a/an)...	**Minulla on...**	**min**noollah oan
asthma	**astma**	**ahst**mah
backache	**selkä|särkyä**	**sayl**kæ**sær**kewæ

cold	**nuha**	**noo**hah
cough	**yskä**	**ews**kæ
cramps	**kouristuksia**	**koa**°°ristooksiah
earache	**korva|särky**	**koar**vahsærkew
hay fever	**heinä|nuha**	**hay**'næ**noo**hah
headache	**pään|särky**	**pææn**særkew
indigestion	**ruoan|sulatus|häiriö**	r°°oahn**soo**lahtoos**hæ**iriur
nosebleed	**veren|vuotoa nenästä**	**vay**raynv°°**oa**toaah nay**næ**stæ
palpitations	**sydämen|tykytystä**	**sew**dæmayn**tew**kewtewstæ
rheumatism	**reumatismi**	**ray**°°mahtismi
sore throat	**kurkku|kipu**	**koor**kkookippoo
stiff neck	**niska jäykkänä**	**nis**kah yæ**ᵉʷ**kkænæ
stomach ache	**vatsa|kipuja**	**vaht**sahkippooyah
sunstroke	**auringon|pisto**	**ah**°°ringoanpistoa
I have difficulties breathing.	**Minulla on hengitys|vaikeuksia.**	**min**noollah oan **hayng**ittews**vah**ᶦkayooksiah
I have chest pains.	**Minulla on rinta|kipuja.**	**min**noollah oan **rin**tahkippooyah
I had a heart attack... years ago.	**Minulla oli sydän|kohtaus... vuotta sitten.**	**min**noollah oali **sew**dænkoahtah°°ss... v°°attah sittayn
My blood pressure is too high/too low.	**Veren|paineeni on liian korkea/ matala.**	**vay**raynpah¯nāyni oan leeahn koarkayah/ mahtahlah
I'm allergic to...	**Olen allerginen... -lle.**	**oa**layn ah**l**layrgginayn... -llay
I'm diabetic.	**Minulla on sokeri-tauti**	**min**noollah oan **soa**kayri**tah**°°ti

Women's section *Naisten osasto*

I have period pains.	**Minulla on kuukautis|kipuja.**	**min**noollah oan kōōkah°°tiskippooyah
I have a vaginal infection.	**Minulla on emätin|tulehdus**	**min**noollah oan aymætin**too**layhdooss
I'm on the pill.	**Käytän ehkäisy|pillereitä.**	**kæ**ᵉʷtæn ayhkæisew**pil**layray'tæ
I haven't had a period for 2 months.	**Minulla ei ole ollut kuukautisia 2:een kuukauteen.**	**min**noollah ayᶦ oalay oalloot kōōkah°°tissiah kahtāyn kōōkah°°tāyn
I'm (3 months) pregnant.	**Olen (3:tta kuukautta) raskaana.**	**oa**layn (koalmahttah kōōkah°°ttah) rahskaanah

Kuinka kauan teillä on ollut näitä oireita?	How long have you been feeling like this?
Onko tämä teillä ensimmäistä kertaa?	Is this the first time you've had this?
Mittaan lämpönne/veren|paineen.	I'll take your temperature/blood pressure.
Käärikää hihanne, olkaa hyvä.	Roll up your sleeve, please.
Riisuuntukaa. (Riisukaa ylä|ruumis paljaaksi.)	Please undress (down to the waist).
Käykää makuulle tänne.	Please lie down over here.
Suu auki.	Open your mouth.
Hengittäkää syvään.	Breathe deeply.
Yskikää.	Cough, please.
Mihin koskee?	Where does it hurt?
Teillä on...	You've got (a/an)...
umpi|lisäkkeen tulehdus	appendicitis
rakko|tulehdus	cystitis
maha|katarri	gastritis
flunssa	flu
tulehtunut...	inflammation of...
ruoka|myrkytys	food poisoning
kelta|tauti	jaundice
keuhko|kuume	pneumonia
tuhka|rokko	measles
suku|puoli|tauti	venereal disease
Se ei ole tarttuvaa.	It's (not) contagious.
Se on allergiaa.	It's an allergy.
Annan teille ruiskeen.	I'll give you an injection.
Tarvitsen teiltä veri|/uloste|/virtsa|näytteen.	I want a specimen of your blood/stools/urine.
Teidän täytyy pysyä vuoteessa... päivää.	You must stay in bed for... days.
Annan teille lähetteen erikois|lääkärille.	I want you to see a specialist.
Lähetän teidät sairaalaan yleis|tarkastukseen.	I want you to go to the hospital for a general check-up.

Prescription—Treatment *Lääke|määräys—Hoito*

This is my usual medicine.	**Tavallisesti käytän tätä lääkettä.**	tahvahllissaysti **kæ**ytæn tætæ **læ**kayttæ
Can you give me a prescription for this?	**Voitteko antaa minulle reseptin tätä varten?**	**voa**'ttaykoa ahntaa minnoollay **ray**sayptin tætæ **vahr**tayn
Can you prescribe a/an/some...?	**Voitteko kirjoittaa reseptin... varten?**	**voa**'ttaykoa **keer**yoa'ttaa **ray**sayptin... **vahr**tayn
antidepressant	**jotain piristävää**	**yoa**tah'n pirristævæ
sleeping pills	**uni|tabletteja**	**oon**itahblayttayyah
tranquillizer	**jotain rauhoittavaa**	**yoa**tah'n **rah**°°hoa'ttahvaa
I'm allergic to penicillin/certain antibiotics.	**Olen allerginen penisilliinille/tiety-ille anti|biooteille.**	**oa**layn ahllayrgginnayn paynissilleenillay/ t'aytew'llay ahnttib**ioa**taillay
I don't want anything too strong.	**En halua mitään vahvaa.**	ayn **hah**looah mittæn vahvaa
How many times a day should I take it?	**Montako kertaa päivässä minun pitää ottaa sitä?**	**moan**tahkoa **kayr**taa **pæi**væssæ minnoon pittæ **oat**taa sittæ
Must I swallow them whole?	**Täytyykö ne niellä kokonaisina?**	**tæ**°°tewkur nay n'ayllæ **koa**koanah'sinnah

Mitä hoitoa saatte?	What treatment are you having?
Mitä lääkkeitä otatte?	What medicine are you taking?
Ruiskeena vai suun kautta?	By injection or orally?
Ottakaa... tee|lusikallista tätä lääkettä...	Take... teaspoons of this medicine...
Ottakaa yksi pilleri vesi|lasillisen kanssa...	Take one pill with a glass of water...
joka...-s tunti	every... hours
... kertaa päivässä	... times a day
ennen ateriaa/aterian jälkeen	before/after each meal
aamulla/illalla	in the morning/at night
jos on kipuja	if there is any pain
... päivää	for... days

CHEMIST'S, see page 107

Fee *Maksu*

| How much do I owe you? | **Paljonko olen velkaa?** | pahlyoankoa oalayn tay^lllay vaylkaa |

How much do I owe you? / **Paljonko olen velkaa?** / pah^lyoankoa oalayn tay^lllay vaylkaa

May I have a receipt for my health insurance? / **Voinko saada kuitin sairaus|vakuutustani varten?** / voa^lnkoa saadah koo^ltin sah^lrah°°svahkōōtoostahni vahrtayn

Can I have a medical certificate? / **Voinko saada lääkärin|todistuksen?** / voa^lnkoa saadah lǣkærintoadistooksayn

Would you fill in this health insurance form, please? / **Täyttäisittekö tämän sairaus|vakuutus|lomakkeen.** / tæ^{ew}ttæissittaykur tæmæn sah^lrah°°svahkōōtoosloa mahkkāēn

Hospital *Sairaala*

Please notify my family. / **Ilmoittaisitteko perheelleni.** / ilmoa^lttah^lsittaykoa payrhāyllayni

What are the visiting hours? / **Mitkä ovat vierailu|ajat?** / mitkæ oavaht v^layrah^llooahyaht

When can I get up? / **Milloin voin nousta ylös?** / milloa^ln voa^ln noa°°stah ewlurs

When will the doctor come? / **Milloin lääkäri tulee?** / milloa^ln lǣkæri toolāy

I'm in pain. / **Minulla on tuskia.** / minnoollah oan tooskiah

I can't eat/sleep. / **En voi syödä./En saa unta.** / ayn voa^l s^{ew}urdæ/ayn saa oontah

Where is the bell? / **Missä on soitto|kello?** / missæ oan soa^lttoakaylloa

nurse	**hoitaja**	hoa^ltahyah
patient	**potilas**	poatillahs
anaesthetic	**puudutus|aine**	pōōdootoosah^lnay
blood transfusion	**veren|siirto**	vayraynseertoa
injection	**ruiske**	roo^lskay
operation	**leikkaus**	lay^lkkah°°s
bed	**vuode**	v°°oaday
bedpan	**alus|astia**	ahloosahstiah
thermometer	**lämpö|mittari**	læmpurmittahri

Dentist *Hammaslääkäri*

Can you recommend a good dentist?	**Voitteko suositella hyvää hammas|lääkäriä?**	voa'sittaykoa s°°asittayllah hewvǣ hahmmahslǣkæriæ
Can I make an appointment to see Dr... as soon as possible?	**Voinko päästä tohtori...-n vas- taan|otolle?**	voa'nkoa pǣstæ toahtoari vahstaanoatoallay
Couldn't you make it earlier?	**Eikö löytyisi aikai- sempaa aikaa?**	ay'kur lur°⁰tew'si
I have a broken tooth.	**Minulta on murtu- nut hammas.**	minnooltah oan moortoonoot hahmmahs
I have toothache.	**Hammastani sär- kee.**	hahmmahstahni særkāy
I have an abscess.	**Minulla on märkä|pesäke.**	minnoollah oan mærkæpaysækay
This tooth hurts.	**Tätä hammasta särkee.**	tætæ hahmmahstah særkāy
at the top	**ylhäällä**	ewlhǣllæ
at the bottom	**alhaalla**	ahlhaallah
at the front	**edessä**	aydayssæ
at the back	**takana**	tahkahnah
Can you fix it temporarily?	**Voitteko paikata sen väli|aikaisesti?**	voa'ttaykoa pah'kahtah sayn væliah'kah'saysti
I don't want it pulled out.	**En halua, että se vedetään pois.**	ayn hahlooah ayttæ say vaydaytǣn poa'ss
Could you give me an anaesthetic?	**Voitteko antaa puudutuksen?**	voa'ttaykoa ahntaa pōōdootooksayn
I've lost a filling.	**Minulta on pudon- nut paikka.**	minnooltah oan poodoannoot pah'kkah
My gums...	**Ikeneni...**	ikkaynayni
are very sore	**ovat hyvin arat**	oavaht hewvin ahraht
are bleeding	**vuotavat verta**	v°°oatahvaht vayrtah
I've broken my dentures.	**Hammas|proteesini on rikki.**	hahmmahsproatāysinni oan rikki
Can you repair my dentures?	**Voitteko korjata hammas|protee- sini?**	voa'ttaykoa koaryahtah hahmmahsproatāysinni
When will they be ready?	**Milloin ne ovat valmiit?**	milloa'n nay oavaht vahlmeet

Reference section

Where do you come from? *Mistä olette kotoisin?*

Africa	**Afrikka**	ahfrikkah
Asia	**Aasia**	aassiah
Australia	**Australia**	ah°°straaliah
Europe	**Eurooppa**	ay°°rōāppah
North America	**Pohjois-Amerikka**	poahyoa's-ahmayrikkah
South America	**Etelä-Amerikka**	aytaylæ-ahmayrikkah
Austria	**Itävalta**	itævahltah
Belgium	**Belgia**	baylgiah
Belorus	**Valkovenäjä**	vahlkoavaynæyæ
Canada	**Kanada**	kahnahdah
China	**Kiina**	keenah
Commonwealth of Independent States (CIS)	**Itsenäisten valtioiden yhteisö (IVY)**	itsaynæistayn vahltioa'dayn ewhtay'sur (IVY)
Denmark	**Tanska**	tahnskah
England	**Englanti**	aynglahnti
Estonia	**Viro**	virroa
Finland	**Suomi**	s°°oami
France	**Ranska**	rahnskah
Germany	**Saksa**	sahksah
Great Britain	**Iso-Britannia**	isoa-britahnniah
Greece	**Kreikka**	kray'kkah
Ireland	**Irlanti**	eerlahnti
Italy	**Italia**	itahliah
Latvia	**Latvia**	lahtviah
Lithuania	**Liettua**	l*ytttooah
Netherlands	**Hollanti**	hoallahnti
New Zealand	**Uusi-Seelanti**	ōosi-sāylahnti
Norway	**Norja**	noaryah
Portugal	**Portugali**	poartoogahli
Russia	**Venäjä**	vaynæyæ
Scotland	**Skotlanti**	skoatlahnti
Slovakia	**Slovakia**	sloavahkiah
South Africa	**Etelä-Afrikka**	eataylæ-ahfrikkah
Spain	**Espanja**	ayspahnyah
Sweden	**Ruotsi**	r°°oatsi
Switzerland	**Sveitsi**	svay'tsi
Ukraine	**Ukraina**	ookrah'nah
United States	**USA (Yhdys|vallat)**	ōōæssaa (ewhdewsvahl-laht)
Wales	**Wales**	vay'ls

Numbers *Luvut*

0	nolla	noallah
1	**yksi**	**ew**ksi
2	**kaksi**	**kahk**si
3	**kolme**	**koal**may
4	**neljä**	**nayl**yæ
5	**viisi**	**vee**ssi
6	**kuusi**	**koo**ssi
7	**seitsemän**	**say**'tsaymæn
8	**kahdeksan**	**kahh**dayksahn
9	**yhdeksän**	**ewh**dayksæn
10	**kymmenen**	**kewm**maynayn
11	**yksi**|**toista**	**ew**ksitoa'stah
12	**kaksi**|**toista**	**kahk**sitoa'stah
13	**kolme**|**toista**	**koal**maytoa'stah
14	**neljä**|**toista**	**nayl**yætoa'stah
15	**viisi**|**toista**	**vee**ssitoa'stah
16	**kuusi**|**toista**	**koo**ssitoa'stah
17	**seitsemän**|**toista**	**say**'tsaymæn**toa**'stah
18	**kahdeksan**|**toista**	**kahh**dayksahn**toa**'stah
19	**yhdeksän**|**toista**	**ewh**dayksæn**toa**'stah
20	**kaksi**|**kymmentä**	**kahk**si**kewm**mayntæ
21	**kaksi**|**kymmentä**|**yksi**	**kahk**si**kewm**mayntæ**ewk**si
22	**kaksi**|**kymmentä**|**kaksi**	**kahk**si**kewm**mayntæ**kahk**si
23	**kaksi**|**kymmentä**|**kolme**	**kahk**si**kewm**mayntæ**koal**may
24	**kaksi**|**kymmentä**|**neljä**	**kahk**si**kewm**mayntæ**nayl**yæ
25	**kaksi**|**kymmentä**|**viisi**	**kahk**si**kewm**mayntæ**vee**ssi
26	**kaksi**|**kymmentä**|**kuusi**	**kahk**si**kewm**mayntæ**koo**ssi
27	**kaksi**|**kymmentä**|**seitsemän**	**kahk**si**kewm**mayntæ**say**'tsaymæn
28	**kaksi**|**kymmentä**|**kahdeksan**	**kahk**si**kewm**mayntæ**kahh**dayksahn
29	**kaksi**|**kymmentä**|**yhdeksän**	**kahk**si**kewm**mayntæ**ewh**dayksæn
30	**kolme**|**kymmentä**	**koal**may**kewm**mayntæ
31	**kolme**|**kymmentä**|**yksi**	**koal**may**kewm**mayntæ**ewk**si
32	**kolme**|**kymmentä**|**kaksi**	**koal**may**kewm**mayntæ**kahk**si
33	**kolme**|**kymmentä**|**kolme**	**koal**may**kewm**mayntæ**koal**may
40	**neljä**|**kymmentä**	**nayl**yæ**kewm**mayntæ
41	**neljä**|**kymmentä**|**yksi**	**nayl**yæ**kewm**mayntæ**ewk**si
42	**neljä**|**kymmentä**|**kaksi**	**nayl**yæ**kewm**mayntæ**kahk**si
43	**neljä**|**kymmentä**|**kolme**	**nayl**yæ**kewm**mayntæ**koal**may
50	**viisi**|**kymmentä**	**vee**ssi**kewm**mayntæ
51	**viisi**|**kymmentä**|**yksi**	**vee**ssi**kewm**mayntæ**ewk**si
52	**viisi**|**kymmentä**|**kaksi**	**vee**ssi**kewm**mayntæ**kahk**si
53	**viisi**|**kymmentä**|**kolme**	**vee**ssi**kewm**mayntæ**koal**may
60	**kuusi**|**kymmentä**	**koo**ssi**kewm**mayntæ
61	**kuusi**|**kymmentä**|**yksi**	**koo**ssi**kewm**mayntæ**ewk**si
62	**kuusi**|**kymmentä**|**kaksi**	**koo**ssi**kewm**mayntæ**kahk**si

63	**kuusi|kymmentä|kolme**	**koo̅ssikewm**mayntæ**koal**may
70	**seitsemän|kymmentä**	**say'tsaymænkewm**mayntæ
71	**seitsemän|kymmentä|yksi**	**say'tsaymænkewm**mayntæ**ewk**si
72	**seitsemän|kymmentä|kaksi**	**say'tsaymænkewm**mayntæ**kahk**si
73	**seitsemän|kymmentä|kolme**	**say'tsaymænkewm**mayntæ**koal**may
80	**kahdeksan|kymmentä**	**kahdayksahnkewm**mayntæ
81	**kahdeksan|kymmentä|yksi**	**kahdayksahnkewm**mayntæ**ewk**si
82	**kahdeksan|kymmentä|kaksi**	**kahdayksahnkewm**mayntæ**kahk**si
83	**kahdeksan|kymmentä|kolme**	**kahdayksahnkewm**mayntæ**koal**may
90	**yhdeksän|kymmentä**	**ewhdayksænkewm**mayntæ
91	**yhdeksän|kymmentä|yksi**	**ewhdayksænkewm**mayntæ**ewk**si
92	**yhdeksän|kymmentä|kaksi**	**ewhdayksænkewm**mayntæ**kahk**si
93	**yhdeksän|kymmentä|kolme**	**ewhdayksænkewm**mayntæ**koal**may

100	**sata**	**sah**tah
101	**sata|yksi**	**sah**tah**ewk**si
102	**sata|kaksi**	**sah**tah**kahk**si
110	**sata|kymmenen**	**sah**tah**kewm**maynayn
120	**sata|kaksi|kymmentä**	**sah**tah**kahk**si**kewm**mayntæ
130	**sata|kolme|kymmentä**	**sah**tah**kol**may**kewm**mayntæ
140	**sata|neljä|kymmentä**	**sah**tah**naylyækewm**mayntæ
150	**sata|viisi|kymmentä**	**sah**tah**vees**si**kewm**mayntæ
160	**sata|kuusi|kymmentä**	**sah**tah**koo̅s**si**kewm**mayntæ
170	**sata|seitsemän|kymmentä**	**sah**tah**say'tsaymænkewm**mayntæ
180	**sata|kahdeksan|kymmentä**	**sah**tah**kahdayksahnkewm**mayntæ
190	**sata|yhdeksän|kymmentä**	**sah**tah**ewhdayksænkewm**mayntæ
200	**kaksi|sataa**	**kahk**si**sah**taa
300	**kolme|sataa**	**koal**may**sah**taa
400	**neljä|sataa**	**naylyæsah**taa
500	**viisi|sataa**	**vees**si**sah**taa
600	**kuusi|sataa**	**koo̅s**si**sah**taa
700	**seitsemän|sataa**	**say'tsaymænsah**taa
800	**kahdeksan|sataa**	**kahhdayksahnsah**taa
900	**yhdeksän|sataa**	**ewhdayksænsah**taa

1000	**tuhat**	**too**haht
1100	**tuhat sata**	**too**haht **sah**tah
1200	**tuhat kaksi|sataa**	**too**haht **kahk**si**sah**taa
2000	**kaksi|tuhatta**	**kahk**si**too**hahttah
5000	**viisi|tuhatta**	**vees**si**too**hahttah

10,000	**kymmenen|tuhatta**	**kewm**maynayn**too**hahttah
50,000	**viisi|kymmentä|tuhatta**	**vees**si**kewm**mayntæ**too**hahttah
100,000	**sata|tuhatta**	**sah**tah**too**hahttah
1,000,000	**miljoona**	**mil**yo̅anah
1,000,000,000	**miljardi**	**mil**yahrdi

first	**ensimmäinen**	aynsimmæinayn
second	**toinen**	toa'nayn
third	**kolmas**	koalmahss
fourth	**neljäs**	naylyæss
fifth	**viides**	veedayss
sixth	**kuudes**	kōōdayss
seventh	**seitsemäs**	say'tsaymæss
eighth	**kahdeksas**	kahhdayksahs
ninth	**yhdeksäs**	ewhhdayksæs
tenth	**kymmenes**	kewmmaynayss
once/twice	**kerran/kahdesti**	kayrrahn/kahhdaysti
three times	**kolme kertaa**	koalmayh kayrtaa
a half	**puolikas**	p°°oalikkahs
half a...	**puoli...-a**	p°°oali...-ah
half of...	**puolet...-sta**	p°°oalayt...-stah
half (adj.)	**puoli**	p°°oali
a quarter/one third	**neljännes (neljäs|osa)/kolmannes (kolmas|osa)**	naylyǽnnays(naylyæsoa ssah)/koalmahnnays (koalmahsoassah)
a pair of	**pari...-a**	pahri
a dozen	**tusina**	toossinnah
one per cent	**yksi prosentia**	ewksi proasaynttiah
3.49%	**3,49%**	koalmay pilkkoo naylyæ kewmmayntæewh- dayksæn proasaynttiah
1981	**tuhat yhdeksän|sataa|kahdeksan-|kymmentä|yksi**	toohaht ewhdayksænsah- taakahhdayksahnkewm- mayntæewksi
1995	**tuhat yhdeksän-|sataa|yhdeksän-|kymmentä|viisi**	toohaht ewhdayksænsah- taaewhdayksænkewm- mayntæveessi
2009	**kaksi tuhatta-|yhdeksän**	kahksi toohahttah ewhdayksæn

Year and age *Vuosi ja ikä*

year	**vuosi**	v°°oassi
leap year	**karkaus|vuosi**	kahrkah°°sv°°oassi
decade	**vuosi|kymmen**	v°°oassikewmmayn
century	**vuosi|sata**	v°°oassisahtah
this year	**tämä vuosi**	tæmæ v°°oassi
last year	**viime vuosi**	veemay v°°ooassi
next year	**ensi vuosi**	aynssi v°°oassi
each year	**joka vuosi**	yoakah v°°oassi
2 years ago	**kaksi vuotta sitten**	kahksi v°°oattah sittayn

in one year	**yhden vuoden kuluttua**	ewhdayn v°°oadayn kooloottooah
in the eighties	**kahdeksan-|kymmentä-|luvulla**	kahhdayksahnkewm-mayntæloovoollah
the 16th century	**1500-luku**	toohatveessisahtaalookoo
in the 20th century	**tuhat|yhdeksän-|sataa|luvulla**	toohahtewhdayksænsah-taaloovoollah
How old are you?	**Kuinka vanha olet(te)?**	koo'nkah vahnhah oalayt(tay)
I'm 30 years old.	**Ole 30 vuotias.**	oalayn koalmaykewm-mayntæ v°°oatiahss
He/She was born in 1960.	**Hän on syntynyt vuonna 1960.**	hæn oan sewntewnewt v°°oanah toohahtewh-dayksænsahtaakōōssi kewmmayntæ
What is his/her age?	**Minkä ikäinen hän on?**	minkæ ikæinayn hæn oan
Children under 16 are not admitted.	**Kielletty lapsilta alle 16.**	k'ayllayttew lahpsiltah ahl-lay kōōssitoa'stah

Seasons *Vuoden\|ajat*

spring/summer	**kevät/kesä**	kayvæt/kayssæ
autumn/winter	**syksy/talvi**	sewksew/tahlvi
in spring	**keväällä**	kayvǣllæ/kayssællæ
during the summer	**kesä|aikana**	kayssæeah'kahanah
in autumn	**syksyllä**	sewksewllæ
during the winter	**talvi|aikana**	tahlviah'kaan
high season	**sesonki|aika**	saysoankiah'kah
low season	**hiljainen aika**	hillyah'nayn ah'kah

Months *Kuukaudet*

January	**tammi|kuu**	tahmmikkōō
February	**helmi|kuu**	haylmikōō
March	**maalis|kuu**	maalisskōō
April	**huhti|kuu**	hoohtikkōō
May	**touko|kuu**	toa°°koakōō
June	**kesä|kuu**	kayssækōō
July	**heinä|kuu**	hay'nækōō
August	**elo|kuu**	ayloakōō
September	**syys|kuu**	sēwskōō
October	**loka|kuu**	loakahkōō
November	**marras|kuu**	mahrrahskōō
December	**joulu|kuu**	yoa°°lookōō

in September	**syys|kuussa**	sēwskōossah
since October	**loka|kuusta asti.**	loakahkōostah ahsti
the beginning of January	**tammi|kuun alku**	tahmmikkōon ahlkoo
the middle of February	**helmi|kuun puoli|väli**	hayImikkōon p°°oalivæli
the end of March	**maalis|kuun loppu**	maaliskōon loappoo

Days and Date *Päivät ja päivämäärät*

What day is it today?	**Mikä päivä tänään on?**	mikkæ pæivæ tænææn oan
Sunday	**sunnuntai**	soonnoontah[i]
Monday	**maanantai**	maanahntah[i]
Tuesday	**tiistai**	teestah[i]
Wednesday	**keski|viikko**	kayskiveekkoa
Thursday	**torstai**	toarstah[i]
Friday	**perjantai**	payryahntah[i]
Saturday	**lauantai**	lah°°ahntah[i]
It's...	**Nyt on...**	newt oan
July 1	**ensimmäinen heinä|kuuta**	aynsimmæ[i]nayn hay[i]næ-k°°tah
March 10	**maalis|kuun kymmenes**	maaliskōon kewm maynayss
in the morning	**aamulla**	aamoollah
during the day	**päivällä**	pæ[i]vællæ
in the afternoon	**ilta|päivällä**	iltahpæ[i]vællæ
in the evening	**illalla**	illahllah
at night	**yöllä**	ew""llæ
the day before yesterday	**toissa|päivänä**	toa[i]ssahpæ[i]vænæ
yesterday	**eilen**	ay[i]layn
today	**tänään**	yænææn
tomorrow	**huomenna**	h°°oamaynnah
the day after tomorrow	**yli|huomenna**	ewlih°°oamaynnah
the day before	**edellisenä päivänä**	aydayllisaynæ pæ[i]vænæ
the next day	**seuraavana päivänä**	say°°raavahnah pæ[i]vænæ
two days ago	**kaksi päivää sitten**	kahksi pæ[i]væ sittayn
in three days' time	**kolmessa päivässä**	koalmayssæ pæ[i]væssæ
last week	**viime viikolla**	veemay veekoallah
next week	**ensi viikolla**	aynsi veekoallah
for a fortnight (two weeks)	**kahden viikon ajan**	kahhdayn veekoan ahyahn
birthday	**syntymä|päivä**	sewntewmæpæ[i]væ
day off	**vapaa|päivä**	vahpaapæ[i]væ

holiday	**loma|päivä**	loamahpæ'væ
holidays/vacation	**loma**	loamah
week	**viikko**	veekkoa
weekend	**viikon|loppu**	veekoanloappoo
working day	**työ|päivä**	tew⁺'pæ'væ
on weekdays	**arkisin**	ahrkissin

Public holidays *Yleiset vapaa\|päivät*

January 1	**uuden|vuoden |päivä**	New Year's Day
May 1	**vappu**	Labour Day
December 6	**itsenäisyys|päivä**	National Day
December 24	**joulu|aatto**	Christmas Eve
December 25	**joulu|päivä**	Christmas Day
December 26	**tapanin|päivä**	St Stephen's Day

Greetings and wishes *Tervehdykset ja toivotukset*

Merry Christmas!	**Hyvää Joulua!**	hewvææ yoa°°looah
Happy New Year!	**Onnellista Uutta Vuotta!**	oannayllistah ōōttah v°°oattah
Happy Easter!	**Iloista Pääsiäistä!**	illoa'stah pæsiæ'stæ
Happy birthday!	**Hyvää syntymä-|päivää!**	hewvææ sewntewmæpæ'-væ
Best wishes	**Parhain terveisin**	pahrhah'n tayrvay'ssin
Congratulations!	**Onneksi olkoon!**	oannayksi oalkōān
Good luck/All the best!	**Onnea!**	oannaea
Have a good trip!	**Hauskaa matkaa!**	hah°°skaa mahtkaa
Have a good holiday!	**Hauskaa lomaa!**	hah°°skaa loamaa
Best regards from ...	**Terveisiä ...-lta.**	tayrvay's'æ ...-ltah
My regards to ...	**Terveiset ...-lle.**	tayrvay'sayt ...-llay

What time is it? *Mitä kello on?*

In Finland, for everyday speech people often prefer the 12-hour clock but in all official or even semi-official contexts the 24-hour clock is used.

| Excuse me. Can you tell me the time? | **Anteeksi. Voitteko sanoa, mitä kello on?** | ahntāȳksi voa'ttaykoa sah-noah mittæ kaylloa oan |

It's...	Se on...	say oan
(exactly) one	(tasan) yksi	(tahsahn) ewksi
five past one	viittä yli yksi	veettæ ewli ewksi
ten past two	kymmentä yli kaksi	kewmmayntæ ewli kahksi
a quarter past three	neljännestä/vartin yli kolme	naylyænnaystæ/vahrtin ewli koalmay
twenty past four	kahta|kymmentä yli neljä	kahhtahkewmmayntæ ewli naylyæ
twenty-five past five	viittä vaille puoli kuusi	veettæ vah'llay p°°oali k°°ossi
half past six	puoli seitsemän	p°°oali say'tsaymæn
twenty-five to seven	kahta|kymmentä-|viittä vaille seitsemän	kahhtahkewmmayntæveet-tæ vah'llay say'tsaymæn
twenty to eight	kahta|kymmentä vaille kahdeksan	kahhtahkewmmayntæ vah'llay kahhdayksahn
a quarter to nine	viisitoista minuuttia vaille yhdeksän	veesitoa'stah minoottiah vah'llay ewhhdayksæn
ten to ten	kymmentä vaille kymmenen	kewmmayntæ va'llay kewmmaynayn
five to eleven	viittä vaille yksi-|toista	veettæ vah'llay ewksitoa's-tah
twelve o'clock (noon/midnight)	kaksitoista (keski-|päivällä/keski-|yöllä)	kahksitoa'stah (kayski-pæ'vællæ/kayskiew°°llæ)
in the morning	aamulla	aamoollah
in the afternoon	päivällä	pæ'vællæ
in the evening	illalla	illahllah
The train leaves at...	Juna lähtee kello...	yoonah læhtay kaylloa
13.04 (1.04 p.m.)	kolme|toista nolla neljä	koalmaytoa'stah noallah naylyæ
0.40 (0.40 a.m.)	nolla neljä-|kymmentä	noallah naylyækewm-mayntæ
in five minutes	viiden minuutin päästä	veedayn minnootin pæstæ
in a quarter of an hour	viidentoista minuutin kuluttua	veedayntoa'stah minootin koaloottooah
half an hour ago	puoli tuntia sitten	p°°oali toontiah sittayn
about two hours	noin kaksi tuntia	noa'n kahksi toontiah
more than 10 minutes	yli 10 minuuttia	ewli kewmmaynayn minnoottiah
less than 30 seconds	alle 30 sekunttia	ahllay koalmaykewm-mayntæ saykoonttiah
The clock is fast/slow.	Kello edistää/jätät-tää	kaylloa aydistæ/yætættæ

Common abbreviations *Yleisiä lyhenteitä*

ap.	aamu|päivällä	a.m.
as.	asema	railway station
esim.	esi|merkiksi	for instance
fil. tri	filosofian tohtori	Ph.D.
Hki	Helsinki	Helsinki
HKL	Helsingin Kaupungin Liikenne |laitos	Helsinki Municipal Transport Company
hra	herra	Mr.
huom.	huomaa, huomautus	note
hv	hevos|voima(a)	horsepower
ip.	ilta|päivällä	p.m
J.K, P.S.	jälki|kirjoitus	postscript
jne.	ja niin edelleen	etc.
joht.	johtaja	director
klo	kello	o'clock
kpl	kappaletta	pieces
ks.	katso	see
lääket. tri	lääke|tieteen tohtori	MD/GP
mk	markka(a)	Finnish mark(s)
n.	noin	approximately
nro	numero	number
nti	neiti	Miss
os.	osoite	address
OY	osake|yhtiö	Ltd., Inc.
p	penni(ä)	penni (100 = 1 mark)
puh.	puhelin	telephone
pvm.	päivä|määrä	date
rva	rouva	Mrs.
s, ss.	sivu, sivut	page(s)
t, h	tunti(a)	hour(s)
v.	vuosi, vuonna	year
VP	vastausta pyydetään	RSVP
VR	Valtion Rauta|tiet	Finnish State Railways
YK	Yhdistyneet Kansa|kunnat	United Nations
ym.	ynnä muuta	etc.

Signs and notices *Kylttejä ja varoituksia*

Alas	Down
Alennus|myynti/Ale	Sale
Avoinna	Open
Älkää tukkiko sisään|käyntiä	Do not block entrance
Ei saa häiritä	Do not disturb
Ei saa koskea	Do not touch
Epä|kunnossa	Out of order
(Hengen|)vaara	Danger (of death)
Hissi	Lift
Hätä|/Vara|ulos|käytävä	Emergency exit
Kassa	Cash desk
... kielletty	... forbidden
Koputtamatta sisään	Enter without knocking
Kuuma	Hot
Kylmä	Cold
Loppuun|myyty	Sold out
Läpi|kulku (sakon uhalla) kielletty	Tresspassers will be prosecuted
Miehille	Gentlemen
Myydään	For sale
Naisille	Ladies
Neuvonta	Information
Odottakaa	Please wait
Pääsy kielletty	No admittance
Roskaaminen kielletty	No littering
Sisään(|käynti)	Entrance
Soitto|kello/Soittakaa	Please ring
Tupakointi kielletty	No smoking
Työnnä	Push
Täynnä	No vacancies
Ulos(|käynti)	Exit
Vapaa	Vacant
Vapaa pääsy	Free admittance
Varattu	Occupied/Reserved
Varo(kaa)	Caution
Varokaa koiraa	Beware of the dog
Vasta maalattu	Wet paint
Vedä	Pull
Vuokralle tarjotaan	To let
Vuokrataan	For hire
Yksityis|tie	Private road
Ylös	Up

Emergency *Hätä|tilanne*

Call the police.	**Kutsukaa poliisi.**	ko_ts_ookaa poaleessi
Consulate	**Konsulaatti**	koansoolaatti
DANGER!	**VAARA!**	vaarah
Embassy	**Lähetystö**	læhaytewstur
FIRE!	**TULI|PALO!**	toolipahloa
Gas	**Kaasua**	kaassooah
Get a doctor.	**Hakekaa lääkäri.**	hahkaykaa lǣkæri
Go away!	**Menkää tiehenne!**	maynkǣ t'aynaynnay
HELP!	**APUA!**	ahpooah
Get help quickly!	**Hakekaa apua– nopeasti!**	hahkaykaa ahpooah noapayahsti
I'm ill.	**Olen sairas.**	oalayn sah'rahs
I'm lost.	**Olen eksynyt.**	oalayn ayksewnewt
Leave me alone!	**Jättäkää minut rauhaan!**	yættækǣ minnoot rah°°haan
LOOK OUT!	**VAROKAA!**	vahroakaa
Poison	**Myrkkyä**	mewrkkewæ
POLICE!	**POLIISI!**	poaleesi
Stop that man/ woman!	**Pysäyttäkää tuo mies/nainen!**	pewsæ^ewttækǣ t°°oa m'ays/nah'nayn
STOP THIEF!	**OTTAKAA VARAS KIINNI!**	oattahkaa vahrahs keenni

Emergency telephone numbers *Hätä|puhelin|numerot*

In Helsinki dial 000 to report police, fire and medical emergencies. In other towns, hotels and tourist offices keep lists of local emergency numbers.

Lost property—Theft *Kadonnut omaisuus—Varkaus*

Where's the...?	**Missä on...?**	missæ oan
lost property (lost and found) office	**löytö|tavara- |toimisto**	lur^ew turtahvahrahtoa'- mistoa
police station	**poliisi|asema**	poaleesiahsaymah
I want to report a theft.	**Tekisin ilmoituksen varkaudesta**	taykissin ilmoa'tooksayn vahrkah°°daystah
My... has been stolen.	**...-ni on varastettu**	-ni oan vahrahstayttoo
I've lost my...	**Olen kadotta- nut...-ni.**	oalayn kahdoattahnoot...-ni
handbag	**käsi|laukku**	kæssilah°°kkooni
passport	**passi**	pahssi
wallet	**lompakko**	loampahkkoa

CAR ACCIDENTS, see page 78

Yleistä

Conversion tables

Centimetres and inches

To change centimetres into inches, multiply by .39.
To change inches into centimetres, multiply by 2.54.

	in.	feet	yards
1 mm	0.039	0.003	0.001
1 cm	0.39	0.03	0.01
1 dm	3.94	0.32	0.10
1 m	39.40	3.28	1.09

	mm	cm	m
1 in.	25.4	2.54	0.025
1 ft.	304.8	30.48	0.304
1 yd.	914.4	91.44	0.914

(32 metres = 35 yards)

Temperature

To convert Centigrade into degrees Fahrenheit, multiply Centigrade by 1.8 and add 32.

To convert degrees Fahrenheit into Centigrade, subtract 32 from Fahrenheit and divide by 1.8.

Kilometres into miles

1 kilometre (km.) = 0.62 miles

km.	10	20	30	40	50	60	70	80	90	100	110	120	130
miles	6	12	19	25	31	37	44	50	56	62	68	75	81

Miles into kilometres

1 mile = 1.609 kilometres (km.)

miles	10	20	30	40	50	60	70	80	90	100
km.	16	32	48	64	80	97	113	129	145	161

Fluid measures

1 litre (l.) = 0.88 imp. quart or 1.06 U.S. quart
1 imp. quart = 1.14 l.   1 U.S. quart = 0.95 l.
1 imp. gallon = 4.55 l.   1 U.S. gallon = 3.8 l.

litres	5	10	15	20	25	30	35	40	45	50
imp. gal.	1.1	2.2	3.3	4.4	5.5	6.6	7.7	8.8	9.9	11.0
U.S. gal.	1.3	2.6	3.9	5.2	6.5	7.8	9.1	10.4	11.7	13.0

Weights and measures

1 kilogram or kilo (kg.) = 1000 grams (g.)

100 g. = 3.5 oz.	½ kg. = 1.1 lb.
200 g. = 7.0 oz.	1 kg. = 2.2 lb.
1 oz. =	28.35 g.
1 lb. =	453.60 g.

CLOTHING SIZES, see page 114/YARDS AND INCHES, see page 111

Basic Grammar

Finnish, which belongs to the small Finno-Ugrian group of languages, is very different from English, Swedish or Russian, which all belong to the big Indo-European group of languages.*

Finnish uses many more suffixes (word endings) than is usual in European languages. Because of a certain melodic logic, the suffixes are not attached mechanically to words. Vowel harmony and some sound changes associated with inflexional suffixes, although quite regular, complicate the grammar.

Nouns

Finnish has no grammatical gender and no definite or indefinite article.

Finnish nouns can have four kinds of suffixes. They always follow the same order: number + case + possessive + particle.

To simplify presentation here, the sign = indicates a vowel which is the same as the nearest preceding vowel.

1. **Number:** If plural, then -**t** in the nominative case and -**i**- in other cases (between two vowels this plural -**i**- changes to -**j**-).

2. **Case**:

The cases used mainly as subject or object:

case	suffix	basic meaning	example	meaning
nominative	–, (pl. -**t**)	(basic form)	auto	a/the car
genitive	-**n**, (pl. -**en**, -**den**, -**ten**)	possession	auto**n**	of the car
partitive	-**a**, -**ta**, -**tta**	indefinite quantity	auto**a**	(some) car

* Finnish is similar to some of the languages around the Gulf of Finland, Estonian being the most widely-spoken. The difference between Finnish and Hungarian, the most widely-spoken of Finno-Ugrian languages, is greater than that between Swedish and Italian.

The local cases:

inessive	**-ssa**	inside	auto**ssa**	in the car
elative	**-sta**	out of	auto**sta**	out of the car
illative	**-=n, -h=n, -seen, -siin**	into	auto**on**	into the car
adessive	**-lla**	on	auto**lla**	at the car
ablative	**-lta**	off	auto**lta**	from the car
allative	**-lle**	onto	auto**lle**	to the car

The cases expressing a state:

essive	**-na**	in a state	auto**na**	as a car
translative	**-ksi**	into a state	auto**ksi**	to (become) a car

There are another *three* cases in Finnish but these are rarely used.

Cases are used in many other ways in Finnish and this is just the briefest outline of their use with nouns.

3. **Possessive:** Instead of possessive determiners ('my', 'your' etc.) Finnish uses the genitive forms of the personal pronouns (see table). These are not always necessary, because possessive suffixes indicate the owner.

	singular			plural		
1st person	**-ni**	auto**ni**	my car	**-mme**	auto**mme**	our car
2nd person	**-si**	auto**si**	your car	**-nne**	auto**nne**	your car
3rd person	**-nsa**	auto**nsa**	his/her car	**-nsa**	auto**nsa**	their car

4. **Particle:** Some particles are added to words as suffixes. The most important of these is **-ko** which is used to form direct questions. The question word (usually a verb) appears first in the sentence e.g:

Tuletko?	Are you coming?
Autollako tulet?	Are you coming by car?

Other common suffix particles are -**kin** ('also/too') and -**kaan** ('also' in negative sentences), e.g. Minä**kin**! 'Me too!'

Suffixes are also added to pronouns, adjectives, numbers and some forms of verbs. As attributes these almost always agree with the headword in number and case.

Personal pronouns

You will notice that Finnish has only one word for 'he' and 'she' - **hän**.

subject		object			possessive	
nominative			accusative	partitive	genitive	
I	**minä**	me	**minut**	**minua**	mine	**minum**
you	**sinä**	you	**sinut**	**sinua**	yours	**sinum**
he/she	**hän**	him/her	**hänet**	**hantä**	his/hers	**hänen**
we	**me**	us	**meidät**	**meitä**	ours	**meidän**
you	**te**	you	**teidät**	**teitä**	yours	**teidän**
they	**he**	them	**heidät**	**heitä**	theirs	**heidän**

The 2nd person plural (**te**) is also used as a polite singular 'you' form. When using this form, verbs and suffixes must of course be in the plural form that corresponds to **te**.

Verbs

Subject pronouns in the 1st and 2nd person are often omitted (sometimes also in the 3rd person), because the ending of the verb is enough to indicate the subject. The verb endings are:

I	-n	we	-mme
you	-t	you	-tte
he/she	two vowels*	they	-vat

* the last vowel of the stem is doubled, if it is not the second vowel of a long vowel or a diphthong.

To form the negative in Finnish a special *verb* is used. This negative verb inflects according to the subject of the sentence just like any other verb. The 'action' verb does not change. This construction is similar to the way 'do not, does not' are used as a negative auxiliary in English.

I	en	we	emme
you	et	you	ette
he/she	ei	they	eivät

Verbs in Finnish can be divided into four groups for inflection:

Present tense:

	ostaa (to buy)	tuoda (to bring)	tulla (to come)	pelata (to play)
I	ostan	tuon	tulen	pelaan
you	ostat	tuot	tulet	pelaat
he/she/it	ostaa	tuo	tulee	pelaa
we	ostamme	tuomme	tulemme	pelaamme
you	ostatte	tuotte	tulette	pelaatte
they	ostavat	tuovat	tulevat	pelaavat

Present tense negative:

I	en osta	en tuo	en tule	en pelaa
you	et osta	et tuo	et tule	et pelaa
he/she/it	ei osta	ei tuo	ei tule	ei pelaa
we	emme osta	emme tuo	emme tule	emme pelaa
you	ette osta	ette tuo	ette tule	ette pelaa
they	eivät osta	eivät tuo	eivät tule	eivät pelaa

Past tense:

The ending for the past tense is -i-. It causes many vowel and consonant changes.

I	ostin	toin	tulin	pelasin
you	ostit	toit	tulit	pelasit
he/she/it	osti	toi	tuli	pelasi
we	ostimme	toimme	tulimme	pelasimme
you	ostitte	toitte	tulitte	pelasitte
they	ostivat	toivat	tulivat	pelasivat

Irregular verbs

olla (to be)				
Present tense		Present tense negative	Past tense	
I am	(minä) olen	en ole	I was	olin
you are	(sinä) olet	et ole	you were	olit
he/she is	hän on	hän ei ole	he/she was	hän oli
it is	se on	se ei ole	it was	se oli
we are	(me) olemme	emme ole	we were	olimme
you are	(te) olette	ette ole	you were	olitte
they are	he ovat	he eivät ole	they were	he olivat

The personal pronouns in brackets are used for emphasis only. Normally they are required only with the 3rd person singular and plural forms.

To have

There is no corresponding verb for 'to have' in Finnish. Instead the possessor appears in the adessive case combined with the 3rd person singular of the verb **olla** (to be) in the appropriate tense:

I have a card.	**Minu*lla* *on* kortti.**
Do you have money?	**Onko sinu*lla*/tei*llä* rahaa?**
He does not have time.	**Häne*llä* *ei ole* aikaa.**
We had fun.	**Mei*llä* *oli* hauskaa.**
They have had fun.	**Hei*llä* *on ollut* hauskaa.**

Some adverbs of place

Missä?	Where?	Mistä?	From where?	Minne?	Where to?
siellä	there (place mentioned before)	sieltä	from there	sinne	(in) there
täällä	here	täältä	from there	tänne	(in) here
tuoola	there (place pointed to)	tuolta	from there	tuonne	(in) there

Dictionary
and alphabetical index

English-Finnish

itr intransitive *tr* transitive

A

abbey luostari 80
abbreviation lyhennys 154
about *(approximately)* noin 153
above yllä, yli 15; yläpuolella 63
abscess märkäpesäke 145
absorbent cotton vanu 108
accept, to ottaa 61; hyväksyä 102
accessories asusteet 115; lisälaitteet 125
accident onnettomuus 78, 139
account tili 130
ache särky 141
adaptor adapteri, sovitin 118
address osoite 21, 31, 76, 79, 102
address book osoitekirja 104
adhesive liima 104, 105
adhesive tape teippi 104
admission (sisään)pääsy 82, 90, 155
admitted päästää sisään 150
Africa Afrikka 146
after jälkeen 15, 77
after-shave lotion partavesi 109
afternoon, in the iltapäivällä 151, 153
again uudelleen 96, 136
against vastaan 140
age ikä 149, 150
ago sitten 149, 151
air bed ilmapatja 106
air conditioning ilmastointi 23, 28
air mattress ilmapatja 106
airmail lentoposti 132
airplane lentokone 65
airport lentokenttä 16, 21; lentoasema 65
aisle seat käytävä-paikka 65
alarm clock herätyskello 121
alcohol alkoholi 37, 58
alcoholic alkoholi 58
all kaikki 103
allergic allerginen 141, 143

almond manteli 53
alphabet aakkoset 9
also myös 15
alter, to *(garment)* korjata 114
altitude sickness lentopahoinvointi 107
amazing hämmästyttävä 83
amber meripihka 122
ambulance ambulanssi 79
American amerikkalainen 93, 105, 126
American plan täysihoito 24
amethyst ametisti 122
amount summa 61, 131
amplifier vahvistin 118
anaesthetic puudutusaine 144; puudutus 145
analgesic kipua lievittävä 108
anchovy anjovis 44
and ja 15
animal eläin 85
aniseed anis 51
ankle nilkka 139
anorak anorakki 115
another toinen 56, 123
answer vastaus 136
antibiotic antibiootti 143
antidepressant piristävä lääke 143
antique shop antiikkikauppa 98
antiques antiikki 83
antiseptic cream antiseptinen voide 108
any yhtään 14
anyone kukaan 12, 16
anything mitään 17, 25, 101, 112
anywhere jossain, missään 89
apartment huoneisto 23
aperitif aperitiivi 57
appendicitis umpilisäkkeen tulehdus 142
appendix umpilisäke 138
appetizer alkuruoka 41

behind takana, taakse 15, 77
beige beige 112
Belgium Belgia 146
bell *(electric)* soittokello 144
below alla, alle 15
belt vyö 116
berth makuupaikka 69; vuodepaikka 70
better parempi 14, 25, 101
between välissä, välillä 15
bicycle (polku)pyörä 74
big suuri 14; iso 101, 117
bilberry mustikka 53
bill lasku 28, 31, 61, 102
bill *(banknote)* seteli 130
billion *(Am.)* miljardi 148
binoculars kiikari 123
bird lintu 85
birth syntymä 26
birthday syntymäpäivä 151, 152
biscuit *(Br.)* keksi 63
bitter kitkerä 61
black musta 112
black and white *(film)* mustavalkoinen 124, 125
black coffee kahvi mustana 40, 60
blackcurrant musta viinimarja 53
bladder virtsarakko 138
blade terä 109
blanket peitto 27
bleed, to vuotaa verta 139, 145
blind *(window shade)* kaihdin 29
blister rakko 139
blocked tukossa 29
blood veri 142
blood pressure verenpaine 141, 142
blood transfusion verensiirto 144
blouse pusero 115
blow-dry föönaus 30
blue sininen 112
blueberry mustikka 53
blusher poskipuna 109
boat vene, lautta, alus 73, 74
bobby pin hiusneula 110
body ruumis 138
boil paise 139
boiled keitetty 47
boiled egg keitetty muna 40
bone luu 138
book kirja 12, 104
booking office lippumyymälä 19; lipunmyynti 67
bookshop kirjakauppa 98, 104
boot saapas 117
boring ikävystyttävä 83

born syntynyt 150
botanical gardens kasvitieteellinen puutarha 80
botany kasvitiede 83
bottle pullo 17, 57
bottle-opener pullonavaaja 120
bottom alaosa 145
bow tie rusetti 115
bowel suoli 138
boxing nyrkkeily 89
boy poika 111, 128
boyfriend poikaystävä 93
bra rintaliivit 115
bracelet rannekoru 121
braces *(suspenders)* henkselit 115
braised haudutettu 47
brake jarru 75
brake fluid jarruneste 75
brandy konjakki 58
bread leipä 36, 40, 63
break down, to mennä epäkuntoon 78
break, to mennä rikki 29, 118, 123; murtua 139, 145
breakdown konerikko 78
breakdown van hinausauto 78
breakfast aamiainen 24, 27, 40
bream lahna 44
breast rinta 138
breathe, to hengittää 141, 142
bridge silta 85
bring down, to tuoda alas 31
bring, to tuoda 13, 57
British britti 93
broiled *(Am.)* grillattu 47
broken rikki 118, 123; murtunut 139, 140
brooch rintakoru 121
brother veli 93
brown ruskea 112
bruise mustelma 139
brush harja 110
Brussels sprouts ruusukaali 49
bubble bath kylpyvaahto 109
bucket ämpäri 120, 128
buckle solki 116
build, to rakentaa 83
building rakennus 81, 83
building blocks/bricks rakennuspalikat 128
bulb *(light)* lamppu 29, 75, 118
burn palohaava 139
burn out, to *(bulb)* palaa (loppuun) 29
bus bussi 18, 19, 65, 72, 80
bus stop bussipysäkki 72, 73
business liikeasia 16; liike- 130

business class business-luokka 65
business district liikekeskus 81
business trip liikematka 94
busy (muussa) puuhassa 96
but mutta 15
butane gas butaani, nestekaasu 32, 106
butcher's lihakauppa 98
butter voi 36, 40, 64
button nappi 29, 116
buy, to ostaa 82, 100, 104, 123

C

cabana uimakoppi 91
cabbage kaali 49
cabin (ship) hytti 74
cable sähke 133
cable release lankalaukaisin 125
café kahvio, kahvila 33
cake kakku 37, 54, 63
calculator laskin 104
calendar kalenteri 104
call (phone) puhelu 134, 136
call back, to soittaa takaisin 136
call, to (give name) nimittää 11
call, to (phone) soittaa 134, 136
call, to (summon) kutsua 78, 156
calm tyyni 90
cambric hieno palttina 113
camel-hair kamelinkarva 113
camera kamera 124, 125
camera case kameralaukku 125
camera shop valokuvausliike 98
camp site leirintäalue 32
camp, to leiriytyä 32
campbed telttasänky 106
camping leirintä 32
camping equipment leirintävarusteet 106
can (be able to) voida 12
can (container) purkki, tölkki 119
can opener purkinavaaja 120
Canada Kanada 146
Canadian kanadalainen 93
cancel, to peruuttaa 65
candle kynttilä 120
candy makeinen 126
candy store makeiskauppa 98
cap lakki 115
capers kapris 51
capital (finance) pääoma 131
car auto 19, 20, 32, 75, 78
car hire auton vuokraus 20

car mechanic (auton)korjaaja 78
car park pysäköintialue 77
car racing kilpa-ajot 89
car radio autoradio 118
car rental auton vuokraus 20
carat karaatti 121
caravan asuntovaunu 32
caraway kumina 51
carbon paper hiilipaperi 104
carbonated (fizzy) hiilihapollinen 59
carburettor kaasutin 78
card kortti 131
card game korttipeli 128
cardigan neuletakki, villatakki 115
carrot porkkana 49
carry, to kantaa 21
cart (työntö)kärry 18
carton (of cigarettes) kartonki 17, 126
cartridge (camera) kasetti 124
case kotelo 123; laukku 125
cash desk kassa 103, 155
cash, to vaihtaa rahaksi 130; lunastaa 133
cassette kasetti 118, 127
cassette recorder kasettinauhuri 118
castle linna 81
catacombs katakombit 81
catalogue luettelo 82
cathedral tuomiokirkko 81
Catholic katolinen 84
cauliflower kukkakaali 49
caution varo 155
cave luola 81
celery selleri 49
cemetery hautausmaa 81
centimetre senttimetri 111
centre keskusta 19, 21, 76, 81
century vuosisata 149
ceramics keramiikka 83
cereal hiutaleita 40
certificate todistus 144
chain (jewellery) ketju 121
chain bracelet rannekoru 121
chair tuoli 106
chamber music kamarimusiikki 128
change (money) vaihtoraha 62, 130; kolikoita 77
change, to vaihtaa 60, 68, 73, 75, 123; muuttaa 65
change, to (money) vaihtaa 18, 130
chapel kappeli 81
charcoal grillihiili 106
charge maksu 20, 32, 77, 89, 136
charge, to veloittaa 25, 130
charm (trinket) amuletti 121

DICTIONARY

charm bracelet ranneketju 121
cheap halpa 14, 101
cheaper halvempi 24, 25, 101
check *(money)* shekki 130, 131
check *(restaurant)* lasku 61
check in, to *(airport)* ilmoittautua (lähtöön) 65
check out, to lähteä (ilmoittautua lähteväksi) 31
check, to tarkistaa 75, 123
check, to *(luggage)* lähettää matkatavara 71
check-up *(medical)* tarkastus 142
cheers! kippis 56
cheese juusto 51, 64
chemist's apteekki 98, 107
cheque shekki 130, 131
cherry kirsikka 52
chervil kirveli 51
chess set shakkipeli 128
chest rintakehä 138, 141
chestnut kastanja 52
chewing gum purukumi 126
chewing tobacco purutupakka 126
chicken kana 48, 62
chicken breast kanan rinta 48
chicory endive 49
chiffon shifonki 113
child lapsi 24, 60, 82, 93, 139, 150
children's doctor lastenlääkäri 137
China Kiina 146
chips ranskalaiset perunat 62; perunalastut 63
chives ruoholaukka 51
chocolate suklaa 64, 119, 126
chocolate *(hot)* kaakao 40, 60
chocolate bar suklaapatukka 64
choice valinta 39
chop *(meat)* kyljys 46
Christmas joulu 152
chromium kromi 122
church kirkko 81, 84
cigar sikaari 126
cigarette savuke 17, 95, 126; tupakka 121
cigarette case savukekotelo 121, 126
cigarette holder imuke 126
cigarette lighter (tupakan) sytytin 121, 126
cinema elokuva 86, 96
cinnamon kaneli 51
circle *(theatre)* parveke 87
city kaupunki 81
city centre kaupungin keskusta 81
classical klassinen 128

clean puhdas 61
clean, to puhdistaa 29, 76
cleansing cream puhdistusvoide 109
cliff jyrkänne 85
cloakroom vaatesäilö 87
clock kello 121; aika 153
clock-radio kelloradio 118
close, to sulkea *tr* 11, 82, 107, 132
closed suljettu 155
clothes vaatteet 29, 115
clothes peg/pin pyykkipoika 120
clothing vaatetus 111
cloud pilvi 94
clove mausteneilikka 51
coach *(bus)* linja-auto 71
coast rannikko 85
coat takki 115
coconut kookospähkinä 52
cod turska 44
coffee kahvi 40, 60, 64
coin (metalli)raha 83
cold kylmä 14, 25, 40, 61, 94, 155
cold *(illness)* vilustuminen 107, 141
cold cuts leikkeleet 64
collar kaulus 116
collect call vastaanottaja maksaa-puhelu 134
colour väri 103, 111, 124, 125
colour chart värikartta 30
colour rinse värihuuhtelu 30
colour shampoo värishampoo 110
colour slide väridia 124
colourfast väripäästämätön 113
comb kampa 110
come, to tulla 36, 92, 95, 137, 144, 146
comedy komedia 86
commission *(fee)* välityspalkkio 130
common *(frequent)* yleinen 154
compact disc CD-levy 127
compartment *(train)* vaunuosasto 70
compass kompassi 106
complaint valitus 60
concert konsertti 87
concert hall konserttisali, talo 81, 88
condom kondomi 108
conductor *(orchestra)* kapellimestari 88
confectioner's makeiskauppa 98
conference room kokoushuone 24
confirm, to vahvistaa 65
confirmation vahvistus 23
congratulation onnittelu 152
connection *(transport)* yhteys 65, 67
constipation ummetus 140
consulate konsulaatti 156

Sanakirja

contact lens kontaktilinssi 123
contagious tarttuva 142
contain, to sisältää 37
contraceptive ehkäisyväline 108
contract sopimus 131
control tarkastus 16
convent nunnaluostari 81
cookie keksi 64
cool box kylmäkassi 106
copper kupari 122
coral koralli 122
corduroy vakosametti 113
corn (Am.) maissi 49
corn (foot) liikavarvas 108
corn plaster liikavarvaslaastari 108
corner kulma 21, 77; nurkka 36
cosmetics kosmetiikka 109
cost kustannukset 131, 136
cost, to maksaa 11, 80, 133
cot lapsen sänky 24
cotton puuvilla 113
cotton wool vanu 108
cough yskä 107, 141
cough drops yskänlääke 108
cough syrup yskänlääke 108
cough, to yskiä 142
counter luukku 133
country maa 93, 146
countryside maaseutu 85
courgette munakoiso 49
court house oikeustalo 81
cousin serkku 93
cracker voileipäkeksi 64
cramp kouristus 141
crayfish (river) rapu 44
crayon värikynä 104
cream kerma 60
cream (toiletry) voide 109
crease resistant rypistymätön 113
credit luotto 130
credit card luottokortti 20, 31, 62, 102, 130
crepe kreppi 113
crockery astiat 120
cross risti 121
cross-country skiing murtomaahiihto 91
crossing (maritime) ylitys 74
crossroads tienhaara 77
cruise risteily 73
crystal kristalli 122
cucumber kurkku 49
cuff link kalvosinnappi 121
cuisine keittiö 34
cup kuppi 36, 60, 120

curler papiljotti 110
currency valuutta 129
currency exchange office valuutanvaihto(toimisto) 18, 67, 129
current virtaus 90
curtain verho 29
customs tulli 16, 102
cut (wound) (viilto)haava 139
cut glass hiottu lasi 122
cut off, to (interrupt) mennä poikki 135
cut, to (with scissors) leikata 30
cuticle remover kynsinauhavesi 109
cutlery ruokailuvälineet 120, 121
cutlet kotletti 46
cycling pyöräily 89
cystitis rakkotulehdus 142

D
dairy maitokauppa 98
dance tanssi 88, 96
dance, to tanssia 88, 96
danger vaara 155, 156
dangerous vaarallinen 90
dark pimeä 25; tumma 101, 111, 112
date (appointment) treffit 95
date (day) päivä 26; päivämäärä 151
date (fruit) taateli 53
daughter tytär 93
day päivä 20, 25, 80, 94, 150, 151
day off vapaapäivä 151
daylight päivänvalo 124
decade vuosikymmen 149
decaffeinated kafeiinitonta 40, 60
December joulukuu 150
decision päätös 25, 102
deck (ship) kansi 74
deck chair kansituoli 90
declare, to (customs) ilmoittaa tullattavaksi 17
deep syvä 142
degree (temperature) aste 140
delay myöhässä 68
delicatessen herkkumyymälä 98
delicious herkullinen 62
deliver, to toimittaa 102
delivery toimitus 102
denim farkkukangas 113
Denmark Tanska 146
dentist hammaslääkäri 98, 145
denture hammasproteesi 145
deodorant deodorantti 109
department (museum) osasto 83
department (shop) osasto 100

emergency hätä 156
emergency exit hätäuloskäynti 28, 99
emery board hiekkapaperiviila 109
empty tyhjä 14
enamel emali 122
end loppu 150
engaged (phone) varattu 136
engagement ring kihlasormus 122
engine (car) moottori 78
England Englanti 134, 146
English englantilainen 93, 126
English (language) englanti 11, 16, 80,
 82, 84, 104, 105
enjoy oneself, to pitää hauskaa 96
enjoyable viihtyisä 31
enlarge, to suurentaa 125
enough tarpeeksi 14, 68
entrance sisään(käynti) 67, 99, 155
entrance fee pääsymaksu 82
envelope kirjekuori 104
equipment varusteet 90, 91, 106
eraser pyyhekumi 104
estimate (cost) (kustannus)arvio 78,
 131
Estonia Viro 146
Eurocheque euroshekki 130
Europe Eurooppa 146
evening ilta 95, 96
evening dress iltapuku 88
evening dress (woman's) iltapuku 115
evening, in the illalla 151, 153
every joka 143
everything kaikki 31, 61
examine, to tutkia 137
exchange rate vaihtokurssi 18, 130
exchange, to vaihtaa 103
excursion retki 80
excuse me anteeksi 11, 152
excuse, to antaa anteeksi 11
exercise book kirjoitusvihko 104
exhaust pipe pakoputki 78
exhibition näyttely 81
exit ulos(käynti) 67, 99, 155
expect, to odottaa 130
expenses kulut 131
expensive kallis 14, 19, 25, 101
exposure (photography) kuva 124, 125
exposure counter kuvalaskuri 125
express pika 132
expression ilmaisu 10, 100
expressway moottoritie 76
extension (phone) alanumero 135
extension cord/lead jatkojohto 118
extra lisä 27
eye silmä 138, 139

eye drops silmätipat 108
eye shadow luomiväri 109
eye specialist silmälääkäri 137
eyebrow pencil kulmakynä 109
eyesight näkö 123

F

fabric (cloth) kangas 112
face kasvot 138
face pack kasvonaamio 30
face powder kasvopuuteri 109
factory tehdas 81
fair messut, markkinat 81
fall (autumn) syksy 150
fall, to kaatua 139
family perhe 93, 144
fan belt tuulettimen hihna 75
far kaukana 14, 100
fare (ticket) maksu 67, 73
farm maatalo 85
fast herkkä (nopea) 124
fat (meat) rasva 37
father isä 93
faucet vesihana 28
fax faksi 133
February helmikuu 150
fee (doctor's) maksu 144
feeding bottle tuttipullo 110
feel, to (physical state) tuntea 140, 142
felt huopa 113
felt-tip pen huopakärkikynä 104
ferry lautta 74
fever kuume 140
few harva 14
few (a few) muutama 14
field pelto 85
fifteen viisitoista 147
fifth viides 149
fifty viisikymmentä 147
file (tool) viila 109
fill in, to täyttää 26, 144
filling (tooth) paikka 145
filling station bensiiniasema 75
film filmi 86, 124, 125
film winder filminkelaaja 125
filter suodatin 125
filter-tipped suodattimella 126
find, to löytää tr 11, 12, 76; löytyä itr
 84, 100
fine (OK) hyvin 11, 92; hyvä 25, 92
fine arts taide-esineet 83
finger sormi 138
Finland Suomi 146

genuine aito 117
geology geologia 83
Germany Saksa 146
get off, to nousta pois 73
get past, to päästä ohi 69
get to, to päästä 19, 76
get up, to nousta ylös 144
get, to (find) saada 11, 19, 21, 32; hankkia 21
gherkin suolakurkku 64
gift lahja 17
gin gini 58
gin and tonic gintonic 58
ginger inkivääri 51
girdle (naisten) liivit 115
girl tyttö 111, 128
girlfriend tyttöystävä 93
give, to antaa 13, 123, 135; saada 63, 75, 126, 130
gland rauhanen 138
glass lasi 36, 57, 60
glasses silmälasit 123
gloomy synkkä 83
glove hansikas 115
glue liima 104
go away! menkää tiehenne! 156
go back, to palata 77
go out, to lähteä ulos 96
go, to mennä 72; ajaa 21, 77; lähteä 96
gold kulta 121, 122
gold plated kullattu 122
golden kullanvärinen 112
golf golf 89
golf course golf-rata 89
good hyvä 14, 86, 101
good afternoon (hyvää) päivää 10
good evening (hyvää) iltaa 10
good morning (hyvää) huomenta 10
good night hyvää yötä 10
goodbye näkemiin 10
goose hanhi 48
gooseberry karviaismarja 52
gram gramma 119
grammar kielioppi 159
grammar book kielioppi 105
grandfather isoisä 93
grandmother isoäiti 93
grape viinirypäle 53, 64
grapefruit greippi 52
grapefruit juice greippimehu 40, 59
gray harmaa 112
graze raapaisu, verinaarmu 139
greasy rasvainen 30, 110
great (excellent) hieno, oikein mukava 95

Great Britain Iso-Britannia 146
Greece Kreikka 146
green vihreä 112
greengrocer's vihannesmyymälä 98
greeting tervehdys 10, 152
grey harmaa 112
grilled grillattu 45, 47
grocer's sekatavarakauppa 98, 119
groundsheet telttapatja 106
group ryhmä 82
guesthouse matkustajakoti 19, 23
guide opas 80
guidebook opaskirja 82, 104, 105
gum (teeth) ikenet 145
gynaecologist gynekologi 137, 141

H
habit tapa 34
hair hiukset 30, 110
hair dryer hiustenkuivaaja 118
hair gel hiusgeeli 30, 110
hair lotion hiusvesi 110
hair slide hiussolki 110
hair spray hiuslakka 30, 110
hairbrush hiusharja 110
haircut tukanleikkuu 30
hairdresser kampaaja 30, 98
hairgrip hiussolki 110
hairpin hiusneula 110
half (a) puoli 149
half an hour puoli tuntia 153
half board puolihoito 24
half, a puolikas 149
hall (large room) sali, halli 81, 88
hall porter portieeri 27
ham kinkku 40, 64
ham and eggs kinkkua ja munia 40
hammer vasara 120
hammock riippumatto 106
hand käsi 138
hand cream käsivoide 109
hand washable käsinpestävä 113
handbag käsilaukku 115, 156
handicrafts käsityö(tuotteet) 83, 127
handkerchief nenäliina 115
handmade käsitehty 112
hanger vaateripustin 27
happy onnellinen 152
harbour satama 73, 81
hard kova 123
hard-boiled (egg) kovaksi keitetty 40
hardware store kodinkonemyymälä 98

hare jänis 48
hat hattu 115
have to, to *(must)* on -ttava 17, 68; täytyy 68, 77, 95, 140
have, to -lla on 163
hay fever heinänuha 107, 141
hazelnut hasselpähkinä 52
he hän 161
head pää 138, 139
head waiter hovimestari 61
headache päänsärky 141
headphones kuulokkeet 118
health food shop luontaistuotemyymälä 98
health insurance *(company)* sairausvakuutus 144
health insurance form sairausvakuutuslomake 144
heart sydän 138
heart attack sydänkohtaus 141
heat, to lämmittää 90
heavy raskas 14; painava 101
heel korko 117
helicopter helikopteri 74
hello hei, terve 10, 135
help apu 156
help! apua! 156
help, to auttaa 13, 21, 70, 100, 134
help, to *(oneself)* ottaa (itse) 119
her hän 161
herb tea yrttitee 59
herbs yrtit 51
here täällä 14
herring silli 44
hi hei, terve 10
high korkea 85, 90, 141
high season sesonkiaika 150
highlights raidat 30
hill mäki 85
hire vuokraus 20, 74
hire, to vuokrata 19, 20, 74, 90, 91, 119, 155; palkata 80
his hänen 161
history historia 83
hitchhike, to liftata 74
hold on! *(phone)* hetkinen 136
hole reikä 30
holiday lomapäivä, loma 152
holidays loma 16; lomapäivä 152
home koti 96
home address kotiosoite 31
home town kotikaupunki 26
home-made kotitekoinen 39
honey hunaja 40
hope, to toivoa 96

horseback riding ratsastus 89
hospital sairaala 98, 142, 144
hot *(warm)* kuuma 14, 24, 25, 40, 94, 155
hot water kuuma vesi 24, 28
hot-water bottle kuumavesipullo 28
hotel hotelli 19, 21, 22, 26, 80, 96, 102
hotel directory/guide hotelliopas 19
hotel reservation hotellin varaus 19
hour tunti 80, 143, 153
house talo 83, 85
household article taloustarvike 119
how kuinka 11
how far kuinka kaukana 11, 76, 84
how long *(time)* kuinka kauan 11, 25
how many kuinka monta 11
how much kuinka paljon 11; paljonko 24, 80
hundred sata 148
hungry nälkäinen 13, 35
hunting metsästys 90
hurry, to be in a on kiire 21
hurt *(to be)* loukata 139
hurt, to koskee 139, 140, 142; särkee 145
husband aviomies 93
hydrofoil kantosiipialus 74

I
I minä 161
ice jää 95
ice cream jäätelö 54
ice cube jääkuutio 28
ice pack jääpussi 106
iced tea jäätee 60
if jos 143
ill sairas 140
illness tauti 140
important tärkeä 13
imported maahantuotu 112
impressive vaikuttava 83
in sisässä, sisällä 15
include, to sisällyttää 24, 31, 32, 80
included sisältyy 20, 61; 31, 32, 80
indigestion ruoansulatushäiriö 141
indoor sisä 90
inexpensive edullinen 35; huokea 124
infected tulehtunut 140
infection tulehdus 141
inflammation tulehdus 141
inflation inflaatio 131
inflation rate inflaatiotaso 131
influenza influenssa 142

information neuvonta 67, 155
injection ruiske 142, 143, 144
injure, to loukata 139
injured loukkaantunut 79, 139
injury vamma 139
ink muste 105
inquiry tiedustelu 67
insect bite hyönteisen pistos 108, 139
insect repellent hyttysöljy 108
insect spray hyönteissuihke 106
inside sisässä, sisälle 15
instead of asemasta 37
insurance vakuutus 20, 144
insurance company vakuutusyhtiö 79
interest (finance) korko 131
interested, to be olla kiinnostunut 83, 96
interesting mielenkiintoinen 83
international kansainvälinen 133, 134
interpreter tulkki 131
intersection risteys 77
introduce, to esitellä 92
introduction (social) esittely 92
investment investointi 131
invitation kutsu 95
invite, to kutsua 94
invoice lasku 131
iodine jodi 108
Ireland Irlanti 146
Irish irlantilainen 93
iron (for laundry) silitysrauta 118
iron, to silittää 29
ironmonger's rautakauppa 98
Italy Italia 146
ivory norsunluu 122

J
jacket (lyhyt) takki, pusakka 115
jade jade 122
jam (preserves) hillo 40
jam, to juuttua kiinni 29, 125
January tammikuu 150
jar (container) purkki 119
jaundice keltatauti 142
jaw leuka 138
jazz jatsi 128
jeans farmarihousut 115
jersey villatakki 115
jewel box korulipas 121
jeweller's kultaseppä 98, 121
joint nivel 138
journey matka 71
juice mehu 37, 40, 59

July heinäkuu 150
jumper villapusero 115
June kesäkuu 150
just (only) vain 16, 37, 100

K
keep, to pitää 62
kerosene valopetroli 106
key avain 27
kidney munuainen 138
kilo(gram) kilo 119
kilometre kilometri 20, 78
kind ystävällinen 95
kind of, what (type) minkä lajin 85;
 millainen 140
knee polvi 138
kneesocks polvisukat 115
knife veitsi 36, 60, 120
knock, to koputtaa 155
know, to tietää 16, 25, 96; tuntea 113

L
label nimilappu 105
lace pitsi 113
lady nainen 155
lake järvi 81, 85, 90
lamb (meat) lammas 46
lamp lamppu 29, 106, 118
lamprey nahkiainen 44
lane (traffic) kaista 79
language kieli 104
lantern lyhty 106
large suuri 20, 130; suurta kokoa 101
last viimeinen 14, 68, 73; viime 149, 151
last name sukunimi 26
late myöhäinen 14
late, to be olla myöhässä 153
later myöhemmin 135
Latvia Latvia 146
laugh, to nauraa 95
launderette itsepalvelupesula 29
laundry (clothes) pesula 29
laundry (place) pesula 29, 98
laundry service pyykkipalvelu 24
laxative ulostuslääke 108
lead (theatre) pääosa 86
leap year karkausvuosi 149
leather nahka 113, 117
leave, to lähteä 31; 68, 95
leave, to (deposit) jättää (talteen) 26

leave, to *(leave behind)* jättää 20, 70
leeks purjo(sipuli) 49
left vasen 21, 68, 77
left-luggage office matkatavaran säilytys 67, 70
leg sääri 138
lemon sitruuna 37, 40, 53, 59
lemonade limonaadi 59
lens *(camera)* objektiivi 125
lens *(glasses)* linssi 123
lentils linssit 49
less vähemmän 14
lesson (oppi)tunti 90
let, to *(hire out)* antaa vuokralle 155
letter kirje 132
letter box postilaatikko 132
letter of credit remburssi 130
lettuce lehtisalaatti 49
library kirjasto 81, 99
licence *(driving)* ajokortti 20, 79
lie down, to käydä makuulle 142
life belt pelastusliivi 74
life boat pelastusvene 74
life guard *(beach)* hengenpelastaja 90
lift *(elevator)* hissi 28, 100
light valo 28, 124
light *(weight)* kevyt 14, 55, 101
light *(colour)* vaalea 101, 112
light *(for cigarette)* tuli 95
light meter valotusmittari 125
lighter sytytin 126
lighter fluid/gas sytytinbensiini, sytytinkaasu 126
lightning salama 94
like kuten 111
like, to haluta 13, 20, 23, 112; pitää 61
like, to *(please)* pitää 25, 102; on mukavaa 92
linen *(cloth)* pellava 113
lip huuli 138
lipsalve huulirasva 109
lipstick huulipuna 109
liqueur likööri 58
listen, to kuunnella 128
Lithuania Liettua 146
litre litra 75, 119
little *(a little)* vähän 14
live, to elää 83
liver maksa 138
lobster hummeri 42
local paikallinen 36
long pitkä 115
long-sighted kaukonäköinen 123
look for, to hakea 13
look out! varokaa! 156

look, to katsella 100; katsoa 123, 139
loose *(clothes)* väljä 114
lose, to hukata 123; kadottaa 156
loss tappio 131
lost eksynyt 13
lost and found office/lost property office löytötavaratoimisto 67, 156
lot *(a lot)* paljon 14
lotion neste, vesi 109
loud *(voice)* kova 135
love to, to mielellään 95
lovely ihana 94
low matala 141
low season hiljainen kausi 150
lower ala(vuode) 69, 70
luck onni 135, 152
luggage matkatavarat 17, 18, 21, 26, 31, 71
luggage locker säilytyslokero 18, 67, 70
luggage trolley (työntö)kärry 18, 70
lump *(bump)* kyhmy 139
lunch lounas 34, 80, 95
lung keuhko 138

M
machine *(washable)* konepestävä 113
mackerel makrilli 44
magazine aikakauslehti 105
magnificent komea 84
maid siivooja 27
mail posti 28, 133
mail, to postittaa 28
mailbox postilaatikko 132
main tärkein 100
make up, to *(prepare)* sijata 29; laittaa kuntoon 70
make, to ottaa 131; tehdä 162
make-up meikki 109
make-up remover pad meikinpoistovanu 109
mallet nuija 106
man mies 156
manager johtaja 27
manicure käsien hoito 30
many monta 15
map kartta 76, 105
March maaliskuu 150
marinated marinoitu 45
marjoram meirami 51
mark *(currency)* markka 18
market *(kauppa)tori 81, 99
marmalade marmelaadi 40

married naimisissa 93
mass *(church)* messu 84
match *(matchstick)* tulitikku 106, 120, 126
match *(sport)* ottelu 89
match, to *(colour)* sopia yhteen 111
matinée varhaisnäytäntö 87
matt *(finish)* mattapintainen 125
mattress patja 106
May toukokuu 150
may *(can)* saada 12
meadow niitty 85
meal ateria 24, 34, 143
mean, to tarkoittaa 11, 26
means väline 74
measles tuhkarokko 142
measure, to mitata 113
meat liha 37, 46, 47, 60
meatball lihapyörykkä 46
mechanic korjaaja 78
mechanical pencil lyijytäytekynä 105, 121
medical certificate lääkärintodistus 144
medicine lääketiede 83
medicine *(drug)* lääke 143
medium *(meat)* keski-kypsä 47
medium-sized keskikokoinen 20
meet, to tavata 96
melon melooni 53
memorial muistomerkki 81
mend, to korjata 75
mend, to *(clothes)* korjata 29
menthol *(cigarettes)* mentholi 126
menu ruokalista 36, 38, 39
merry iloinen 152
message viesti 28, 136
metre metri 111
mezzanine *(theatre)* parveke 87
middle keski(vuode) 69; puoliväli 150
midnight keskiyö 153
mild *(light)* mieto 126
mileage kilometrimäärä 20
milk maito 40, 60, 64
milkshake pirtelö 59
million miljoona 148
mineral water mineraalivesi 59
minister *(religion)* pappi 84
mint minttu 51
minute minuutti 21, 68, 153
mirror peili 114, 123
miscellaneous sekalaista 127
Miss neiti 10
miss, to puuttua 18, 29; uupua 60
mistake virhe 31, 61, 102; erehdys 60

moccasin mokkasiini 117
modified American plan puolihoito 24
moisturizing cream kosteusvoide 109
monastery munkkiluostari 81
Monday maanantai 151
money raha 18, 130, 156
money order maksumääräys 133
month kuukausi 16, 150
monument monumentti 81
moon kuu 94
moped mopo 74
more enemmän 12, 14; lisää 15, 37
morning, in the aamulla 143, 151, 153
mortgage kiinnitys 131
mosque moskeija 84
mosquito net hyttysverkko 106
motel motelli 22
mother äiti 93
motorbike moottoripyörä 74
motorboat moottorivene 91
motorway moottoritie 76
mountain vuori 85
mountaineering vuoristokiipeily 89
moustache viikset 31
mouth suu 138, 142
mouthwash suuvesi 108
move, to liikuttaa 139
movie elokuva 86
movies elokuva 86, 96
Mr. herra 10
Mrs. rouva 10
much paljon 11, 14
mug muki 120
muscle lihas 138
museum museo 81
mushroom sieni 49
music musiikki 83, 128
musical musikaali 86
mussel sinisimpukka 44
must *(have to)* täytyä 31, 60, 95, 142
my minun 161
myself *(minä)* itse 119

N

nail *(human)* kynsi 109
nail brush kynsiharja 109
nail clippers kynsileikkuri 109
nail file kynsiviila 109
nail polish kynsilakka 109
nail polish remover kynsilakanpoistoaine 109
nail scissors kynsisakset 109
name nimi 23, 26, 79, 92, 131, 136

napkin lautasliina 36, 120
nappy vaippa 110
narrow kapea 117
nationality kansallisuus 26, 93
natural luonnon 83
natural history luonnonhistoria 83
nauseous pahoinvointi, kuvotus 140
near lähellä, lähelle 14, 15
nearby lähellä 32, 77
nearest lähin 75, 78, 98
neat *(drink)* sekoittamaton 58
neck niska 30; kaula (ja niska) 138
necklace kaulakoru 121
need, to tarvita 29, 90, 137
needle neula 28
negative negatiivi 124, 125
nephew veljen/sisaren poika 93
nerve hermo 138
Netherlands Hollanti 146
never ei koskaan 15
new uusi 14
New Year uusi vuosi 152
New Zealand Uusi-Seelanti 146
newsagent's lehtimyymälä 99
newspaper sanomalehti 104, 105
newsstand lehtimyymälä 19, 67;
   lehtikioski 99, 104
next seuraava 14, 65, 68, 73, 76, 151;
   ensi 149, 151
next time ensi kerralla 95
next to vieressä 15, 77
nice *(beautiful)* kaunis 94
niece veljen/sisaren tytär 93
night yö 10, 25, 151
night cream yövoide 109
night, at yöllä 151
nightclub yökerho 88
nightdress/-gown yöpaita 115
nine yhdeksän 147
nineteen yhdeksäntoista 147
ninety yhdeksänkymmentä 148
ninth yhdeksäs 149
no ei 10
noisy meluisa 26
nonalcoholic alkoholiton 59
none ei yhtään 15
nonsmoker ei-tupakoijille 36;
   tupakointi kielletty 69
noon puolipäivä 31; keskipäivä 153
normal normaali 30
north pohjoinen 77
North America Pohjois-Amerikka 146
Norway Norja 146
nose nenä 138
nose drops nenätipat 108

nosebleed verenvuoto nenästä 141
not ei 15
note *(banknote)* seteli 130
note paper kirjoituspaperi 105
notebook muistikirja 105
nothing ei mitään 15, 17
notice *(sign)* varoitus 155
notify, to ilmoittaa 144
November marraskuu 150
now nyt 15
number numero 26, 65, 135, 136, 147
nurse hoitaja 144
nutmeg muskotti 51

O

occupation *(profession)* ammatti 26
occupied varattu 14, 155
October lokakuu 150
office myymälä 19; myynti 67;
   toimisto 80, 99, 132, 156
oil öljy 37, 75, 110
oily *(greasy)* rasvainen 30, 110
old vanha 14
old town vanha kaupunki 81
on päällä, päälle 15
on foot jalan 76
on time aikataulussa 68
once kerran 149
one yksi 147
one-way *(traffic)* yksisuuntainen 77
one-way ticket menolippu 65, 69
onion sipuli 49
only vain 15, 25, 80, 87, 108
onyx onyks 122
open avoin 14; auki 82, 142; avoinna
   155
open, to aueta *itr* 11, 107, 132; avata *tr*
   17, 130
open-air ulko 90
opera ooppera 88
opera house oopperatalo 81, 88
operation leikkaus 144
operator keskus 134
operetta operetti 88
opposite vastapäätä 77
optician optiko 99, 123
or tai 15
orange appelsiini 52, 64
orange *(colour)* oranssi 112
orange juice appelsiinimehu 40, 59
orangeade appelsiinilimonaadi 59
orchestra orkesteri 88
orchestra *(seats)* etupermanto 87

order *(goods, meal)* tilaus 102
order, to *(goods, meal)* tilata 60, 102, 103
oregano oregano 51
ornithology lintutiede 83
other muu 74, 101
our meidän 161
out of order epäkunnossa 136, 155
out of stock ei varastossa 103
outlet *(electric)* (sähkö)pistorasia 27
outside ulkona, ulos 15; ulkoa 36
oval soikea 101
overalls haalarit 115
overdone *(meat)* ylikypsä 60
overheat, to *(engine)* ylikuumeta 78
owe, to olla velkaa 144
oyster osteri 44

P

pacifier *(baby's)* tutti 110
packet rasia 126
pail ämpäri 128
pain kipu 140, 141; tuska 144
painkiller särkylääke 140, 144
paint maali 155
paint, to maalata 83
paintbox vesivärirasia 105
painter taidemaalari 83
painting maalaus 83
pair pari 115, 117, 149
pajamas pyjama 115
palace palatsi 81
palpitations sydämen tykytys 141
panties pikkuhousut 115
pants *(trousers)* housut 115
panty girdle housuliivit 115
panty hose sukkahousut 115
paper paperi 105
paper napkin paperilautasliina 105, 120
paperback taskukirja 105
paperclip liitin 105
paraffin *(fuel)* valopetroli 106
parcel paketti 132, 133
pardon, I beg your (pyydän) anteeksi 11
parents vanhemmat 93
park puisto 81
park, to pysäköidä 26, 77
parka sadepusakka 115
parking pysäköinti 77, 79
parking disc pysäköintikiekko 77
parking meter pysäköintimittari 77
parliament building eduskuntatalo 81

parsley persilja 51
part osa 138
partridge peltopyy 48
party *(social gathering)* kutsut 95
pass *(mountain)* sola 85
pass through, to kulkea läpi 16
passport passi 16, 17, 25, 26, 156
passport photo passikuva 124
paste *(glue)* liima 105
pastry shop konditoria 99
patch, to *(clothes)* paikata 29
path polku 85
patient potilas 144
pattern kuvioitus 112
pay, to maksaa 17, 31, 62, 100, 102, 136
payment maksu 102, 131
pea herne 49
peach persikka 53
peak huippu 85
peanut maapähkinä 52
pear päärynä 53
pearl helmi 122
pedestrian jalankulkija 155
peg *(tent)* telttapuikko 106
pen kynä 105
pencil lyijykynä 105
pencil sharpener kynänteroitin 105
pendant riipus 121
penicillin penisilliini 143
penknife kynäveitsi 120
pensioner eläkeläinen 82
people ihmiset 92
pepper pippuri 37, 40, 51, 64
per cent prosentti 149
per day päivältä 20, 32, 89
per hour tunnilta 77, 89
per night yöltä 24
per person hengeltä 32
per week viikolta 20, 24
percentage prosentti 131
perch ahven 44
perform, to *(theatre)* esittää 86
perfume hajuvesi 109
perhaps ehkä 15
period *(monthly)* kuukautiset 141
period pains kuukautiskivut 141
perm(anent) permanentti 30
permit lupa 90
person henki(lö) 32
personal henkilökohtainen 17, 130
personal call/person-to-person call henkilöpuhelu 134
personal cheque henkilökohtainen shekki 130

DICTIONARY

Sanakirja

petrol bensiini, bensa 75, 78
pewter tina 122
pharmacy apteekki 107
pheasant fasaani 48
photo valokuva 82, 124, 125
photocopy valokopio 131
photograph, to valokuvata 82
photographer valokuvaamo 99
photography valokuvaus 124
phrase sanonta 12
pick up, to *(person)* hakea 80, 96
picnic piknik 62
picnic basket eväskori 106
picture *(painting)* taulu 83
picture *(photo)* (valo)kuva 82
piece kappale 18; pala 63, 119
pike hauki 44
pill pilleri 141; tabletti 143
pillow tyyny 28
pin neula 109, 110, 121
pineapple ananas 52
pink vaaleanpunainen 112
pipe piippu 126
pipe cleaner piipun puhdistin 126
pipe tobacco piipputupakka 126
pipe tool piippukalu 126
place paikka 26, 76
place of birth syntymäpaikka 26
place, to *(call)* tilata 134
plaice punakampela 44
plain *(colour)* yksivärinen 112
plane lento(kone) 65
planetarium planetaario 81
plaster kipsi 140
plastic muovi 120
plastic bag muovikassi 120
plate lautanen 36, 60 120
platform *(station)* laituri 67, 68, 69
platinum platina 122
play *(theatre)* näytelmä 86
play, to esittää 86; soittaa 88; pelata 89, 93
playground leikkikenttä 32
playing card pelikortti 105
please olkaa hyvä 10
plimsolls kumitossu 117
plug *(electric)* pistoke 29, 118
plum luumu 52
pneumonia keuhkokuume 142
poached keitetty 45
pocket tasku 116
pocket calculator taskulaskin 105
pocket watch taskukello 121
point of interest *(sight)* nähtävyys 80
point, to osoittaa 12

poison myrkky 108, 156
poisoning myrkytys 142
pole *(ski)* sauva 91
pole *(tent)* telttaseiväs 106
police poliisi 78, 79, 156
police station poliisiasema 99, 156
pond lampi 85
poplin popliini 113
pork porsaanliha 46
port *(harbour)* satama 73
portable kannettava 118
porter kantaja 18, 26, 70
portion annos 37, 54, 60
Portugal Portugali 146
possible, (as soon as) mahdollista, (niin pian kuin) 137
post *(mail)* posti 28, 133
post office posti(toimisto) 19, 99, 132
post, to postittaa 28
postage kirjemaksu 132
postage stamp postimerkki 28, 126, 132, 133
postcard postikortti 105, 126; 132
poste restante poste restante 133
pottery savenvalanta 83
poultry lintu 48
pound punta 18, 102, 130
powder puuteri 109
powder compact puuterirasia 122
powder puff puuterihuisku 109
prawn katkarapu 44
pregnant raskaana 141
premium *(gasoline)* korkeaoktaaninen 75
prescribe, to kirjoittaa resepti 143
prescription resepti 107; lääkemääräys 143
press stud painonappi 116
press, to *(iron)* prässätä 29
pressure paine 75, 141
pretty sievä 84
price hinta 24
priest *(katolinen)* pappi 84
print *(photo)* kuva 125
private oma 24; yksityinen 80, 155
processing *(photo)* kehitys 125
profession ammatti 26
profit voitto 131
programme ohjelma 87
pronounce, to ääntää 12
pronunciation ääntäminen 6
propelling pencil lyijytäytekynä 105, 121
Protestant protestanttinen 84
provide, to järjestää, hankkia 131

prune kuivattu luumu 52
public holiday yleinen vapaapäivä 152
pull, to vetää 155
pull, to *(tooth)* vetää pois 145
pullover villapaita 115
pump pumppu 106
purchase osto 131
pure täyttä (puhdasta) 113
purple sinipunainen 112
push, to työntää 155
put, to tuoda 24
pyjamas pyjama 116

Q

quality laatu 103, 112
quantity määrä 14
quarter of an hour neljännestunti 153
quartz kvartsi 122
question kysymys 11
quick(ly) nopea(sti) 14, 79, 137, 156
quiet hiljainen 24; rauhallinen 25

R

rabbi rabbi 84
race kilpailu 89
race course (track) kilparata 89
racket *(sport)* maila 90
radiator *(car)* jäähdyttäjä 78
radio radio 23, 28, 118
radish retiisi 49
railway station rautatieasema 19, 21, 66, 69
rain sade 94
rain, to sataa 94
raincoat sadetakki 117
raisin rusina 53
rangefinder etäisyysmittari 125
rare *(meat)* raaka 47, 61
rash ihottuma 139
raspberry vadelma 52
rate *(inflation)* taso 131
rate *(of exchange)* vaihtokurssi 18, 130
rate *(price)* hinta 20
razor partakone 109
razor blades partakoneen terä 109
read, to lukea 39
reading lamp lukulamppu 28
ready valmis 30, 117, 123, 125, 145
real *(genuine)* aito 117, 121
rear takana 69; 75

receipt kuitti 103, 144
reception vastaanotto 23
receptionist vastaanotto 27
recommend, to suositella 35, 36, 80, 86, 88, 137, 145
record *(disc)* levy 127, 128
record player levysoitin 118
recorder nauhuri 118
rectangular suorakulmainen 101
red punainen 105, 112
red *(wine)* puna 57
reduction alennus 24, 82
refill *(pen)* säiliö 105
refund *(to get a)* maksun palautus 103
regards terveiset 152
region alue 92
register, to *(luggage)* lähettää matkatavara 71
registered mail kirjattu lähetys 132
registration kirjoittautuminen 26
registration form matkustajakortti 26
regular *(petrol)* matalaoktaaninen 75
religion uskonto 83
religious service jumalanpalvelus 84
rent, to vuokrata 19, 20, 74, 90, 91, 119, 155
rental vuokraus 20, 74
repair korjata 125
repair, to korjata 29, 117, 118, 121, 123, 125, 145
repeat, to toistaa 12
report, to *(a theft)* tehdä ilmoitus 156
required vaaditaan 88
requirement tarve 27
reservation varaus 19, 23, 65, 69
reservations office paikanvaraus 67
reserve, to varata 19, 23, 35, 69, 87
reserved varattu 155
rest loput 130
restaurant ravintola 19, 32, 33, 35, 67
return ticket menopaluu 65, 69
return, to *(come back)* palata 21, 80
return, to *(give back)* palauttaa 103
rheumatism reumatismi 141
rib kylkiluu 138
ribbon värinauha 105
right *(correct)* oikea 14
right *(direction)* oikea 21, 68, 77
ring *(jewellery)* sormus 122
ring, to *(doorbell)* soittaa 155
river joki 85, 90
river cruise jokiristeily 74
road tie 76, 77, 85
road assistance tiepalvelu 78
road map tiekartta 105

shampoo and set pesu ja kampaus 30
shape muoto 103
share *(finance)* osake 131
sharp *(pain)* pistävä 140
shave parranajo 31
shaver parranajokone 27, 118
shaving brush partasuti 109
shaving cream partavaahdoke 109
she hän 161
shelf hylly 119
ship laiva 74
shirt paita 116
shiver puistatus 140
shoe kenkä 117
shoe polish kengänkiilloke 117
shoe shop kenkäkauppa 99
shoelace kengännauha 117
shoemaker's suutari 99
shop myymälä, kauppa, liike 98
shop window näyteikkuna 100
shopping ostos 97
shopping area ostosalue 81, 100
shopping centre ostoskeskus 99
short lyhyt 30, 114
short-sighted likinäköinen 123
shorts shortsit 116
shoulder olkapää, hartiat 138
shovel lapio 128
show näytös 87; ohjelma 88
show, to näyttää 12, 13, 76, 100, 101, 103, 118, 124
shower suihku 23, 32
shrimp katkarapu 44
shrink, to kutistua 113
shut suljettu 14
shutter *(camera)* suljin 125
shutter *(window)* ikkunaluukku 29
sick *(ill)* sairas 140
sickness *(illness)* sairaus 140
side sivu 31
sideboards/-burns pulisongit 31
sight nähtävyys 80
sightseeing kiertoajelu 80
sightseeing tour nähtävyyskierros 80
sign *(notice)* viitta 77; merkki 77, 79; kyltti 155
sign, to allekirjoittaa 26, 131
signature allekirjoitus 26
signet ring sinettisormus 122
silk silkki 113
silver hopea 121, 122
silver *(colour)* hopeanvärinen 112
silver plated hopeoitu 122
silverware hopeaesineitä 122
simple yksinkertainen 124

since alkaen 15; -sta asti 151
sing, to laulaa 88
single *(ticket)* menolippu 65, 69
single *(unmarried)* naimaton 93
single cabin yhden hengen hytti 74
single room yhden hengen huone 19, 23
sister sisko 93
sit down, to istuutua 95
six kuusi 147
sixteen kuusitoista 147
sixth kuudes 149
sixty kuusikymmentä 147
size koko 113, 117, 124
skate luistin 91
skating rink luistinrata 91
ski suksi 91
ski boot hiihtokengät 91
ski lift hiihtohissi 91
ski run latu 91
ski, to hiihtää 91
skiing hiihto 89, 91
skiing equipment hiihtovarusteet 91, 106
skiing lessons hiihtotunti 91
skin iho 138
skin-diving sukellus 91
skin-diving equipment sukellusvarusteet 90, 106
skirt hame 116
sky taivas 94
sleep, to nukkua 144
sleeping bag makuupussi 106
sleeping car makuuvaunu 68, 69, 70
sleeping pill unitabletti 108, 143
sleeve hiha 116, 142
sleeveless hihaton 116
slice siivu 119
slide *(photo)* dia 124
slip *(underwear)* alushame 116
slipper tohveli 117
slow hidas 14
slowly, more hitaammin 21, 135
small pieni 14, 20, 25, 101, 117, 130
smoke, to polttaa 95
smoked savustettu 45
smoker tupakoitsija 69
snack välipala 62
snack bar pikabaari 67
snap fastener painonappi 116
sneaker kumitossu 117
snorkel snorkkeli 128
snow lumi 94
snow, to sataa lunta 94
snuff nuuska 126

soap saippua 28, 110
soccer jalkapallo 89
sock (nilkka)sukka 116
socket *(electric)* (sähkö)pistorasia 27
soft pehmeä 123
soft drink (alkoholiton) juoma 64
soft-boiled *(egg)* pehmeäksi keitetty 40
sold out loppuunmyyty 87
sole *(fish)* meriantura 44
sole *(shoe)* pohja 117
soloist solisti 88
some hieman 14
someone joku 96
something jotain 30, 36, 107, 111, 112, 139
somewhere jossain 87
son poika 93
song laulu 128
soon pian 15
sore *(painful)* arka 145
sore throat kurkkukipu 141
sorry anteeksi 11, 16; valitettavasti 87, 103
sort *(kind)* laatu 119
soup keitto 42
south etelä 77
South Africa Etelä-Afrikka 146
South America Etelä-Amerikka 146
souvenir muistoesine 127
souvenir shop matkamuistmyymälä 99
spade lapio 128
Spain Espanja 146
spare tyre vararengas 75
spark(ing) plug sytytystulppa 76
sparkling *(wine)* kuohu 57
speak, to puhua 11, 12, 16, 84; tavata (puhutella) 135
speaker *(loudspeaker)* kaiutin 118
special erikois 20; 37
special delivery pikajakelu 132
specialist erikoislääkäri 142
speciality erikoisuus 39
specimen *(medical)* näyte 142
spectacle case simälasikotelo 123
speed nopeus 79
spell, to tavata 12
spend, to kuluttaa 101
spice mauste 51
spinach pinaatti 49
spine selkäranka 138
sponge pesusieni 110
spoon lusikka 36, 60, 120
sport urheilu 89

sporting goods shop urheiluvälinekauppa 99
sports jacket urheilupusero 116
sprained nyrjähtänyt 140
spring *(season)* kevät 150
spring *(water)* lähde 85
square neliskulmainen 101
square *(town)* tori 81
stadium stadion 81
staff *(personnel)* henkilökunta 27
stain tahra 29
stainless steel ruostumaton teräs 120
stalls *(theatre)* etupermanto 87
stamp *(postage)* postimerkki 28, 126, 132, 133
staple niitti 105
star tähti 94
start, to alkaa 80, 86; *(car)* käynnistyä 78
starter *(meal)* alkuruoka 41
station *(railway)* (rautatie)asema 19, 21, 66, 69
station *(underground/subway)* asema 71
stationer's paperikauppa 99, 104
statue patsas 81
stay oleskelu 31, 92
stay, to viipyä 16, 25, 26; pysyä 142
stay, to *(reside)* asua 94
steak pihvi 46
steal, to varastaa 156
steamed höyryssä keitetty 45
stewed muhennettu 47
stiff neck niska jäykkänä 141
still *(mineral water)* hiilihapoton 59
sting pistos 139
sting, to pistää 139
stitch, to ommella 29; 117
stock exchange pörssi 81
stocking (naisten) sukka 116
stomach maha, vatsa 138
stomach ache vatsakipu 141
stools uloste 142
stop *(bus)* pysäkki 72, 73
stop thief! varas kiinni! 156
stop! seis! 156
stop, to pysähtyä *itr* 21, 68; seisoa 70; pysäyttää *tr* 156
store *(shop)* myymälä, kauppa, liike 98
straight *(drink)* sekoittamaton 58
straight ahead suoraan eteenpäin 21, 77
strange outo 84
strawberry mansikka 52
street katu 26, 77

than kuin 14
thank you kiitos 10
thank, to kiittää 10, 96
that tuo 11, 100
theatre teatteri 81, 86
theft varkaus 156
their heidän 161
then sitten 15
there tuolla 14
thermometer lämpömittari 108, 144
they he 161
thief varas 156
thigh reisi 138
thin ohut 113
think, to (believe) taitaa olla 31, 61, 102; luulla 94
third kolmas 149
third, one kolmannes 149
thirsty, to be janoinen 13, 35
thirteen kolmetoista 147
thirty kolmekymmentä 147
this tämä 11, 100
thousand tuhat 148
thread lanka 28
three kolme 147
throat kurkku 138, 141
throat lozenge kurkkutabletti 108
through läpi 15
through train suora (juna)yhteys 67
thumb peukalo 138
thumbtack piirustusnasta 105
thunder ukkonen 94
thunderstorm ukkosmyrsky 94
Thursday torstai 151
thyme tinjami 51
ticket lippu 65, 69, 72, 87, 89
ticket office lipputoimisto 67
tie solmio, kravatti 116
tie clip solmion pidike 122
tie pin solmioneula 122
tight (close-fitting) tiukka 114
tights sukkahousut 116
time aika 68, 80; kello 152
time (occasion) kerta 95, 142, 143
timetable (trains) aikataulu 68
tin (container) tölkki 119
tint hiusväri 110
tinted värjätyt 123
tire rengas 75, 76
tired väsynyt 13
tissue (handkerchief) paperipyyhe 110
tissue paper silkkipaperi 105
to luokse 15
to get (fetch) hankkia 31; hakea 137
to get (go) päästä 100

to get (obtain) saada 90, 107; päästä 134
toast paahtoleipä 40
tobacco tupakka 126
tobacconist's tupakkakauppa 99, 126
today tänään 29, 151
toe varvas 138
toilet paper vessapaperi 110
toilet water eau de toilette 110
toiletry kosmetiikka 109
toilets WC:t 24, 28, 37, 67; vessat 32
tomato tomaatti 49
tomato juice tomaattimehu 59
tomb hauta 81
tomorrow huomenna 29, 96, 151
tongue kieli 138
tonic water tonic-vesi 59
tonight tänä iltana 29, 86, 87, 96
tonsils kitarisat 138
too liiaksi 14
too (also) myös 15
too much liiaksi 14
tools työkalut 120
tooth hammas 145
toothache hammassärky 145
toothbrush hammasharja 110, 118
toothpaste hammastahna 110
top, at the päällä 30; ylhäällä 145
torch (flashlight) taskulamppu 106
torn revähtänyt 140
touch, to koskea 155
tough (meat) sitkeä 60
tour kierros 73, 80
tourist office matkailutoimisto 19, 23, 80
tourist tax matkailijavero 32
tow truck hinausauto 78
towards kohti 15
towel pyyhe 27, 110
towelling (terrycloth) pyyhekangas 113
tower torni 81
town kaupunki 19, 76, 88
town centre kaupungin keskusta 21, 72, 76
town hall kaupungintalo, raatihuone 82
toy leikkikalu 128
toy shop lelukauppa 99
tracksuit verryttelypuku 116
traffic liikenne 79
traffic light liikennevalo 77
trailer asuntovaunu 32
train juna 66, 68, 69, 70, 153
tram raitiovaunu 72

tranquillizer rauhoittava lääke 108, 143
transfer *(finance)* siirto 131
transformer muuntaja 118
translate, to kääntää 12
transport, means of kulkuväline 74
travel agency matkatoimisto 99
travel guide matkaopas 105
travel sickness matkapahoinvointi 107
travel, to matkustaa 93
traveller's cheque matkashekki 18, 60, 102, 130
travelling bag (matka)laukku 18
treatment hoito 143
tree puu 85
tremendous valtava 84
trim, to *(a beard)* siistiä 31
trip matka 71, 94, 152
trolley (työntö)kärry 18, 70
trousers (pitkät) housut 116
trout taimen 44
try on, to sovittaa 114
try, to yrittää 135
tube putkilo 119
Tuesday tiistai 151
tumbler juomalasi 120
tuna tonnikala 44
tunny tonnikala 44
turbot kampela 45
turkey kalkkuna 48
turn, to *(change direction)* kääntyä 21, 77
turnip nauris 49
turquoise *(colour)* turkoosi 112
turquoise *(gem)* turkoosi 122
turtleneck poolo-kaulus 115
tweezers pinsetit 110
twelve kaksitoista 147
twenty kaksikymmentä 147
twice kahdesti 149
twin beds kaksi vuodetta 23
two kaksi 147
typewriter konekirjoittaja 27
typing paper konekirjoituspaperi 105
tyre rengas 75, 76

U
ugly ruma 14, 84
umbrella sateenvarjo 116
umbrella *(beach)* aurinkovarjo 90
uncle setä 93
unconscious tajuton 139
under alla, alle 15

underdone *(meat)* puolikypsä 47, 61
underground *(railway)* metro 71
underpants (miesten) alushousut 116
undershirt aluspaita 116
understand, to ymmärtää 12, 16
undress, to riisua 142
United States USA (Yhdysvallat) 146
university yliopisto 82
unleaded lyijytön 75
until asti 15
up ylhäällä, ylös 15
upper ylä(vuode) 69
upset stomach vatsavaiva 107
upstairs yläkerrassa 15
urgent kiire 13
urine virtsa 142
use käyttö 17, 108
use, to käyttää 78, 134
useful hyödyllinen 15
usually tavallisesti 94, 143

V
V-neck V-aukko 116
vacancy vapaa huone 23
vacant vapaa 14, 155
vacation loma 152
vaccinate, to rokottaa 140
vacuum flask termospullo 120
vaginal infection emätintulehdus 141
valley laakso 85
value arvo 131
value-added tax liikevaihtovero 24, 102
vanilla vanilja 54
VAT *(sales tax)* liikevaihtovero 24, 102
veal vasikanliha 46
vegetable vihannes 49
vegetable store vihanneskauppa 99
vegetarian kasvissyöjä 37
vein suoni 138
velvet sametti 113
velveteen puuvillasametti 113
venereal disease sukupuolitauti 142
venison hirvenliha 48
vermouth vermutti 59
very tosi 15
vest aluspaita 116
vest *(Am.)* (miesten) liivit 116
veterinarian eläinlääkäri 99
video camera videokamera 124
video cassette videokasetti 118, 124, 127
video recorder videonauhuri 118

view *(panorama)* näköala 23, 25
village kylä 76, 85
vinegar viinietikka 37
vineyard viinitarha 85
visit käynti 92
visit, to tulla käymään 95
visiting hours vierailuajat 144
vitamin pill vitamiinipilleri 108
vodka vodka 59
volleyball lentopallo 89
voltage jännite 27, 118
vomit, to oksentaa 140

W

waist vyötärö 142
waistcoat liivi, hihaton (villa)takki 116
wait, to odottaa 21, 96, 107
waiter tarjoilija 26, 36
waiting room odotushuone 67
waitress tarjoilija 27, 36
wake, to herättää 27, 70
Wales Wales 146
walk, to kävellä 74, 85
wall muuri 85
wallet lompakko 156
walnut saksanpähkinä 53
want, to haluta 13, 101, 102
warm lämmin 94
wash, to pestä 29, 113
washable pestävä 113
washbasin pesuallas 29
washing powder pesupulveri 120
washing-up liquid nestemäinen pesuaine 120
watch kello 121, 122
watchmaker's kelloseppä 99, 121
watchstrap kellon hihna 122
water vesi 24, 28, 32, 40, 90; neste 75
water flask kenttäpullo 106
water melon vesimelooni 53
water-skis vesisukset 91
waterfall vesiputous 85
waterproof vedenpitävä 122
wave aalto 90
way tie 76
we me 161
weather sää 94
weather forecast säännuste 94
wedding ring vihkisormus 122
Wednesday keskiviikko 151
week viikko 16, 20, 25, 80, 92, 151
weekday arkipäivä 151

weekend viikonloppu 20
well hyvin 10, 140
well-done *(meat)* hyvin/kypsäksi paistettu 47
west länsi 77
what mitä 11
wheel pyörä 78
when milloin 11
where missä 11
where from mistä 92, 146
which mikä, kumpi 11
whipped cream kermavaahto 54
whisky viski 17, 58
white valko 57; valkoinen 112
who kuka 11
whole kokonainen 143
why miksi 11
wick sytyttimen sydän 126
wide leveä 117
wide-angle lens laajakulmaobjektiivi 125
wife vaimo 93
wig peruukki 110
wild boar villisika 48
wind tuuli 94
window ikkuna 29, 36, 65, 69, 100, 111
windscreen/shield tuulilasi 76
windsurfer purjelauta 91
wine viini 56, 57, 61
wine list viinilista 56
wine merchant's viinimyymälä, alkoholiliike 99
winter talvi 150
winter sports talviurheilu 91
wiper *(car)* pyyhkijän sulka 76
wish toivotus 152
with kanssa 15
withdraw, to *(from account)* nostaa 130
withdrawal otto 130
without ilman 15
woman nainen 156
wonderful ihana 96
wood metsä 85
wool villa 113
word sana 12, 15, 133
work, to toimia 28, 118
working day työpäivä 152
worse huonompi 14
worsted kampalankaa 113
wound haava 139
wrap up, to panna pakettiin 103
wrapping paper käärepaperi 105
wrinkle-free rypistymätöntä 113
wristwatch rannekello 122

Suomi hakemisto

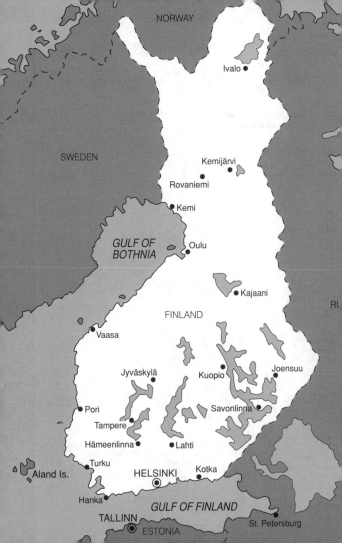